IFIP Advances in Information and Communication Technology 334

IFIP – The International Federation for Information Processing

IFIP was founded in 1960 under the auspices of UNESCO, following the First World Computer Congress held in Paris the previous year. An umbrella organization for societies working in information processing, IFIP's aim is two-fold: to support information processing within its member countries and to encourage technology transfer to developing nations. As its mission statement clearly states,

> *IFIP's mission is to be the leading, truly international, apolitical organization which encourages and assists in the development, exploitation and application of information technology for the benefit of all people.*

IFIP is a non-profitmaking organization, run almost solely by 2500 volunteers. It operates through a number of technical committees, which organize events and publications. IFIP's events range from an international congress to local seminars, but the most important are:

- The IFIP World Computer Congress, held every second year;
- Open conferences;
- Working conferences.

The flagship event is the IFIP World Computer Congress, at which both invited and contributed papers are presented. Contributed papers are rigorously refereed and the rejection rate is high.

As with the Congress, participation in the open conferences is open to all and papers may be invited or submitted. Again, submitted papers are stringently refereed.

The working conferences are structured differently. They are usually run by a working group and attendance is small and by invitation only. Their purpose is to create an atmosphere conducive to innovation and development. Refereeing is less rigorous and papers are subjected to extensive group discussion.

Publications arising from IFIP events vary. The papers presented at the IFIP World Computer Congress and at open conferences are published as conference proceedings, while the results of the working conferences are often published as collections of selected and edited papers.

Any national society whose primary activity is in information may apply to become a full member of IFIP, although full membership is restricted to one society per country. Full members are entitled to vote at the annual General Assembly, National societies preferring a less committed involvement may apply for associate or corresponding membership. Associate members enjoy the same benefits as full members, but without voting rights. Corresponding members are not represented in IFIP bodies. Affiliated membership is open to non-national societies, and individual and honorary membership schemes are also offered.

Marijn Janssen   Winfried Lamersdorf
Jan Pries-Heje   Michael Rosemann (Eds.)

E-Government, E-Services and Global Processes

Joint IFIP TC 8 and TC 6 International Conferences
EGES 2010 and GISP 2010
Held as Part of WCC 2010
Brisbane, Australia, September 20-23, 2010
Proceedings

 Springer

Volume Editors

Marijn Janssen
Delft University of Technology
Section of Information & Communication Technology
Jaffalaan 5, 2628 BX Delft, The Netherlands
E-mail: m.f.w.h.a.janssen@tudelft.nl

Winfried Lamersdorf
University of Hamburg, Computer Science Department
Vogt-Kölln-Str. 30, 22527 Hamburg, Germany
E-mail: lamersdorf@informatik.uni-hamburg.de

Jan Pries-Heje
The IT University of Copenhagen
Rued Langgaards vej 7, 2300 Copenhagen, Denmark
E-mail: jph@itu.dk

Michael Rosemann
Queensland University of Technology, Business Process Management Group
126 Margaret Street, Brisbane, QLD 4000, Australia
E-mail: m.rosemann@qut.edu.au

Library of Congress Control Number: 2010932602

CR Subject Classification (1998): K.5.2, K.4.4, C.2, E.3, H.4, J.1

ISSN   1868-4238
ISBN-10   3-642-15345-3 Springer Berlin Heidelberg New York
ISBN-13   978-3-642-15345-7 Springer Berlin Heidelberg New York

springer.com

© IFIP International Federation for Information Processing 2010
Printed in Germany

Typesetting: Camera-ready by author, data conversion by Scientific Publishing Services, Chennai, India
Printed on acid-free paper   06/3180

IFIP World Computer Congress 2010 (WCC 2010)

Message from the Chairs

Every two years, the International Federation for Information Processing (IFIP) hosts a major event which showcases the scientific endeavors of its over one hundred technical committees and working groups. On the occasion of IFIP's 50th anniversary, 2010 saw the 21st IFIP World Computer Congress (WCC 2010) take place in Australia for the third time, at the Brisbane Convention and Exhibition Centre, Brisbane, Queensland, September 20–23, 2010.

The congress was hosted by the Australian Computer Society, ACS. It was run as a federation of co-located conferences offered by the different IFIP technical committees, working groups and special interest groups, under the coordination of the International Program Committee.

The event was larger than ever before, consisting of 17 parallel conferences, focusing on topics ranging from artificial intelligence to entertainment computing, human choice and computers, security, networks of the future and theoretical computer science. The conference History of Computing was a valuable contribution to IFIPs 50th anniversary, as it specifically addressed IT developments during those years. The conference e-Health was organized jointly with the International Medical Informatics Association (IMIA), which evolved from IFIP Technical Committee TC-4 "Medical Informatics".

Some of these were established conferences that run at regular intervals, e.g., annually, and some represented new, groundbreaking areas of computing. Each conference had a call for papers, an International Program Committee of experts and a thorough peer reviewing process of full papers. The congress received 642 papers for the 17 conferences, and selected 319 from those, representing an acceptance rate of 49.69% (averaged over all conferences). To support interoperation between events, conferences were grouped into 8 areas: Deliver IT, Govern IT, Learn IT, Play IT, Sustain IT, Treat IT, Trust IT, and Value IT.

This volume is one of 13 volumes associated with the 17 scientific conferences. Each volume covers a specific topic and separately or together they form a valuable record of the state of computing research in the world in 2010. Each volume was prepared for publication in the Springer IFIP Advances in Information and Communication Technology series by the conference's volume editors. The overall Publications Chair for all volumes published for this congress is Mike Hinchey.

For full details of the World Computer Congress, please refer to the webpage at http://www.ifip.org.

June 2010
Augusto Casaca, Portugal, Chair, International Program Committee
Phillip Nyssen, Australia, Co-chair, International Program Committee
Nick Tate, Australia, Chair, Organizing Committee
Mike Hinchey, Ireland, Publications Chair
Klaus Brunnstein, Germany, General Congress Chair

Introduction

This book contains the proceedings of two of the IFIP conferences that took place at the IFIP World Computer Congress 2010 in Brisbane, Australia.

The proceedings of each conference are allocated separate parts in this book each with their own editors.

Organization

E-Government and E-Services
(EGES 2010)

EGES Co-chairs

Marijn Janssen	Delft, The Netherlands
Winfried Lamersdorf	Hamburg, Germany
Lalit Sawhney	Bangalore, India
Leon Strous	Helmond, The Netherlands

EGES Reviewers

Agarwal Ashok	ACS Technologies Ltd., Bhoopal, India
Mark Borman	University of Sydney, Australia
Erwin Fielt	Queensland University of Technology, Brisbane, Australia
Ernest Foo	Queensland University of Technology, Brisbane, Australia
M.P. Gupta	Indian Institute of Technology Delhi, India
Paul Henman	The University of Queensland, Australia
Ralf Klischewski	German University, Cairo, Egypt
Christine Leitner	Donau-Universität Krems, Austria
Miriam Lips	Victoria University of Wellington, New Zealand
Zoran Milosevic	Deontic, Brisbane, Australia
Oystein Sabo	University of Agder, Norway
Jochen Scholl	University of Washington, Seattle, USA
Leif Skiftenes	University of Agder, Norway
Weerakoddy Vishanth	Brunel University Business School, West London, UK
Dirk Werth	DFKI, Saarbrücken, Germany
Maria Wimmer	University Koblenz-Landau, Germany

EGES Subreviewers

Alexandra Chapko, Andreas Emrich and Marc Graessle
German Research Center for Artificial Intelligence, Saarbrücken, Germany

Kristof Hamann, Kai Jander, Ante Vilenica and Sonja Zaplata
University of Hamburg, Germany

Global Information Systems Processes (GISP 2010)

GISP Co-chairs

Jan Pries-Heje   Roskilde University, Denmark
Michael Rosemann   Queensland University of Technology,
                            Brisbane, Australia

GISP Reviewers

Richard Baskerville   Georgia State University, USA
Josef Basl   Charles University Prague, Czech Republic
Irwin Brown   University of Cape Town, South Africa
Sven Carlsson   University of Lund, Sweden
Kevin Crowston   Syracuse University, USA
Dirk Deschoolmeester   Vlerick Management School, Belgium
Steve Elliot   University of Sydney, Australia
Theo Hrder   University of Kaiserslautern, Germany
Juhani Iivari   University of Oulu, Finland
Anders G. Nilsson   Karlstad University, Sweden
Marijn Janssen   Delft University of Technology, The Netherlands
George M. Kasper   Virginia Commonwealth University, Richmond, USA
Karlheinz Kautz   Copenhagen Business School, Denmark
John Krogstie   NTNU, Norway
Tor J. Larsen   Norwegian School of Management
Michael Myers   University of Auckland, New Zealand
Bill Olle   Representative, British Computer Society in
                            IFIP TC 8
Barbara Pernici   Politecnico di Milano, Italy
Yves Pigneur   University of Lausanne, Switzerland
Maria Raffai   Szechenyi Istvan University, Hungary
Jolita Ralyte   University of Geneva, Switzerland
Isabel Ramos   University of Minho, Portugal
Krassen Stefanov   University of Sofia, Bulgaria
A. Min Tjoa   Vienna University of Technology, Austria
Maria Wimmer   Koblenz University, Germany
Doug Vogel   City University, Hong Kong

Table of Contents

EGES Session 4: Back-End Transformation

EGES Session 5: New Applications

Part 2: Global Information Systems Processes (GISP)

GISP Session 1: Global Case Studies on Process Design Issues

GISP Session 2: Globalized Process Design

Part 1

E-Government and E-Services (EGES)

EGES Preface

The E-Government and E-Services (EGES) Conference at WCC 2010 was a co-operation of a number of groups that already have well-established activities in the field of e-government, e-governance, e-business, etcetera. Notably IFIP working group 8.5 (Information Systems in Public Administration) IFIP working group 6.11 (Communication, Information and Security Aspects of E-Business, E-services and E-society) and the CSI SIG on E-Governance (Computer Society of India Special Interest Group on E-Governance) joined forces with the Program Co-chairs to make this stream of the IFIP World Computer Congress indeed outstanding and challenging. At this event, contributions with perspectives from researchers, practitioners and policymakers were presented. Looking at these three angles has led to new perspectives and a better understanding of the challenges and opportunities that come with developing and implementing e-government services and applications. With this new area of IT applications, there is a great need to share good practices across different parts of the world – the developed world and the emerging economies, the domains of government and business, and also to promote academic and research work to build the theoretical foundations for this field. This field has great potential to improve delivery of services from governments to citizens and interaction between different parts of government and public administration, between government and businesses, and of course between government and citizens. We hope this conference will be seen a step towards addressing the digital divide and rural–urban divide.

Twelve papers from seven countries, one invited speaker and a panel session addressed a wide spectrum of interesting topics, divided into five themes: interoperability, participation, adoption and diffusion, back end transformation and new applications. The number of papers was limited due to a strict reviewing process which ensured high-quality contributions. The acceptance rate for EGES 2010 was 33%. We thank all contributors, the Program Committee members and all reviewers for their efforts and commitment. Without them EGES would not have happened.

We refrain from mentioning the details of the papers and from highlighting a few of them. They are all worth reading and therefore we encourage the reader to do just that. We would also like to mention the effort it takes to compile the proceedings, a valuable document that provides worthwhile reading and an archival document of the event. Similar to compiling a high-quality program, producing high-quality proceedings like the one you are reading now is a challenge. We thank the colleagues that took up this challenge and succeeded.

As mentioned above, EGES 2010 was a co-operation between different working groups and specialist groups. E-government in all its aspects is a typical example of an interdisciplinary issue that deserves such co-operation. Let us continue with this.

September 2010

Marijn Janssen
Winfried Lamersdorf
Lalit Sawhney
Leon Strous

EGES Session 1:
Interoperability

Narrowing the Gap between Open Standards Policy and Practice: The Dutch E-Government Experience

Rutger Lammers[1,2], Erwin Folmer[1, 2,3], and Michel Ehrenhard[2]

[1] The Netherlands Open in Connection, The Hague, The Netherlands
[2] University of Twente, Enschede, The Netherlands
[3] TNO Information and Communication Technology, Enschede, The Netherlands
{rutger.lammers,erwin.folmer}@noiv.nl

Abstract. Interoperability in the public sector can be improved by the use of open standards. Nonetheless, the openness of standards in government policies is debatable. This paper introduces the Dutch government policy on open standards, and will introduce a multi-dimensional view (and model) on openness rather than a one-dimensional strict definition. Applicability of the multi-dimensional model is tested in a case study, which demonstrates that this model has value for standardization organizations active in the government domain. In future cases the model helps in understanding how government-related standardization organizations can influence openness in a situation-specific way and the model therefore narrows the gap between open standards policy and practice.

Keywords: standards, standardization, open, e-government, policy, interoperability.

1 Introduction

High on the Dutch government's agenda is the creation of an innovative, competitive and enterprising economy. To achieve this goal the government has developed a policy in which it states that the governments needs to be a service-oriented and a client-friendly partner [1][2][11][15]. Important for the realization of this policy is that the IT infrastructure of the public sector is flexible [15]. To achieve flexibility, interoperability between governments and businesses, between governments and citizens and between government bodies themselves is an essential condition [2][15]. We define interoperability as the degree to which an information system is able to exchange information with other systems, in such a way that the meaning of information (semantics) does not change [2][15]. Interoperability provides a environment in which various systems can communicate with each other, not only syntactical, but also shared semantics. Therefore interoperability implies a common language between systems, which results in governmental supplier-independence, digital sustainability and transparency [11][15].

1.1 Purpose of This Paper

Within this paper open standards are seen as a mean to achieve the goal of interoperability. We will explain why a more sophisticated approach is needed than just a strict

M. Janssen et al. (Eds.): EGES/GISP 2010, IFIP AICT 334, pp. 7–18, 2010.

definition of what constitutes an open standard. Every situation is unique and a situation-specific process will results in a better fit of a standard. The purpose of this paper is to gain more insight in the openness of standards. Therefore, the central question of this paper is: "How can the openness of an open standard be influenced?" The unit of analysis in this report is a standard, but since the openness of a standards greatly depends on the process surrounding the standard, the framework may be generalized to the degree of openness of the standard developing organization (SDO) as a whole.

In this paper we answer this question by

1) Introducing the Dutch policy on open standards (chapter 2);
2) Defining a model on openness (chapter 3);
3) Operationalizing the model to make it useful for practice (chapter 4);
4) Using the operationalized model to analyze the openness of the StUF standard.
5) Discussing the results of this case study and drawing conclusions.

However, first the concepts of interoperability and open standards will be discussed briefly.

1.2 Interoperability

Interoperability within the public sector can be achieved via various mechanisms. One way to achieve interoperability is by only using information systems from a single vendor [2]. These systems will most probably be able to perfectly exchange information with each other, by means of a proprietary interface between the systems. But, as the current IT portfolio of the public sector is very heterogeneous, and the sector is characterized by a plethora of different systems, this is not a realistic solution [11][15]. Moreover, single-vendor interoperability will not contribute to supplier-independence because the use of an proprietary interface by another vendor is usually a costly and complex process. Another mechanism to achieve interoperability is the use of open standards [11][18]. Standards are about collectively agreeing on the specifications for the interfaces between application, services, systems and networks that interact. Open standards differ from proprietary standards because participating in the process of developing, using and maintaining such a standard is in principle open to and freely accessible for everyone. The Dutch government has chosen to prefer open standards above proprietary standard, mainly to achieve interoperability within its IT architecture [1][2][11]. This paper focuses on standards for data exchange. These standards relate to technical and semantic interoperability and not so much to organizational interoperability [20].

1.3 Open Standards

'Open standard' is a broad term and in literature many definitions of an open standard are given [5][3][10]. There is a need for a more sophisticated approach to describing and examining open standards than just a one-dimensional and rigid definition. For the Dutch government it is essential to understand which parameters play an essential role in the openness of a standard. Understanding the parameters of openness contributes to the founded and deliberate selection and/or development of an open standard. The requirements to the parameters of openness will depend on the situation, since not every standard needs to be open on all aspects. For instance, the TCP/IP protocol does not need to have a very open change process, since most people are only interested in the open use of this standard. But there are also standards for which other aspects of openness are more important [5].

Standards are developed and maintained by a standard developing organization (SDO's). Many SDOs exist, ranging from formal standardization organizations such as ISO to fora such as W3C. The internal process of developing and maintaining a standard within these organizations varies. Naturally, the degree of openness of the process influences the degree of openness of a standard.

2 Dutch Policy on Open Standards

To stimulate the use of open standards and to guide the change process, the Dutch government has initiated the action plan "The Netherlands Open in Connection" (Dutch abbreviation: NOiV), which consists of several action lines resulting in three objectives [1][11]:

1. Increase interoperability of information system in the Dutch public sector by accelerating the use of open standards
2. Reduce dependence on suppliers in the use of ICT through faster introduction of open standards
3. Promote a level playing field in the software market by using open standards

The Dutch government intends to encourage the use of open standards within the public and semi-public sector. The key focus is: use open standards, unless there is a very good reason why this is not possible, and indicate when open standards will indeed be implemented. This is the principle of 'comply or explain, and commit'. Through this principle the use of open standards will be given a firm foundation.

2.1 Actors Related to Dutch Policy

Figure 1 gives more insight in the relations between organizations that are concerned with the execution of the Dutch policy on the use of open standards.

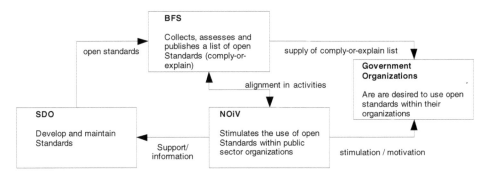

Fig. 1. Actors related to Dutch policy

2.1.1 The Bureau Forum Standardization (BFS)

In order to be able to implement the government's policy, a process of selecting and applying open standards based on a clear framework for interoperability should be determined. This is done by the Bureau Forum Standardization (BFS) [2][12]: a program office that selects the open standards that fall under the rule 'comply or explain, and commit'. BFS selects standards for the 'comply or explain, and commit' list. BFS maintains two separate lists of open standards:

1. A list of 'comply-or-explain' standards. These standards are often not yet widely used within the Dutch public sector, but the use of these standards is mandatory. The standards on this list are usually semantic standards, like SETU (procurement), XBRL (finance) and StUF (administrative) and these standards are often a specific instance of a global standard (like SETU, which is a location-specific version of HR-XML).
2. A list of "frequently applied standards", standards which are widely used in the architecture of information systems. These 'defacto' standards are often technical, world-wide standards located at the lower layers in the OSI reference model, like the TCP/IP-protocol, SMTP et cetera. This list helps purchasers in the public sector in tendering among others.

2.1.2 NOiV and Action Lines

The Dutch policy on the use of open standards consists of several action lines organized in the program NOiV [11]. Together these action lines contribute to the three objectives of the government's policy on open standards. Relevant action lines[1] are discussed shortly.

Action line 1 – The Bureau Forum Standardization (BFS) publishes a basis list of open standards which is necessary for implementation of the 'comply or explain, and commit' principle [12][2].

Action line 2 – Institutions in the public and semi-public sector will introduce the 'comply or explain, and commit' principle for ICT orders. Public sector bodies and institutions are themselves responsible for the application of 'comply or explain, and commit', using self self-policing measures.

- Comply: apply established open standards to orders for new IT systems or rebuilds and IT contract extension.
- Explain: exception criteria are: no open standard is available for the desired functionality; the open standard is not supported by multiple suppliers and on several platforms; conduct of business and/or service provision would be unacceptably jeopardized, including in terms of security or international agreements would be broken.
- Commit: give preference to the application of open standards so that an exception criterion is no longer applicable.

---

[1] The action plan also includes action lines on the adoption of open source software (action line 7-13). But, as this paper only considers open standards, these action lines will not be discussed further.

Action line 3 – BFS prepares a Dutch interoperability framework.
Action line 4 – IT orders can be voluntarily examined for advice.
Action line 5 – Enforcement via monitoring and ranking.
Action line 6 – Central governments support ODF.

In summary, this Dutch policy makes the use open standards mandatory for all (semi) public organizations.

3   Open Standards Definitions and Models

Openness is not a black or white situation, and whatever definition is chosen, it is arbitrary. For example, take the criterion of the free or nominal fee for a standard, also discussed by Rada [17]. Imagine that we have to pay 20 euro for a standards specification. Some will call this an open and free specification (nominal price), others will say this does not satisfy the definition of open and free specification. And how will this change if the amount will be changed to 200 or 20.000 euro's? But all agree on that a standard for which 20 euro should be paid is less open than a standard that can be freely downloaded. Although open standards itself are without doubt, a lot of debate is going on about the definition of an open standards. We will not go into that discussion, simply because it distracts attention on how to achieve more open standards. The discussion is also the other way around: it focuses on creating a definition to which many as open perceived standards comply. The definition is adapted to current practice. In our opinion the definition of a standards should be more transparent and adaptable to a specific situation. However we argue that the definition is not that interesting when the government tries to improve the openness of standards. For that use a broad view on openness is needed instead of a strict and small definition of openness.

3.1   Open Standard Definition Used by Dutch Governments

The definition of open standards which is used by Dutch government complies with the definition which is used by the European Commission as set by the IDABC program[2]) [7][11]:

- The standard is approved and will be maintained by a non-profit organization, and ongoing development will be on the basis of an open decision-making process that is accessible for all interested parties.
- The standards is published and the specification document for the standard is freely available or can be obtained for a nominal contribution. It must be possible for everyone to copy it, make it available and use it, free or for a nominal price
- The intellectual property – regarding any patents that may be present – of the standard or parts thereof is irrevocably made available on a royalty-free basis;
- There are no restrictions on reuse of the standard.

---

[2] IDABC stands for Interoperable Delivery of European eGovernment Services to public Administrations, Business and Citizens.

In addition to this definition, the government uses the following two specification in elaborating the action plan:

- Open Specification: an open specification is one that is published and whose specification document is freely available. Alternatively, it may be available for a nominal contribution. It must be possible for everyone to copy it, make it available and use it, free or for a nominal price
- Free Specification: a free specification is an open specification that is free of legal restrictions making its use and distribution difficult. The intellectual property – regarding any patents that may be present – of the standard or parts thereof is irrevocably made available on a royalty-free basis.

3.2   Existing Research on Open Standards

A scan of existing literature on open standards showed that in general there are very few models and definitions that exceed a rigid definition. There is a need for a more sophisticated in-depth model which describes the dimension on which a standards can be positioned. One very useful model on open standards comes from Krechmer [5]. Krechmer introduces ten requirements on open standards. These ten requirements function as dimensions in which a certain open standard can be positioned. This dimensioning helps in shifting the discussion on open standards from a dichotomous black or white situation to a more nuanced situation. This helps in achieving a better task technology fit as discussed in chapter one. However, it remains unclear how Krechmer derives these ten requirements, why there are ten and moreover, each requirements leaves a lot of freedom of interpretation. Another useful model comes from Andersen [4]. This work is related to the ten requirements described by Krechmer. Andersen made an operationalization on the openness of open standards based on desk research. Other definitions and models are introduced in table 1. The dimensions which are used in this table are derived from Krechmer. The work of Krechmer forms the theoretical basis of this research. Since each definition can be mapped to one or more requirements, the requirements of Krechmer is the most complete set of dimensions.

Table 1. Models and definitions on open standards

Dimension (Krechmer) [5]	Andersen [4]	Perens [13]	NOiV [11]	IDABC [7]	Dimension (Krechmer) [5]	Andersen [4]	Perens [13]	NOiV [11]	IDABC [7]
Open Meeting	x	x	x	x	Open Change	x	x		
Consensus	x	x	x	x	Open Documents	x	x	x	x
Due Process	x	x			Open Interface		x		
Open IPR	x	x	x	x	Open Access	x	x	x	x
One World	x				On-going Support	x			

As stated earlier, the current quantity of academic literature on dimensions of open standards is low. When we compare the available literature, the work of Krechmer is the most complete and most cited work. Therefore the ten requirements are already very useful in practice and they will therefore function as the basis of this paper.

4   Operationalization of the Model on Openness

Although defined dimensions are needed, they will become even more valuable when they are operationalized to (measurable) consequences in practice. As shown in table 1, the dimensions which are used by Krechmer to analyze the openness of standards have a broader view than others. Therefore, the operationalization of openness will be based on these ten dimensions (requirements in terms of Krechmer). These ten dimensions can be interpreted as a must-have to be labeled as an open standard and are therefore very useful in determining at a first glance to which degree an open standard is really open. However, if we interpret the ten requirements as ten dimensions on which a standard can be positioned, we need more than just the dimensions. For example, it could be discussed what exactly an open meeting is. Is everybody free to join meetings? How are invitations for these meetings arranged? So, to further improve the usability of the ten requirements on open standards we will make a first step in the operationalization of the requirements, which results in an model useful in practice.

4.1   Method

To identify variables for the ten dimensions on open standards a workshop was organized and also the work of Andersen [4] was used. The first part of the workshop had the character of a informal brainstorm session in which five experts on open standards were invited to come up with variables for the ten dimensions on open standards. These experts have a background in standardization, varying from developers, implementers and users.

The ten dimensions were discussed step-wise, following the format of "if you think of this requirement, what comes up to measure it?" The second part of the workshop consisted of a clustering of the results from the workshop, following the structure of the ten dimensions. During the brainstorm and clustering we followed Langley [19]. This resulted in three to five variables per requirement, which are considered valid by the experts. The results of the workshop were combined with existing literature on openness of standards, especially the work of Andersen. This synthesis resulted in the model on openness of standards.

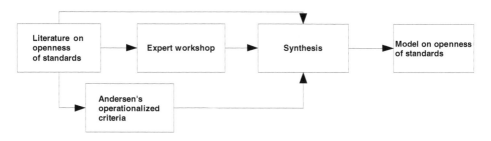

Fig. 2. Process used in this research paper

Table 2. Model derived in this research

Criterion	variables	Score
1. Open meeting	1 No entrance fee	0 / 1 / 2
All may participate in the standards development process.	2 Suitable meeting location	0 / 1 / 2
	3 Open for all	0 / 1 / 2
	4 Open calander	0 / 1 / 2
2. Consensus	1 Open and stated decision process	0 / 1 / 2
During a meeting all interests are discussed and agreement found, no domination.	2 Procedure if no consensus reached	0 / 1 / 2
	3 Equal voting rights	0 / 1 / 2
	4 External review	0 / 1 / 2
	5 Open agenda	0 / 1 / 2
3. Due process	1 Stated appeal process on technology	0 / 1 / 2
Balloting and appeals during process may be used to find resolution.	2 Stated appeal process on process	0 / 1 / 2
	3 Independent chairman	0 / 1 / 2
	4 Higher instance for appeals	0 / 1 / 2
4. Open IPR	1 Right regime published	0 / 1 / 2
IPR related to the standard is available to implementers.	2 Level of IPR (free vs. patents)	0 / 1 / 2
	3 Reciprocal licenses	0 / 1 / 2
5. One world	1 Fit with other standards	0 / 1 / 2
The standard is used for the same capability, world-wide.	2 Location-independent	0 / 1 / 2
6. Open documents	1 Open drafts	0 / 1 / 2
Standards committee drafts and completed standards documents are easily available for implementation and use.	2 Open specifications	0 / 1 / 2
	3 Open meeting notes	0 / 1 / 2
	4 Open procedural documents	0 / 1 / 2
	5 Open redistribution	0 / 1 / 2
7. Open interface	1 Back- and forwards compatible	0 / 1 / 2
Standards supports migration and allows proprietary advantage but standardized interfaces are not hidden or controlled.	2 Implementations compatible with specification	0 / 1 / 2
8. Open access	1 Conformance testing	0 / 1 / 2
Standards is equipped with objective conformance mechanisms for implementation testing and user evaluation.	2 Conformance validation	0 / 1 / 2
	3 Conformance certification	0 / 1 / 2
	4 Disability support	0 / 1 / 2
9. On-going support	1 Support throughout life cycle	0 / 1 / 2
Standards are supported until user interest ceases.		
10. Open change	1 Coverage of other dimensions during change	0 / 1 / 2
All changes in the standards are presented and agreed		

4.2 Results

The synthesis of both workshop results and literature resulted in concrete variables for the ten dimensions on open standards. The result is a method, which is presented in Table 2. The ten dimensions of Table 1 are operationalized in one or more variables (some dimensions could not be operationalized further into two or more variables).

Each variable can be scored, using a three-point scale:

- 0: in documentation related to the standard, nothing can be found regarding this variable or it is explicitly stated no action related to this variable is present.
- 1: documentation related to the standard touches upon this variable in a positive way, but not fully compliant to the line of reasoning behind the variable. Improvement is possible.
- 2: documentation related to the standard explicitly touches upon the line of reasoning behind the variable. Improvement is not necessary.

When using this model to score a standard, the most open source of information will be official documentation by the SDO on a website. So, if information regarding a variable cannot be found on-line at the SDO's website, a 0 is applied. Of course, information stated in official documentation can differ from the actual, real-life situation. This bias can be bypassed by doing observations during meetings et cetera, but this method comprises easily accessible information. Background information on the workshop results and descriptions of the variables can be found on [16].

5 Case Study

To examine to usability and applicability of the operationalized model, it was tested in a case study. For this purpose the open standard STuF was used. STuF is an abbreviation of standard exchange format and it is an open standard which is used by the Dutch government, especially by municipalities, for the purpose of exchanging basic civilian information (like addresses) within and between information systems [14]. STuF is on the list 'comply-or-explain' standards as discussed in chapter two [12]. More information about STuF can be found in [19].

The results are based on information published in official documentation. The official documentation was found on the website of EGEM-ITEAMS, which is the SDO of STuF [14][8][9]. We chose to measure the openness of STuF based only on official on-line documentation since this contributes to the openness of a standards. Maybe the openness of STuF as mentioned in documentation differs from the actual

Table 3. Scores of STuF using the model

Criterion	Average score	Criterion	Average score
Open Meeting	1	Open Documents	1
Consensus	1.8	Open Interface	0.5
Due Process	0.4	Open Access	0.5
Open IPR	2	On-going Support	2
One World	1	Open Change	1.25
Total average	1.1		

openness in practice. This could be overcome by using other techniques like interviews or observations, but these techniques are very intensive and are therefore not appropriate to use in our framework. Some variables are 0, simply because no explicit information could be found in documentation. In practice it could be that a variable is actually implemented correctly, but since it is not documented it scores a 0. Explicit description in documentation contributes to the openness of a standard. The results show that the STuF standards scores well in Open IPR and On-going Support, these are effectively addressed in the STuF standard. Of concern is the Due Process, which scores a 0.4. This can be explained by the fact that in case of disputes no balloting procedures are described. As the adoption STuF is growing, the likelihood of disputes of any kind is rising. Other points of concern are Open Interface and Open Access, both scoring a 0.5. Issues with version management and compatibility are related to score on Open Interface, while the absence of conformance services are related to Open Access.

6 Conclusions

This research shows that standards which – by their SDO – are claimed to be open, are not always fully open. These standards may actually be open on several, but not all, dimensions. For the Dutch government the model which is constructed in this research is useful, because standards that are claimed to be open can be analyzed for their degree of openness. This avoids situations in which the policy (use of open standards) is not in line with practice (open standards that are in fact not that open). In this case, STuF scores a 1.1, whereas this is one of the most important semantic open standards used within the Dutch government. Usage of the model indicates which aspects of STuF can be made more open, and which aspects are really open. The study provides a useful 'checklist' for government bodies in determining whether to put a standard on the 'comply or explain, and commit' list. This narrows the gap between policy on open standards and actual practice.

This research is also useful for SDO's who want to improve the openness of their standards or to have at least a certain idea which parameters are adaptable to influence the openness of their standards. As said earlier, open standards do not always have to be the open in all dimensions, since certain dimensions are not that important in a specific situation. But, apart from the outcomes, all dimensions related to openness should at the very least be discussed.

Next to having a better view on the openness of a standard the model can be used to compare the openness of standards. For example, if an organization chooses to only use open standards for a specific situation, this model could be used to make a well-based choice for an open standard when competing open standards might exist. But also the scoring of the StUF standard would be more valuable when compared to the scoring of other standards.

Another useful application of this model is to rank SDO's organizations. Often, these organizations are concerned with setting standards for the use in public sector situations. For government organizations these standards are often mandatory by law. It might be interesting how `closed' these standards actually are. In certain cases the policy on interoperability might collide with legal obligations. If a government wants to stimulate the use of open standards, this model could be useful by making visible how closed certain mandatory standards really are. This might add momentum to open standards and interoperability.

7 Further Research

This research is a first attempt at operationalizing the dimensions of openness, focusing on the applicability of such an operationalized model. Further improvements and underpinning of the model is needed, including improvement of the measurement scales. For example, more research can be conducted on the degree of mutual exclusiveness and collective exhaustion of the coverage of open standards by the ten dimensions. Also more case studies would be welcome to iteratively improve the model and to gather a database with results.

References

1. Netherlands Ope. In: Connection (NoiV), `http://noiv.nl/`
2. Bureau Forum Standardization (BFS), `http://www.open-standaarden.nl`
3. Rosen, L.: Open Standards,
   `http://www.rosenlaw.com/DefiningOpenStandards.pdf`
4. Andersen, P.: Evaluation of Ten Standard Setting Organizations with Regard to Open Standards. In: Special Study, IDC 2008 (2008)
5. Krechmer, K.: Open standards: a call for change. IEEE Comm. Mag. 47(5), 88–94 (2009)
6. Langley, A.: Strategies for theorizing from process data. Academy of Management Review 24, 691–710 (1999)
7. IDABC. Documentation on the European Interoperability Framework,
   `http://ec.europa.eu/idabc/en/document/3473`
8. EGEM-iteams: Beheermodel StUF, `http://www.egem-iteams.nl/system/files/StUF+Beheermodel+en+releasebeleid.pdf`
9. Bureau Forum Standardization: Expert advice StUF, `http://www.egem-iteams.nl/system/files/Expertadvies_StUF_0.pdf`
10. de Vries, H.: Standards for the Nation. Kluwer Academic Publishers, Dordrecht (1999)
11. NOiV. An action plan for the use of Open Standards and Open Source Software in the public and semi-public sector
12. BFS. List of 'comply or explain, and commit' standards, `http://www.open-standaarden.nl/fileadmin/os/documenten/OS%20lijst%20open%20standaarden%20voor%20pas%20toe%20of%20leg%20uit.pdf`
13. Perens, B.: Open Standards: Principles and Practice,
    `http://perens.com/OpenStandards/Definition.html`
14. EGEM-iteams: website STuF, `http://www.egem-iteams.nl/stuf`
15. Fomin, V.V., Pedersen, M.K., de Vries, H.J.: Open Standards and Government Policy: Results of a Delphi Survey. Communications of the Association for Information Systems, April 22, 459–484 (2008)
16. NOiV: Wiki on Open Standards,
    `http://wiki.noiv.nl/xwiki/bin/view/NOiV/Open+Standaarden`
17. Rada, R., Berg, J.: Standards: Free or Sold? Communications of the ACM 38(2), 23–27 (1995)
18. Zhu, K., Kraemer, K.L., Gurbaxani, V., Xu, S.X.: Migration to Open-Standard Interorganizational Systems: Network Effects, Switching Costs, and Path Dependency. MIS Quarterly (August 2006) (30:Special issue)

19. EGEM-ITEAMS. Intelligent standards for municipalities,
    `http://egem-iteams.nl/system/files/`
    `Boekje_verdieping_Malmo.pdf`
20. Decker, S., Melnik, S., Van Harmelen, F., Fensel, D., Klein, M., Broekstra, J., Erdmann, M., Horrocks, I.: Semantic Web: The roles of XML and RDF. IEEE Internet Computing 4(5), 63–74 (2000)

Appendix – In-depth Scoring of STuF

Variable	0/1/2	Elaboration
1.1	0	No information found in both [9] and [8]
1.2	0	No information found in both [9] and [8]
1.3	2	In principle open for everyone who's interested, [9] page 10, [8] page 7, [8] page 9
1.4	2	Meeting dates can be found on line.[8] multiple pages in appendix A
2.1	2	Decision process is thoroughly described, [8] page 7 [8] multiple pages in appendix A
2.2	2	Majority decides if no consensus, [8] multiple pages in appendix A
2.3	1	Every stakeholder has voting rights, but equality is not explicitly stated, [8] page 16
2.4	2	External reviewers are invited to comment, [8] page 8, [8] page 15
2.5	2	Attendees can put topics on agenda, [8] page 11
3.1	2	Appeals are possible in case of technology issues, [8] page 12 [8] page 16
3.2	0	No information found in both [9] and [8]
3.3	0	No information found in both [9] and [8]
3.4	0	No information found in both [9] and [8]
3.5	0	No information found in both [9] and [8]
4.1	2	Rights regime is published, [8] page 9
4.2	2	Royalty-free, [8] page 9
4.3	2	Licenses on (subsets of) the standard are reciprocal, [8] page 9
5.1	2	The fit with related standard is described, [9] page 11 [8] page 8
5.2	0	No information found in both [9] and [8]
6.1	1	Drafts are published, but it's unsure if this is publicly [8] page 8
6.2	2	All specification can be found online, [8] page 9, [8] page 8
6.3	0	No information found in both [9] and [8]
6.4	2	Procedural documents can be found online, [8] page 9, [8] multiple pages in appendix A
6.5	1	Reciprocal licenses (4.3) imply this, but not explicitly stated
7.1	0	No information found in both [9] and [8]
7.2	2	A conformance certificate is applied. [8] page 17
8.1	0	No information found in both [9] and [8]
8.2	0	No information found in both [9] and [8]
8.3	2	Conformance certification is available, page 11 [8]
8.4	0	Not found
9.1	2	Standard is supported throughout standards life cycle [8] page 19
10.1	0	For example not the dimensions that score low

Evaluation of WS-* Standards Based Interoperability of SOA Products for the Hungarian e-Government Infrastructure

Balázs Simon, Zoltán László, Balázs Goldschmidt, Károly Kondorosi,
Péter Risztics, and László Bacsa

Budapest University of Technology and Economics,
Department of Control Engineering and Information Technology
Magyar tudósok körútja 2,
1117 Budapest, Hungary
{sbalazs,laszlo,balage,kondor}@iit.bme.hu,
{risztics,bacsa}@ik.bme.hu

Abstract. The proposed architecture of the Hungarian e-Government Framework, mandating the functional co-operation of independent organizations, puts special emphasis on interoperability. WS-* standards have been created to reach uniformity and interoperability in the common middleware tasks for web services such as security, reliable messaging and transactions. These standards, however, while existing for some time, have implementations slightly different in quality. In order to assess implementations, thorough tests should be performed, and relevant test cases ought to be accepted. For selecting mature SOA products for e-Government application, a methodology of such an assessment is needed. We have defined a flexible and extensible test bed and a set of test cases for SOA products considering three aspects: compliance with standards, interoperability and development support.

Keywords: Web services, testing; interoperability, WS-* standards, e-Government.

1 Introduction

Similarly to numerous other countries all over the world, Hungary has its own strategy for e-government development [10]. Although Hungary has middle-ranked position in the level of e-government services [11], strategic studies and assessments showed that one of the primary deficiencies is the lack of interoperable, multi- and cross-organizational back-office functionality.

Several interoperability frameworks have been accepted by national, or union-level governments or organizations: e-Government Interoperability Framework (eGIF) in UK, [8], Federal Enterprise Architecture (FEA) in USA, [12], Standards and Architectures for e-Government Applications (SAGA) in Germany [13], European Interoperability Framework (EIF) in EU [7] etc. For interoperable cross-sector collaboration the concept of Seamless e-Government has been introduced to describe the ideal model of delivering public services [9].

M. Janssen et al. (Eds.): EGES/GISP 2010, IFIP AICT 334, pp. 19–31, 2010.
© IFIP International Federation for Information Processing 2010

A similar effort has been started in Hungary by establishing the Hungarian e-Government Framework (HeGF) [14]. The Framework proposes a SOA-based e-Government Service Bus for the implementation of the integrated back-office services. The architecture specifies three layers: process-level layer, service-level layer and message-level layer. The process-level layer orchestrates cross-organizational activities and services. The service-level layer defines interfaces, manages the basic operations, handles security, federated identity and management aspects. It is based on WS-* standards, and a wide variety of products promising conformity to them. The message layer is based on a message oriented middleware to provide reliability.

Early laboratory pilots showed the difficulties of the integration of heterogeneous components on the basis of WS-* standards. In some cases products did not follow the standards, in others poor documentation caused difficulties. Two questions arose at this point: a) are the SOA products mature enough for e-government use; b) how to select the best product at a future tender.

The rest of this paper describes a methodology developed to evaluate the interoperable behavior of SOA products and the quality of the WS-* standards implementations. Our goal was only the evaluation of the proposed methodology itself, not pre-selection of product, or making a ranking at this stage. The test cases copied from the architecture specification in the HeGF are listed in Table 1.

After presenting related work in section II, several SOA products selected for test are introduced in section III. Section IV enlists the tested WS-* standards. Section V describes the test cases. Section VI specifies the test environment. Section VII presents the test results. Section VIII concludes the paper and describes future work.

Table 1. Test cases from HeGF

Requirement		Corresponding test case
Message format	M	HTTP, SOAP 1.2
Exception handling	M	HTTP, SOAP 1.2 faults
Addressing	M	HTTP, SOAP 1.2, WS-A 1.0
Asynchronous messages	M	HTTP, SOAP 1.2, WS-A 1.0, async
Message level security	M	HTTP, SOAP 1.2, WS-A 1.0, WS-SC
Transport level security	M	HTTPS, SOAP 1.2
Binary transmission	R	HTTP, SOAP 1.2, MTOM
Reliable messaging	O	HTTP, SOAP 1.2, WS-A 1.0, WS-RM
Short-term transactions	O	HTTP, SOAP 1.2, WS-A 1.0, WS-AT
Message format	O	HTTP, SOAP 1.1
Addressing	O	HTTP, SOAP 1.1, WS-A 1.0
Addressing	O	HTTP, SOAP 1.1, WS-A 2004/08
Asynchronous messages	O	HTTP, SOAP 1.1, WS-A 1.0
Binary transmission	O	HTTP, SOAP 1.1, MTOM
Short-term transactions	O	HTTP, SOAP 1.1, WS-A 1.0, WS-AT

M=Mandatory, R=Recommended, O=Optional,
WS-A=WS-Addressing, WS-SC=WS-SecureConversation,
WS-RM=WS-ReliableMessaging, WS-AT=WS-AtomicTransaction.

2 Related Work

2.1 WS-I Basic Profile

The various WS-* standards provide too many options from which the implementers can choose what to implement. This freedom makes interoperability much harder since different vendors may choose different options to implement. Therefore the Web Services Interoperability (WS-I) Organization [1] was formed by a wide range of companies and standards development organizations to provide best practices called profiles for a selected set of standards. They also define test cases and create testing tools to verify the various implementations against these profiles. Software vendors participating in WS-I usually implement the test cases in their own products.

WS-I defines profiles for the most important WS-* standards. Basic Profile covers SOAP, WSDL, WS-Addressing and MTOM. Basic Security Profile aims WS-Security with different Security Token Profiles including SAML. Reliable Security Profile deals with WS-ReliableMessaging and WS-SecureConversation. WS-Coordination and WS-AtomicTransaction, however, are not yet included in any profiles.

The advantage of WS-I is that it covers a lot of issues regarding WS-* standards, it resolves ambiguities, it defines a lot of test cases and it also implements them. The source codes are available for public access; they can be downloaded from the WS-I web site. All the major software vendors participate in the WS-I Organization, thus the profiles defined are a results of a consensus and are expected to be supported in their products as well.

The disadvantage of WS-I is that its profiles are a result of a slow agreement process, therefore it always lags behind the newest versions of the WS-* standards. The implementations of the test cases are not up-to-date; they cannot keep up with the acquisitions in the market and the rapid evolution of the products. The test cases focus mainly on verifying the conformance to the profiles and are not derived from real customer needs.

2.2 Interop Events

While Windows Communication Foundation (WCF, codename Indigo) was being developed, Microsoft organized a series of events called Interop Plug-Fests for SOA vendors to implement a set of test cases by every participant and then execute the tests between each other. In the previous years numerous Interop Plug-Fests have been held and the web services endpoints of WCF are still available [2]. The close cooperation of Microsoft and Sun Microsystems has led to a very high level of interoperability between WCF and Metro, the web services stack of Sun.

The advantage of these Interop Plug-Fests is that there were very detailed predefined test cases for the selected WS-* standards and the executed tests resulted in immediate feedbacks to the vendors. The test specifications are still available for download. Unfortunately, most of the web pages about these Plug-Fests are no longer available, the evolution of the products is no longer followed and also the source codes cannot be downloaded.

2.3 Web Services Test Forum

Web Services Test Forum (WSTF) [3] is an open community founded by a couple of software vendors to provide test scenarios and a multi-vendor testing environment. Customers can also join the community to suggest test cases based on their needs. After accepting the test cases members of the community can implement them and provide web services endpoints to the public.

The advantage of WSTF is that it is less formal than a standards body; therefore, it is more flexible. Members of WSTF do not have to wait for the standards development organizations to complete the standards or the final version of SOA products to be released to start implementing the test cases. The source code is also accessible for the community. The current test clients provide a user interface only, no automated tests are defined. Although some test cases are already available for the various WS-* standards, not all of them are implemented yet, since the community was formed at the end of 2008. Unfortunately, Microsoft and Sun Microsystems (although acquired by the community member: Oracle) were not among the founders and Microsoft still has not joined the community yet.

Another similar initiative to WSTF is the Apache Stonehenge project [4] formed earlier than WSTF mainly by open-source vendors (Apache, WSO2, Red Hat), but Microsoft is also a participant and they also welcome other software vendors.

2.4 Other

Senthil et al. [5] examined how WS-I Basic Profile (WS-I BP) 1.0 addresses interoperability issues with the core web services standards (SOAP 1.1 and WSDL 1.1). They found that the efforts point to the right direction, however, there are some limitations, too. The main argument they brought up is that WS-I BP does not deal with such data types as float, decimal, date and time, and this can result in precision loss in interoperability scenarios.

Kuppuraju et al. [6] identified various aspects on how to test interoperability of SOA products based on a case study. They raised the issues but did not provide any solution: testing tools and test report generation are mentioned only as a future work. The main issues are compliance tests against WS-I profiles, integration tests for business processes, and performance tests. They also identified WS-* standards as a key to interoperability.

3 SOA Landscape

This section compares the set of products we selected for testing, but this set is far from complete since there are many more SOA products. The proposed test environment, however, is flexible and mature enough to extend the range of the current study to incorporate further products.

Table II. compares the selected products based on the following aspects: name, vendor name, application server name, Integrated Development Environment (IDE), web service API, web service stack implementation, supported programming languages, configuring WS-* protocols.

Other well-known SOA products subject of further investigation include FUSE from Iona based on CXF, the WSO2 SOA Platform based on Axis2, ActiveVOS from Active Endpoints, Intalio BPM from Intalio and also TIBCO Service Bus and Sonic ESB.

Table 2. Comparison of SOA products

name	vendor name	applica- tion server	IDE	WS API	WS stack	program language	configuration
WCF	Microsoft	IIS	Visual Studio	WCF	WCF	any .NET	custom XML
GlassFishESB	Sun	GlassFish	Netbeans	JAX-WS	Metro	Java	WS-Policy
RAD 7	IBM	WAS 7	RAD 7 (Eclipse based)	JAX-WS		Java	WS-Policy
WebLogic Suite	Oracle	WebLogic Server	JDeveloper	JAX-WS		Java	WS-Policy
JBoss	RedHat	JBoss AS	Eclipse	JAX-WS	Native (RedHat); Metro (Sun); CXF (Iona)	Java	custom XML; WS-Policy
Axis2	Apache	Tomcat	Eclipse	JAX-WS	Axis2 (WSO2)	Java	custom XML

Abbreviations: WCF = Windows Communication Foundation, IIS = Internet Information Services, RAD = Rational Application Developer, WAS = WebSphere Application Server, AS = Application Server.

4 WS-* Standards

This section gives a short overview of WS-* standards specified in the requirements of the Hungarian e-Government Infrastructure.

WS-Addressing (WS-A) raises addressing and routing specifications to message level thus makes them independent of the actual transport layer. The Message Transmission Optimization Mechanism (MTOM) defines how large binary data can be efficiently transmitted as part of a SOAP message. WS-ReliableMessaging (WS-RM) can minimize the impact of network communication problems. It can guarantee exactly-once message delivery and preserving the order of the messages. WS-Coordination and WS-AtomicTransaction (WS-AT) make specifying and committing transactions possible.

WS-Security is responsible for signing and encrypting parts of a SOAP message, and also for transmitting authorization tokens. WS-SecureConversation (WS-SC) is designed to support excessive encrypted message-exchange by maintaining a security context (similarly to SSL). WS-Trust defines means for issuing, renewing, exchanging and revoking security tokens by a Security Token Service (STS) (similarly to Kerberos) and makes federated authorization across security domains also possible mostly through SAML (Security Assertion Markup Language) assertions.

5 Test Aspects and Test Cases

In order to conduct testing three basic tasks were defined; each designed to be capable of assessing the existence or absence of functionalities selected for testing. For each task the functionalities checked and the relevant standards are listed. For compliance and interoperability testing both the input and the expected output parameters have been specified before actual testing was done.

5.1 Test Cases for Compliance

Calculator

The aim of this task is to test compliance with basic protocols and simple fault handling. A calculator application has to be created with the operations: addition, subtraction, multiplication and division. The tested standards are:

- SOAP 1.1 and SOAP 1.2 over HTTP
- SOAP 1.2 over HTTPS
- Fault handling with SOAP 1.2: when dividing by zero, MathFault exception is to be thrown.
- Ws-Addressing 1.0 and Ws-Addressing August 2004
- Ws-ReliableMessaging with SOAP 1.2: order of messages preserved; session properly closed.
- Ws-SecureConversation with SOAP 1.2: message level encryption and digital signature is to be applied, based on Basic256 (AES-256) algorithm. Authenticate both sides with X.509 certificates.
- WS-Trust, SAML: the different operations require different access rights provided by SAML tokens issued by a STS. (test case not yet implemented)

Asynchronous calculator

The aim of this task is the asynchronous version of the Calculator. The tested standards are:

- *WS-Addressing 1.0 with SOAP 1.1 and SOAP 1.2:* the server has to retrieve the addressing headers and use dynamic addressing when calling back the client.

Upload

This test is to check MTOM encoding compliance, by sending a 1MB file to the server. The tested standards are:

- MTOM with SOAP 1.1 and SOAP 1.2

Bank

The aim of the test is to check compliance with transaction standards. The task is to access a database through a web service. The server is a bank which provides services for modifying the balance of an account and getting the account's status. If the account number is non-existent, or during withdrawal the amount is greater than the balance, a specific BankFault exception is to be thrown. For repeatability automated SQL scripts have to be created for setting up the database. The tested standards are:

- *WS-AtomicTransaction and WS-Coordination over SOAP 1.1 and SOAP 1.2:* checking commit, rollback and exceptions. At the end of each transaction the correct amounts have to be found in the database.

5.2 Interoperability

To each service endpoint a corresponding client has to be created that tests this specific service. Clients are also web services and all have the same interface containing a single tester operation accepting the URL of the service to be called. This tester operation executes a functional test on the service observing the correct behavior, handling the expected faults and checking for unexpected exceptions resulting from protocol implementation mismatches. The return value of the operation indicates the success of the test. This method makes it possible to pair each client and each service from all the products corresponding to a given test case, and thus automatic tests can be run to check interoperability.

5.3 Development Support

This aspect refers to how products support development of web services. Different products provide different ways of WS-* protocol configuration. The task was to summarize and evaluate these possibilities.

6 Testing Environment

The testing environment was predefined and every product had to be installed and tested accordingly. This section summarizes the environment and the main problems which had to be solved.

The testing environment was built on five high-performance computers each of them capable of hosting multiple virtual machines. Each SOA product had to be installed on a separate virtual machine to avoid collisions with the others. The primary cause of collisions is that the different application servers use the same HTTP port, although in most cases these ports are reconfigurable.

For security tests X.509 certificates had to be issued for the services, clients and STSs. The certificates were generated as self-signing certificates using OpenSSL. Then they were installed in Windows with special access rights for IIS to access the private keys. The JDK had to be upgraded with the Unlimited Strength Jurisdiction Policy Files to be able to use longer keys for security. The public certificates were imported into the trust-stores of the Java products using keytool from the JDK. To import private certificates into key-stores a separate tool named pkcs12import had to be downloaded. To configure a transaction coordinator for WCF some special packages had to be installed in Windows. Also the WS-AT coordinators required the public certificates of the coordinators to be installed into the other products' trust-stores.

Predefined forms were specified for each task and each test. These forms had to be filled for every implementation. Additional forms were supplied for installation instructions and development problems.

In order to automate tests the clients also had to be created as web services, all of them providing the same interface having a single operation accepting the URL of the service to call. A simple testing tool has been created to pair each client with each service for a given test-case, and the results have been summarized in a table for each test-case.

7   Results and Evaluation

In order to validate the testing environment, including product-dependent components, forms, the automated testing program and testing methodology a series of tests have been performed. The test-cases mentioned in section V were implemented in the selected products. Both the client and service of each test case were realized as web services. The results of the tests based on the testing method described in sub-section V.B. are grouped into the following categories:

- **Passed:** the products participating in the test support the related standards and the result conforms to the expectations
- **Failed:** the products participating in the test support the related standards, but the cooperation between the parties failed for some reason: the client and the service were unable to produce the expected result
- **Not supported:** according to the documentation of the tested version of the product the given function is not supported
- **Not tested:** this feature was not supported or was undocumented in the tested version of the product, but according to the documentation of a newer version, the functionality is now supported

7.1   Compliance

In the first test session both the client and the service came from the same SOA product. This kind of configuration makes it possible to check compliance to the selected functionalities. There were 15 test cases for each of the 6 SOA products. From the 90

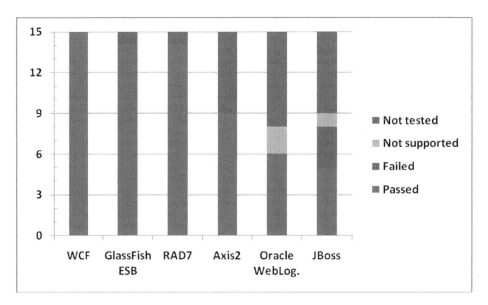

Fig. 1. Number of tests passed, failed, unsupported and untested grouped by products (products tested with themselves)

test runs 63 have passed, and only 3 have failed. The number of unsupported test cases was also 3. The relatively high number (21) of the untested results demonstrates that the SOA products are evolving rapidly.

It can be seen from Fig. 1. that WCF passed all the tests. GlassFish ESB and RAD7 also perform very well. The reason for the many untested results of the other three products is that they lacked detailed documentation at the time of the testing. Since then new versions have been released of them and also their documentations have gone through improvements, therefore, the tests have to be implemented and executed again.

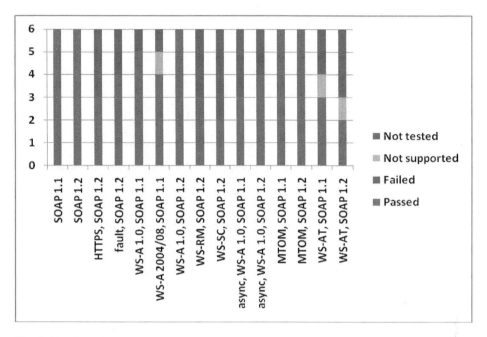

Fig. 2. Number of tests passed, failed, unsupported and untested grouped by test cases (products tested with themselves)

From Fig. 2. it can be inferred that the most supported standards are SOAP 1.1 and 1.2, WS-Addressing 1.0, and MTOM. WS-SC and WS-AT do not perform very well; they had only 2 successful runs each.

7.2 Interoperability

In the second test session the test cases were executed for each client-service pair of the SOA products (including themselves). This configuration can be used to check interoperability between different products. Having 15 test cases for 36 client-service pairs the total sum of tests is 540.

From Fig. 3. it can be seen that the results are very similar to the ones before, but more tests have failed. This means, that although the products perform well with themselves, there are still problems when communicating with the others. Another

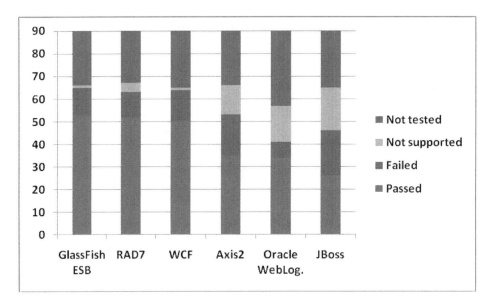

Fig. 3. Number of tests passed, failed, unsupported and untested grouped by products as services (products tested with each other)

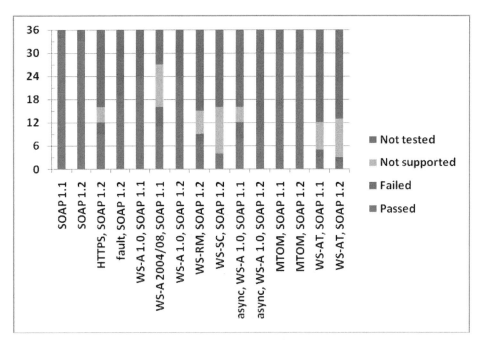

Fig. 4. Number of tests passed, failed, unsupported and untested grouped by test cases (products tested with each other)

interesting thing to note is that GlassFish ESB became the top one and WCF slid down to the third place. The reason for this is that GlassFish ESB is more permissive with the protocols, e.g. if a web service call having multiple MIME parts arrives, it will still be accepted even if MTOM is not enabled. WCF on the other hand is much stricter, and rejects every call that does not conform to the specified configuration.

Fig. 4. shows the results grouped by the test cases. It can be noted that the most and least supported standards are the same as before.

7.3 Development Support

For maintainable and interoperable development it is essential to have support for generating client proxies and service implementations from a WSDL. WCF has a tool named SvcUtil.exe, which generates service contracts as well as application configurations. JDK contains a similar tool named wsimport that does the same (less the configuration files) in the Java world. In the case of Metro the WSDL containing the bindings and policies serves directly as configuration file, too. Other JAX-WS API implementations usually rely also on wsimport, however, in most cases the configuration has to be done manually due to lack of built-in tool support.

WCF and JAX-WS implementations automatically generate WSDL-s for the deployed service endpoints. Authors have found that WS-Policy support is essential for interoperability since more complicated standards like WS-SecureConversation require many parameters, and setting them manually in a custom configuration to match the required values is very difficult and often results in unexpected errors. Some older SOA products lacked WS-Policy support, but the current versions of the examined products all perform very well regarding this aspect.

The different products provide different ways of WS-* standards configuration. These were mentioned during the introduction of the SOA products. The two main methods are either the direct usage of WS-Policy or using a custom XML configuration file. In the former case it is useful to have pre-defined policies or graphical support for policy generation. In the latter case a tool is needed to convert between the custom configuration and WS-Policies.

It is advisable to keep the program code independent of the applied protocols; therefore a separate configuration is useful. In most cases this can be achieved. Unfortunately, JAX-WS raises some protocols to programming level: the SOAP version, MTOM and WS-Addressing features are all selected by Java annotations, however, in some cases these can be overridden in configuration files.

JAX-WS provides a portable API for web services in the Java world, however, configuration of WS-* standards is out of scope resulting in vendor-dependent configuration solutions. This also makes interoperability harder as it is difficult to find the exact match for a specific configuration in another product.

7.4 Evaluation

The applied testing methodology is very similar to the one used in WSTF, but our testing environment supports automated tests, too. The test cases are not intended to formally check conformance to specific standards. The focus is mainly on achieving interoperability based on typical application patterns. From the implementations and documentations of these patterns new applications can be easily created. The test cases cover all the service level requirements of the Hungarian e-Government.

When a new version of a product was released during the testing phase, we immediately switched to that one so that we could always have the most current results. The tests ended at the end of 2008. Newer versions of the products released since then have to be retested, but it would take much less effort than the original tests. Some of the products were already mature enough in 2008 to pass most of the test cases.

Implementing the test cases helped us to learn the peculiarities of the selected products, and now we have a broader view of the different development methods. We have the virtual machines running the products, the source codes of each test case and nearly 400 pages of documentation. Based on this documentation the test environment and all the test cases can be reproduced.

8 Conclusions and Future Work

When selecting mature SOA products for e-Government application, a methodology of assessment, including test-case specifications and a flexible, automated testing environment is needed. This paper has shown a test bed suitable to assess interoperability of SOA products. The test cases are reproducible and the testing environment is flexible enough for adding a new product and having it tested with all the others. The automated tests make collecting the results easier. We also evaluated our results of tests on products of several major vendors.

The test results published in this paper only demonstrate the suitability of the testing framework for assessing interoperability based on WS-* standards. Our intention was not yet the ranking the tested SOA products, although, we have found that some SOA products are mature enough to fulfill the HeGF requirements. We would like to introduce further test aspects such as performance and stress tests.

The tested SOA products use different configuration methods. Based on a product-independent model, a code generator tool could be used to produce directly interoperable configurations. The construction of a meta-model and a tool has been started and some of its functions are already under test. This tool is also for generating common administration and management components, and also functional test cases for e-Government services. The platform-independent models of these services and the code generators producing the required components could be part of a service registry to make development easier.

As it was shown in section II, WSTF has a similar testing methodology. We have the most development experience in WCF and GlassFish ESB, which seem to be a shortage of their profile. Cooperation with them could be mutually beneficial.

References

[1] WS-I Basic Profile, http://www.ws-i.org/ (accessed: June 11, 2009)
[2] Microsoft, Web Services Interoperability Plug-Fest,
      http://www.mssoapinterop.org/ilab/ (accessed: June 11, 2009)
[3] Web Services Test Forum, http://www.wstf.org/ (accessed: June 11, 2009)

[4] Apache, Project Stonehenge,
    http://wiki.apache.org/incubator/StonehengeProposal
    (last access: June 11, 2009)
[5] Senthil Kumar, K.M., Das, A.S., Padmanabhuni, S.: WS-I Basic Profile: a practitioner's
    view. In: Proc. IEEE International Conference on Web Services, pp. 17–24 (2004)
[6] Kuppuraju, S., Kumar, A., Kumari, G.P.: Case Study to Verify the Interoperability of a
    Service Oriented Architecture Stack. In: Proc. IEEE International Conference on Ser-
    vices Computing SCC 2007, pp. 678–679 (2007)
[7] European Interoperability Framework, http://ec.europa.eu/idabc/en/
    document/7728 (accessed: June 11, 2009)
[8] Saekow, A., Boonmee, C.: Towards a Practical Approach for Electronic Government In-
    teroperability Framework (e-GIF). In: Proc. 42nd Hawaii International Conference on
    System Sciences HICSS 2009, pp. 1–9 (2009)
[9] Estevez, E., Janowski, T.: Government-Enterprise Ecosystem Gateway (G-EEG) for
    Seamless e-Government. In: Proc. 40th Annual Hawaii International Conference on Sys-
    tem Sciences HICSS 2007, pp. 101–110 (2007)
[10] E-public administration, Strategy (2010), http://www.ekk.gov.hu/hu/ekk/
    strategia/egovstrategy.pdf (accessed: June 14, 2009)
[11] United Nations e-Government Survey 2008, From e-Government to Connected Govern-
    ance, United Nations, New York (2008)
[12] US Government, Federal Enterprise Architecture,
    http://www.whitehouse.gov/omb/e-gov/fea/ (accessed: June 14, 2009)
[13] German Government, Standards and Architectures for e-Government Applications
    (SAGA) 4.0 (March 2008), http://www.kbst.bund.de/saga (accessed: June 14,
    2009)
[14] E_Közgazgatási Követelménytár (in Hungarian),
    http://kovetelmenytar.complex.hu/ (accessed: June 14, 2009)

Providing Adaptive and Evolving Government E-Services through Citizen-Centric Process Views

Gustav Aagesen and John Krogstie

Norwegian University of Science and Technology, Department of Computer and
Information Science, Sem Sælandsvei 7-9, NO-7491 Trondheim, Norway
{gustav.aagesen,krogstie}@idi.ntnu.no

Abstract. As users of government services, citizens spend much of their time
in transit between government agencies acting in different roles with varying
responsibilities. Government agencies are providers of services virtually connected, but with limited actual integration in practice. We believe that by allowing citizens more direct access to ongoing processes in which they are involved,
it could improve service delivery from the perspective of citizen and the government organization alike. In this paper we discuss the concept of citizen-
centric process views, a conceptual architecture providing channel independent
support for knowledge management and monitoring of cross-organizational
service delivery in transformational government. We will set the stage for the
discussion of requirements for the next generation government infrastructures
and the surrounding organizations in order to support delivery of adaptive and
evolving government services.

Keywords: e-government, services, knowledge management, workflow,
evolving IS.

1 Introduction

E-government is about the continuous improvement of public administration and
service delivery. It is supported through the use of information technology, facilitating
the reorganization and development of new services and with the potential of reorganizing the service administration as well.

Services to the citizens are normally provided from government agencies based on
what could be understood as an optimal service delivery from point of view of the
service provider, and based on historical organization and responsibilities. Individual
government agencies deliver services of similar nature to citizens, and the citizens
receive combined services from different agencies based on the complexity of
the needs of the citizen. From the citizen point of view, orchestration of services appears to be weak, and there is a risk of being caught between uncoordinated service
providers.

By connecting services provided to single citizens, new services and service features supporting the potential for increased value of service delivery can be added.
Examples include updated information improving expectation management, allowing

M. Janssen et al. (Eds.): EGES/GISP 2010, IFIP AICT 334, pp. 32–45, 2010.

proactive interference and better coordination of compound services, better control with customized services fitted to individual needs, and improved organization of services.

The goal of this paper is twofold: First we discuss the motivation and opportunities of a citizen-centric configuration of service delivery, being aware of that the technical and organizational barriers for citizen access to connected government services are extensive [7, 21]. We further know that providing citizen-centric organization of services require changes in technology, changes that can significantly affect the direction and progress of applications development, by either enhancing or limiting choices or functionality [30]. Based on that we will discuss the possibilities of an adaptive infrastructure and organization supporting delivery of evolving e-services.

In section 2 we provide a background on the current status of e-government service delivery and the motivation of our work. This is followed by a description of the citizen-centric process views, the conceptual architecture, and the discussion of the associated knowledge management scenarios. In the related work section we present research relevant to the functional aspects of the implementation followed by discussion and conclusion.

2 Background

Existing stage models for e-government maturity [13, 14, 24] describe the complexity of provided services and the cultural, technological and political prerequisites associated with service delivery on the different stages. The stages depict interactions between government agencies and citizens spanning from the simple availability of online information, to interaction and transaction services and to complex long-running transactions with multiple actors involved. There is both a cultural and a technological gap between the government service provisioning we see today and that of the transformational government scenario described in literature.

The need for further research on the next generation digital government infrastructures has previously been identified [16, 29]. Research areas include among other building a secure and flexible infrastructure, application areas for service provisioning, establishing business models for the component industry as well as the organizational aspects related to the responsibility of development and maintenance of components. The United Nations has identified three priority areas for future development and the improvement of provided services [28]:

- Making efficiency and effectiveness a reality through high user satisfaction with public services through using IT appropriately to reduce the administrative burdens of citizens and businesses
- Using common platforms to achieve efficiency gains
- Improved interoperability between e-government through the use of e-signatures and electronic identification management.

The 2009 *Ministerial Declaration on eGovernment*[6] promotes shared European objectives by 2015 including the development of user-centric services that provide flexible and personalized ways of interacting with the public administration. It further actively seeks collaboration with third parties, for example businesses, civil society or individual citizens, in order to develop user-driven e-government services.

The future strategy and directions for the development of e-government in Norway includes mapping of standard services and their use of central registries as well as planning access to centrally developed components as common platforms, and the use of e-signatures and electronic identification management.

Altinn II, which is an important part of future information infrastructure in Norway, will among other things support service collaboration and several process owners for cross-organizational processes presented as one integrated process for the users.

User centricity implies that the needs of the different users affect the contents and reach of the services provided. User centricity also involves facilitating for the needs of the individual user in terms of customizing the services offered to that particular user, and taking action to improve the service delivery to all users [8]. Examples of improved service delivery for common good involve extending opening hours and reducing the time spent waiting to be served. Through active collaboration between the central state and municipalities, shared service centers [15] are being developed. This promotes a one-stop government and free citizens from being tossed between governmental offices.

There has been a critique of e-government initiatives taking on a techno-centric, rationalist focus, ignoring the value of organizational learning and knowledge management (KM), and that KM is an important aspect of future government strategies [18]. It is further important that e-government strategies for transformation does not move back to organizational re-engineering and an attempt to 'reinventing government', but promote the development of an ICT strategy that underpins the implementation of organizational change [3].

The work presented in this paper is a part of a study on service provisioning based on the transformational government scenario. Constraining factors of the scenario includes the autonomy of actors, the changing government organizations and policies, the necessary support for process innovation and service reorganization, and the changing requirements of users and systems caused by the availability of new technology affordances.

The 'citizen-centric process views' is a suggested artifact created within a scenario of the next generation government infrastructure. It is based on the idea of a (de-) centralized middleware connecting core components, legacy- and government front office systems for the organization of ongoing and completed instances of provided services to the citizen. It does not provide a user-interface and is in that sense channel independent and extendable through various interfaces. It is a 'what if'-scenario, disregarding many cultural, political and technological gaps between the current situation and the envisioned transformational government. At the same time it provides a basis for discussion of the possible utility provided by the technical architecture and the discovery new directions of research.

3   Citizen-Centric Process Views

In this section we will present and discuss a potential development of services and service capabilities provided by what we refer to as citizen-centric process views.

First, we will introduce the main concepts. Then, we will discuss some of the functional capabilities given that the cultural, political, and technological prerequisites for transformational government are met.

3.1 From Organization- and Service-Centric to Citizen-Centric Service Delivery

Using Fig. 1, (I) illustrates a traditional understanding of service delivery between a government agency (A) and the citizens (1-N). Each citizen is served directly and service production is centered on the service provider and the isolated service requests. The scenario in the middle (II) provides a shift in focus and places the citizen (X) in the centre of service delivery, and we can see that the citizen interacts directly with several government agencies (A, B, C) although the coordination of the process and service delivery is still left to the citizen.

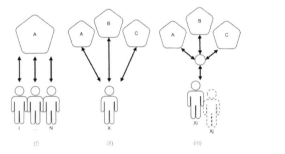

Fig. 1. Service delivery to citizens

The scenario to the right (III) illustrates the conceptual artifact we refer to as a citizen-centric process view: The citizen remains as the main subject, but instead of being the main responsible for coordinating the delivery of services provided, the citizen, government, and non-government agencies are all actors in the choreography of services. These actors are allowed access to review the whole citizen process rather than the individual service stubs in which the process is comprised.

Van der Aalst [33] differentiate enablers of inter-organizational workflows as *capacity sharing*: Tasks are executed by external resources under the control of one workflow manager, *chained execution*: The process is divided into subsequent phases and each partner takes care of one phase, *subcontracting*: A sub-process is executed by another organization, *case transfer*: Each partner uses the same workflow process and cases are transferred from one partner to another, *and loosely coupled*: Each partner takes care of a specified part of the process. Regardless of the internal organization of the service provisioning, the current state of the process should be reported to some central artifact in order for the citizen and involved actors to monitor progress, and by doing that support quality assurance.

3.2 Process Access through Roles

Central to the citizen-centric process view is the citizen and the different roles the citizen has in its various interactions with the government. It is the roles that initiate and require the services, and it is the coordination of the different roles that is important to the citizen. With the roles of a single citizen (Fig. 1, Xi and Xj), come different responsibilities. Some roles might vary depending on the current situation of other citizens related to that particular citizen. The parent role gives access to different services depending on the age and needs of a child, the child role has a different nature when caring for elderly parents and there is a need to take a more active role on behalf of relatives that might not be able to administrate their own rights and responsibilities. Having a certain health condition or being out of work also qualifies for access to particular services. Similarly owning property in different regions might require access to information as well as responsibilities in those regions.

The service providers themselves are not of much importance to the citizen, and the organization and location of government agencies are irrelevant until a service is required. From a citizen point of view, currently utilized services might be chained to connected services located at different providers necessary at a later stage of service provision. Take hospital-services, followed by home-care, borrowing of equipment to support a quick recovery and financial compensation in case of having to be out of work for a longer period. All these services are connected, but provided by different government agencies. The service provider is not important for the citizen, and by connecting the services the citizen will be informed of the required steps and procedures and events. For the government agencies involved in the service provisioning to that particular citizen, the transparency and openness of a channel creates a virtual organization [9] better suited to provide the service efficiently. From the citizen point of view, partly "outsourcing" the coordination of services to a relative or trusted peer as a role in this scenario might serve all involved actors. Alternatively, assigning the support role to a civil servant familiar with the process as responsible for the citizen's interests exclusively, providing online or offline support, will have the potential to compensate for any divide (digital, cultural, etc) the citizen is exposed to.

3.3 Discovery, Customization and Service Interaction

By looking at services commonly used in concert, one could use the service connections to discover eligible services based on the role of the citizen or through current service use. This might typically be related to new regulations opening for extra support for citizens in a given situation. Allowing citizens to discover eligible services using current service configuration could provide value to the citizen and increased efficiency in the service distribution from the government side. Connected services are typically found in collections commonly referred to as life-events [27]. Most life-event approaches to service discovery are based on semantic models of services rather than information about actual use, involved actors or historical data. There can be situations where information about the services themselves might not be sufficient to provide the necessary information in order to discover complimentary or follow-up services. Using process goals for the citizen in addition to the current services it could be less cumbersome to locate replacement services or to validate whether the current service configuration is the best for the given citizen. This would however require that the involved actors should be granted access to information not necessarily limited to the virtual organization created to support the delivery of a single service.

Citizen-centricity can involve customizing single services to each citizen's individual needs. This means that the process view should show the actual planned process of the service in which the particular citizen is receiving, including providers, events and other relevant information. This enables proactive behavior from the citizen as well as providers. In the case of the citizen, by merging the workflow for all processes in which it is involved, it is possible to resolve any conflicts that might occur between different services and allow a timely coordination of services.

For some services, it might also be possible for the citizen to interact with the process model and change the order of occurrence, poll status, spin out additional subprocesses, postpone events or cancel ongoing requests. All in all, the interface of the involved actors should invite to a continuous open dialogue between the government and the citizens. The level of process transparency exposed could depend on the requested or necessary involvement of the different actors as well as the nature of the service provided. In its simplest form, the process view provided to the citizen can be limited to a calendar with the planned occurrence of events with event descriptions, deliveries and locations. And for the citizen, some of the bureaucratic elements of a single process might be more confusing than helpful, and might be better left out of the process-view of the citizen.

The implementation of the centralized component is conceptually similar to the functionality of that of a Public Service Broker found in earlier transaction based e-government initiatives, allowing the citizen to see what government organizations are currently using information about the citizen. The individual user will further have authority over their personal data and can specify what organizations that can access different information [10].

3.4 Simulation, Monitoring and Forecasting

From an administrative perspective, the run-time integration of ongoing processes provides an extensive amount of information for monitoring, analysis and policy development. This includes simulating new regulations on actual data, forecasting service demand and discovering possibilities for new services or improved service delivery.

In discovering new process innovations, the need to allow trial and error is one of the aspects of the innovation toolkits introduced by von Hippel [28]. This involves that the user will be allowed to test any changes done to measure the relative improvement of the changes to the artifact, which in our case in most situations will be a process on the instance-level or policy-level. One approach for trial and error on the policy-level has been to extract data from the execution environment, change the rules/regulations or process flow and re-run the process using actual data. This would provide important information to the modeler on how successful a new policy will be based on an isolated and limited dataset. This approach does however have some limitations: First, it is required and assumed that the only those who are eligible and have applied for a service based on the old policy will be within the window of the new policy. Further, any new policy addressing different properties and criteria from previous policies will not be open for simulation, since the properties required will most probably not be within the data available for simulation. There is further only a particular kind of services which are open for such simulation. Human driven processes might leave traces of information in the system, and would allow some simulation with respect to breadth and reach of the provided services (i.e. who is eligible, and what outputs exists and the economy of each contact). On the instance-level this trial and error might prove more fruitful, since one can assume that the user has knowledge of the instance and can supply data relevant to the trial and error simulation. This would involve measuring the process outcomes in form of delay and cost by alternating process flow.

As for government agencies responsible for later steps in the process chains, the forecasting element is based on current active use of services qualifying for entrance to the services provided by that particular provider. The information produced by this forecasting is primarily important to planning and resource management.

4 Conceptual Architecture

The conceptual architecture of the citizen-centric process views (Fig. 2 illustrates a part of this) is organized around the delivery of a *service* to a single citizen. The service comprises of a single or multiple *process* instances, which contribute to the completion of the *service*. That is, the *process* can be the partial delivery of a compound *service*, a *service* delivery in a chain of subsequently provided *services*, or the delivery of a single *service*. The *service* defines and organizes the *processes* where all work is done. The *service* and *processes* share the same goals, or the *processes* partly fulfill the goals of the *service*.

Each *process* has a set of *actors,* which have defined *roles* in the *process*. The citizen is the *subject* who is the receiver of the *service* produced by the *process*. There can be several *contributors* from government and non-government organizations as well as *caretakers* acting in the interest of the citizen. These *actors* together form a *virtual organization* for the *service* in which the *processes* are defined. In cases of hand-over of control between different contributors there is always defined a temporary owner of the *process* responsible for *service* delivery.

The *process* is created based on a *process template* at the time of instantiation. *Actors* can alter the *process* either directly if authorized or through change requests (*events*) that are accepted or rejected by other actors responsible for the process steps that are requested to be changed or affected by the requested changes.

The *events* contribute to synchronize the current state of the *process* between all involved *actors* in the *virtual organization*. This allows local information systems connected through the system interface to subscribe to events within processes or they can request information about the process. Capabilities defined in the *process* can be implemented through *actors* connected to the *system interface*. This can typically by core components in the national infrastructure or locally defined functionality in the given municipality. This means that the *actors* interact with the *process* through a defined system *interface*, which can be extended to local information systems at the *contributors*, or to various user devices for *caretakers* and *subjects*. The *system interface* can allow access to custom defined modules running within devices connected through the interface. These can provide various views of the process separately or combined for the different actors. Examples of these are alerts on spending, deadlines, regulations; lookups in central registries for explanations or references; support for running what-if scenarios on process changes; process documentation, central reporting, benchmarking or locating similar cases as the given process instance; translation services, or other utilities that prove useful for single actors or the virtual organization as a whole.

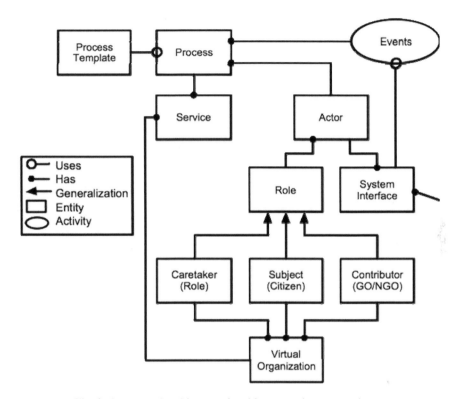

Fig. 2. Conceptual architecture for citizen-centric process views

As we can see from the described conceptual architecture, the citizen-centric process view is a single point of access for the citizen where it can interact with the government on currently provided services. It provides an infrastructure for service collaboration, knowledge management and innovation of service delivery. It supports flexible organization of providers and the different government information systems and with that supports continuous transformation of government services.

5   Adaptive and Evolving Capabilities

In the previous section we discussed the conceptual infrastructure of the citizen-centric process views. As mentioned, an important aspect is not only to provide services based on a fixed configuration, but also to support service delivery in a transformational government scenario. This requires supporting both dynamic aspects in a static environment, and dynamic aspects in an environment that is dynamic itself.

This involves changing process instances at run-time, evolving through updating templates, replacing functional components, or redeploying the process as a whole.

The ability to monitor and learn from how the services are provided is one of the utilities of the citizen-centric process views. It enables knowledge creation on the central, local, service and instance level. This further contributes both to making knowledge visible, and promotes knowledge in the organization; it promotes sharing and a knowledge-intensive culture; supports a knowledge infrastructure of technical systems and a web of connections among people given space, time and tools [1].

Changes made to process templates for the running processes can be monitored centrally and locally. Trends can be identified, which can suggest the need for adjusting the process templates. Actual use can further be observed and new policies can be formed for future process executions. At the service level, virtual organizations providing services using similar systems, configurations or acting on similar policies, or municipalities with similar core characteristics (policies, size, budgets, or key-figures) can share experiences and best-practice and in that way co-evolve and share innovations (Fig. 3.). This means that government agencies providing similar services can collaborate on how their process should evolve. They can also share the expenses of improving the systems supporting the process. Having a shared understanding of how services are delivered and a (executable) process description further simplifies the replacement of system components.

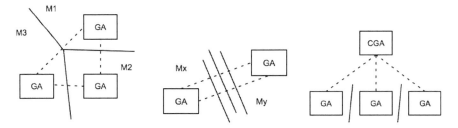

Fig. 3. Co-evolution in virtual organizations or process change coordinated centrally. M: Municipalities; GA: Government Agency; CGA: Central Government Agency.

At the instance level, access to similar scenarios and experiences is functionality the involved actors can benefit from. However, the collaboration of actors and availability of information beyond the isolated task of the single actor is itself a resource that can promote sharing of tacit, individual knowledge of the participating actors and thus improve service delivery.

Using process-mining techniques [33] can also assist the alignment of the formal and actual process, and questionnaire-based pre-process support [32] can help create the process templates and involve the required actors.

6   Related Work

There is a gap between currently available technology affordances, organizational culture and political ambitions required to take on the full implementation of the scenario presented in the last section. Some of these are disregarded on purpose by our work and are not needed when establishing scenario descriptions or working prototypes. Others are currently addressed and are assumed to receive the proper attention by related work. In this section we will look at current concepts and research that we believe is relevant to our scenario. The relevant work includes architecture principles, work within life-events, enterprise interoperability, commercially available applications and research on dynamically adaptable processes.

6.1 Organization around Services

Service Oriented architecture (SOA) is one of the cornerstones to the transformational government infrastructure. "Although SOAs might not be new, they address the fundamental challenges of open systems, which are to operate efficiently and achieve coherence in the face of component autonomy and heterogeneity" [12]. Equally important is the ability to renew, add and remove services dynamically as the requirements of the systems change. Building on the concept of the Enterprise Service Bus, the citizen connects to government agencies and service registries for discovery of services and service interactions. So far, this is similar to the concept of Active Life-Event Portals [27], aiding service discovery based on the life events of the citizen. Further, Bercic and Vintar [2] suggest allowing agents act on behalf of the citizen as proxies in the interaction with the government. We see that the use of agents to discover eligible services and acting on behalf of the citizen is useful. In the case of citizen-centric process views, using agents as proxies in the virtual organization, responding to the occurrence or non-occurrence of events as one of the application areas. The Norwegian LivsIT project (later named Los) started out as a standardization project for semantic interoperability of public services organized around life-events. The life-event focus was later abandoned due to fact that the scope of services related to single life-events is hard to determine. This work is now focused on providing standardization information related to the delivery of single services [5].

6.2 Inter-organizational Collaboration

Due to the autonomy of government agencies, obstacles for inter-agency cooperation on the process level occur when the different agencies use different process description languages. Karagiannis and Hofferer [17] have performed a survey looking at the use of meta-models to integrate processed across organizations. Ziemann et al [30] propose a framework to model and transform cross-organizational business processes to technical process model based on web service protocols. The approach involves establishing process descriptions using Event Process Chains (EPC), which is further converted to BPEL syntax.

Holm Larsen and Klischewski [11] discuss the challenges of process ownership in relation to inter-organizational collaboration. They conclude that there is no recipe or guidance available on how to proceed in situations where there is an absence of an overall process ownership or where the overall process ownership is not desired. Punia and Saxena [22] suggest three approaches involving establishing the super-ordinate role, a common shared workspace or interacting through a third party intermediary. Our suggested approach points towards establishing the third party intermediary in the custody of the citizen-centric process view, but it is important that the overall process ownership is not left up to the citizen, and that a separate role independent from the agencies providing services take the overall process ownership and the promote the interest of the citizen.

6.3 Process Modeling and BPM Oriented Tools

When it comes to the BPM systems, there are several commercially available frameworks. The Itensil dynamic process platform [3] is a solution supporting ad-hoc collaborative process work is different from what found in traditional BPM systems, allowing process change on the fly and version control of individual process instances. Itensil uses a wiki-style framework and AJAX-based user interfaces, supporting effective workspace redistribution. While the Itensil framework is designed for ad-hoc knowledge work in smaller teams, the approach is interesting with respect to large-scale process distribution, innovation and flexibility in government organizations. More traditional BPM-approaches provided in the cloud can be found, e.g. Appian Anywhere[1] and Cordys Process Factory[2]. Cordys also provides support for more informally defined case-processing systems, but this is so far not available "in the cloud".

Lillehagen and Krogstie [20] describe Active Knowledge Modeling and interactive Models. Models are interactive when they are available to the users at run-time and support automatic synchronization of the execution environment and behavior of the system based on changes to the model made by the user . Active knowledge modelling extends enterprise modeling and focus on the knowledge supporting work through models, methods and tools. Systems can evolve with corporate knowledge and users build and manage their own work environment through model-generated workplaces proving process support and access to relevant information [19]. So far these approaches have not been applied in a transformational government setting.

7 Discussion and Conclusion

This paper has introduced the concept of citizen-centric process views for e-government services. The concept is located within work on next generation government infrastructure and the application area for services in the transformational government scenario. It is a (de-)centralized approach connecting core components, legacy- and government front office systems for the organization of ongoing and completed instances of provided services to the citizen. The concept is similar to the one-stop government and active life-events portals where the citizen has online access to discover services. It extends those concepts by focusing on the monitoring, choreography and knowledge management aspects of the actual workflow of ongoing service delivery. The citizen-centric process views create a virtual organization around the citizen and the service provided. In contrast to similar concepts, it suggests that there is knowledge about the optimal service delivery present in the virtual organization that is not formalized and therefore preventing the process from being subject to automated processing. This might

---

[1] http://www.appian.com/bpm-saas.jsp
[2] http://www.theprocessfactory.com/

also be due to the fact that the actual services provided are physical or emotional services, and that the process view acts as a documentation and collaboration space for the involved actors. The models used in the process view can be interactive, and changing the workflow model will affect the actors' involvement and actual workflow of the process in question, supporting the evolution of the overall information system.

The citizen-centric process view is one step closer to the recognition of the e-citizen as a separate entity. Traditional government systems identify individuals through references and variables in information system without any binding to the citizen itself. With the process views the citizen will govern information previously not available and which is not controlled by any government agency. Rech Filho [23] suggests that the development of the e-citizen concept might not be a priority interest of the government and that its function might rather be of commercial interest. We believe that the access to government or non-government actors should be open, or at least that it is a political choice rather than technological limitation whether the access should be open or not. In transformational government, government services might just as well be provided through private contractors. On the question of citizen-centricity, Kolsaker and Lee-Kelley [18] stresses the fact that "if the needs of the citizens are not understood, provision will be designed around the needs of the state; if the needs of the state are prioritized, e-services will only be used where the needs of the citizens and state coincide".

We observe that a majority of the related work within life-events and one-stop government is relatively old. Some of the suggested life-events frameworks rely on semantic operability and interoperability support not yet mature for large-scale implementation. We believe that our approach is similarly relying on cultural interoperability, but additionally take advantage of the knowledge of the people involved in service delivery, rather than that of formalized information stored prior to service execution. This approach is believed to be more agile and should be able to support a dynamic service configuration and changing systems as a result of changing prerequisites caused by political, technological and regulatory change.

The work so far does not involve a prototype nor does it critically evaluate the concept. We will continue our work on the conceptual model before we can take on the development of any prototype and evaluation within the citizen-centric process views.

References

1. Alavi, M., Leidner, D.E.: Review: Knowledge management and knowledge management systems: Conceptual foundations and research issues. MIS Quarterly 25(1), 107–136 (2001)
2. Bercic, B., Vintar, M.: Ontologies, web services, and intelligent agents: ideas for further development of life-event portals. In: Traunmüller, R. (ed.) EGOV 2003. LNCS, vol. 2739, pp. 329–334. Springer, Heidelberg (2003)
3. BPMFocus, 'Itensil Dynamic Process Platform', whitepaperv(2008), http://bpmfocus.wordpress.com/2008/04/15/ itensil-dynamic-process-platform/ (accessed June 29, 2009)
4. Carlson, J.R., Zmud, R.W.: Channel expansion theory and the experiential nature of media richness perceptions. Academy of Management Journal 42(2), 153–170 (1999)

5. Elgesem, D.: Lik tilgang for alle. In: Jansen, A., Wiese Schartum, D. (eds.) Elektronisk forvaltning på Norsk, Fagbokforlaget, pp. 355–368 (2008), ISBN 978-82-450-0770-1
6. Minsterial Declaration on eGovernment, 5th Ministerial eGovernment Conference, Teaming up for the eUnion, Malmö (2009), Downloaded from, http://www.se2009.eu/
7. Estevez, E., Janowski, T.: Government-Enterprise Ecosystem Gateway (G-EEG) for Seamless e-Government. In: 40th Hawaii International Conference on System Sciences (2007)
8. FAD, An Administration for Democracy and Community, Report No. 19 (2008-2009) to the Storting, Norwegian Ministry of Government Administration and Reform (2009)
9. Fountain, J.E.: Building the Virtual State: Information Technology and Institutional Change. Brookings Institution Press, Washington (2001)
10. Golden, W., Hughes, M., Scott, M.: The role of process evolution in achieving Citizen-Centered e-government. In: Ninth Americas Conference on Information Systems, pp. 801–810 (2003)
11. Holm Larsen, M., Klischewski, R.: Process ownership challenges in IT-enabled transformation of interorganizational business processes. In: Proceedings of the 37th Annual Hawaii International Conference on System Sciences (2004)
12. Huhns, M.N., Singh, M.P.: Service-oriented computing: Key concepts and principles. IEEE Internet Computing, 75–81 (2005)
13. Irani, Z., Al-Sebie, M., Elliman, T.: Transaction Stage of e-Government Systems: Identification of its Location & Importance. In: Proceedings of the 39th Hawaii International Conference on System Sciences (2006)
14. Iyer, L.S., Singh, R., Salam, A.F., D'Aubeterre, F.: Knowledge management for Government-to-Government (G2G) process coordination. Electronic Government, an International Journal 3, 18–35 (2006)
15. Janssen, M., Wagenaar, R.: An analysis of a shared services centre in e-government. In: Proceedings of the 37th Annual Hawaii International Conference on System Sciences (2009)
16. Janssen, M., Chun, S.A., Gil-Garcia, J.R.: Building the next generation of digital government infrastructures. In: Government Information Quarterly. Elsevier, Amsterdam (2009)
17. Karagiannis, D., Hofferer, P.: Metamodeling as an Integration Concept. In: Software and Data Technologies: First International Conference, Icsoft 2006, Setubal, Portugal, September 11-14, pp. 37–49. Springer, Heidelberg (2008) (Revised Selected Papers)
18. Kolsaker, A., Lee-Kelley, L.: Citizen-centric e-government: a critique of the UK Model. Electronic Government 3(2), 127–138 (2006)
19. Krogstie, J., Jørgensen, H.: Interactive Models for Supporting Networked Organisations. In: Persson, A., Stirna, J. (eds.) CAiSE 2004. LNCS, vol. 3084, pp. 550–563. Springer, Heidelberg (2004)
20. Lillehagen, F., Krogstie, J.: Active Knowledge Modeling of Enterprises. Springer, Heidelberg (2008)
21. Papazoglou, M.P., Traverso, P., Dustdar, S., Leymann, F., Krämer, B.J.: Service-oriented computing: A research roadmap. International Journal of Cooperative Information Systems 17, 223–255 (2008)
22. Punia, D.K., Saxena, K.B.C.: Managing inter-organisational workflows in eGovernment services. In: Proceedings of the 6th International Conference on Electronic Commerce, pp. 500–505 (2004)
23. Rech Filho, A.: e-Citizen: Why Waiting for the Governments? In: Böhlen, M.H., Gamper, J., Polasek, W., Wimmer, M.A. (eds.) TCGOV 2005. LNCS (LNAI), vol. 3416, pp. 91–99. Springer, Heidelberg (2005)

24. Siau, K., Long, Y.: Synthesizing e-government stage models- a meta-synthesis based on meta-ethnography approach. Industrial Management & Data Systems 105, 443–458 (2005)
25. United Nations, United Nations E-government Survey 2008: From E-government to Connected Governance, Division for Public Administration and Development Management (2007), ISBN 978-92-1-123174-8
26. Van der Aalst, W.: Loosely coupled interorganizational workflows: modeling and analyzing workflows crossing organizational boundaries. Information & Management 37(2), 67–75 (2000)
27. Vintar, M., Leben, A.: The concepts of an active life-event public portal. In: Traunmüller, R., Lenk, K. (eds.) EGOV 2002. LNCS, vol. 2456, pp. 383–390. Springer, Heidelberg (2002)
28. von Hippel, E.A.: Democratizing Innovation. The MIT Press, Cambridge (2005)
29. Wimmer, M., Codagnone, C., Janssen, M.: Future e-government research: 13 research themes identified in the eGovRTD2020 project. In: Proceedings of the 41st Annual Hawaii International Conference on System Sciences, pp. 223 (2008)
30. Ziemann, J., Matheis, T., Werth, D.: Conceiving Interoperability between Public Authorities A Methodical Framework. In: Proceedings of the 41st Annual Hawaii International Conference on System Sciences, pp. 194–205 (2008)
31. Grant, G., Chau, D.: Developing a Generic Framework for E-Government. Journal of Global Information Management 13(1), 1–30 (2005)
32. Gottschalk, F., Wagemakers, T.A.C., Jansen-Vullers, M.H., van der Aalst, W.M.P., La Rosa, M.: Configurable process models: experiences from a municipality case study. In: van Eck, P., Gordijn, J., Wieringa, R. (eds.) CAiSE 2009. LNCS, vol. 5565, pp. 486–500. Springer, Heidelberg (2009)
33. Van der Aalst, W.M.P., Weijters, A.: Process mining: a research agenda. Computers in Industry 53(3), 231–244 (2004)

EGES Session 2: Participation

Hands-On Guideline for E-Participation Initiatives

Sabrina Scherer, Maria A. Wimmer, and Stefan Ventzke

University of Koblenz-Landau, Institute for IS Research, Research Group E-Government,
Universitätsstraße 1, 56070 Koblenz, Germany
{scherer,wimmer,sventzke}@uni-koblenz.de

Abstract. E-participation applications enable online participation of citizens and interested stakeholder groups in political debates and strategic decision-making. The tools, channels and devices through which online participation takes place require proper design to support citizens, politicians and other actors. To incorporate the needs of these actors into the functionalities of an eParticipation platform, this contribution proposes a hands-on guideline for e-participation initiatives. It has been generated from the experiences of two European projects: VoicE and VoiceS. The paper describes the six-step iterative process to successfully plan and realize e-participation initiatives.

Keywords: citizen participation, e-participation, project implementation guideline.

1 Introduction

Although e-participation has been introduced as a new discipline only some years ago, the use of Information and Communication Technologies (ICT) in political participation has a longer tradition. The potential of using this medium to reach many people increased with the spread of the Internet [1]. This development has reached another push with the recent evolution and wide take-up of technologies summed up under the buzzword "Web 2.0". The "participatory web" promised new possibilities for political online participation [2].

Nevertheless till 2010, civic participation has in many countries still not reached the expectations affiliated with the hype of e-participation and Web 2.0. One reason is that the possibilities of e-participation have not yet been sufficiently exploited. Too little interaction takes place between the different parties in the policy life-cycle[1]. While information offerings are often high level, active participation opportunities are hard to find or limited (e.g. in the German Parliament as a study from 2008 evidences [3]). Additionally, often a conceptual integration in the political process is missing: "Participants are unable to understand the purpose of the debate, to identify the addressee of the postings and to see in which form the results are further processed in the political process" ([3] p. 47).

The success of e-participation solutions depends heavily on the organizational planning and the incorporation into the policy making or political processes. Current

---

[1] The stages of the policy life-cycle and levels of participation are detailed in [36].

M. Janssen et al. (Eds.): EGES/GISP 2010, IFIP AICT 334, pp. 49–61, 2010.
© IFIP International Federation for Information Processing 2010

solutions in the area of e-participation suffer from insufficiently responding to requirements specific for e-participation. A successful introduction of e-participation does not only require an adaptation of given processes. Sometimes new participation procedures, which have not existed before, need to be introduced. The lack of a sophisticated guideline with a holistic approach is tackled in the contribution at hand. The paper introduces a hands-on guideline for projects and organisations that build up e-participation initiatives. The guideline is based on a well-defined iterative process. It results from findings of the projects VoicE[2] and VoiceS[3].

The VoicE Internet platform promotes the dialogue between citizens from two European regions (Baden Württemberg, Germany[4] and Valencia, Spain[5]) and policy makers from the European Parliament as well as from other institutions of the European Union (EU) and regional assemblies. In terms of contents, the project focuses on the policy field of consumer protection in the EU. Citizen participation in VoicE is targeted at the legislation proposal formation stage and the debate on draft legislation [4]. In the follow-up project VoiceS, the VoicE platform is improved and complemented by adding a series of new features such as a serious games, semantic search, social networking tools and a toolkit for regional e-participation [5].

To implement such a toolkit, this contribution gives instructions for effective transfer of knowledge and good practice cases and describes a guideline for e-participation knowledge transfer. With it, this paper summarizes results and lessons learned from the VoicE and VoiceS projects. The next section introduces the methodology to construct the guideline for e-participation initiatives. Section 3 describes the guideline in detail. Concluding remarks and an outlook for further research are provided in section 4.

2   Methodology

According to Macintosh et al. [6], the evaluation of e-participation experiments is still in its infancy as the nature of e-participation is fragmented, unfocused and geographically dispersed. A number of researchers and networks started to develop evaluation frameworks (see e.g. [7, 8, 9]). Many approaches provide recommendations usable to establish e-participation or e-democracy policies (see e.g. [10, 11]). Some approaches provide general recommendations or requirements for e-participation, which are usable in practice when first time an e-participation application is to be set up [8, 9, 12].

In this paper, we generalise lessons, experiences and results from VoicE and VoiceS, and we ground them with insights from literature studies. Subsequently, we structure them and make them usable for other e-participation projects in an easy-to-understand step-by-step guideline.

The hands-on guideline for e-participation initiatives gives step-by-step recommendations for e-participation project implementation therewith answering the following questions:

---

[2] VoicE: Giving European people a voice in EU legislation, www.give-your-voice.eu

[3] VoiceS: Integrating semantics, social software and serious games into e-.participation, www.eu-voices.eu

[4] www.bw-voice.eu

[5] www.voice.gva.es

- How can e-participation processes be planned and implemented in an effective way?
- How can actors' needs be incorporated in the design of e-participation features and platform structures, how to choose the appropriate tools, and how to develop the e-participation platform to best fit the actors' needs?
- How to handle the preparation of the information related to topics to be discussed?

Approach to develop the hands-on guideline
Fig. 1 visualises the methodology applied to answer the three questions and ground the experiences of VoicE and VoiceS with literature study. The three lanes in the diagram separate the work performed in the projects from grounding results in literature studies. The boxes represent activities performed as part of the investigations. The shapes for documents represent results achieved and documented. The arrows show the flow of activities or the next usage of a result. Results achieved at a given step are further elaborated in the subsequent steps. The investigations in the projects have always been supported with findings from literature studies.

In order to elaborate the hands-on guideline for e-participation initiatives, the following nine activities have been performed:

1. The VoicE project started with a requirements analysis, which was based on two surveys, one with politicians and one with citizens. It was complemented by use case and goal analysis. The final requirements for the VoicE platform are formulated in the "End users' requirements report" [13].
2. The design process of the VoicE portal was an iterative process, influenced by the heuristic analysis performed by project partners and the empirical testing with pilot users. The results and the applied usability engineering process are documented in [14]. The VoicE usability engineering process intends the involvement of users in different stages of e-participation platform design and implementation. The iterative process consists of a requirements analysis phase, a design, testing and development phase and a deployment phase. Each step is accompanied by an evaluation against usability goals defined in the requirement analysis stage.
3. In a next iteration after the empirical testing phase, field observations with a more recent platform version resulted in a catalogue of critical points and weaknesses of the existing VoicE platform [15].
4. Results from the requirements analysis survey conducted in VoiceS (the follow-up project) have been taken into consideration to generalise and detail requirements and recommendations for e-participation. The interviews and questionnaires aimed to gather the VoiceS' requirements from citizens' point of view. The online questionnaire was filled out by 71 citizens from Spain, Germany and Austria. Additionally 22 interviews were conducted in Germany and Spain to get more detailed answers from the target group [15].
5. In order to fit participation in the VoiceS project to the European decision-making processes and thereof to have the best possible result of participation, a detailed analysis of processes and possible points of participation was conducted. The resulting process and workflow models were used to optimize the VoiceS processes and platform features (for details see [15]). Usefulness of the process models was evaluated through a survey among the project partners [16].

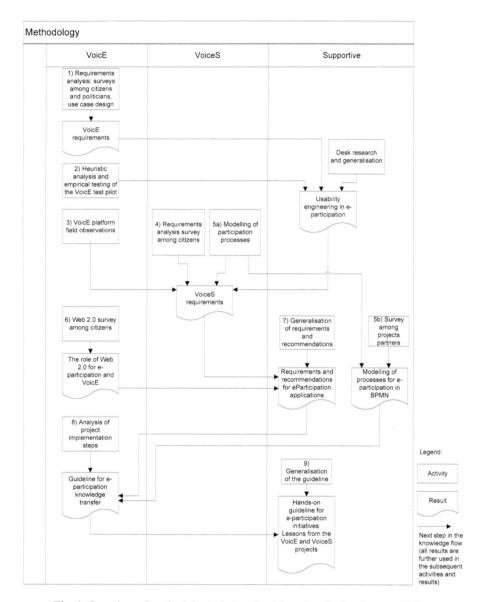

Fig. 1. Overview of methodological steps in elaborating the hands-on guideline

6. A survey among visitors of the German VoicE platform was undertaken in July/August 2009 with the aim to analyse the usage of Web 2.0 features. The survey (filled out by 164 respondents) investigated how the contents and Web 2.0 features were accepted by the users and if the use of such features resulted in an added value to achieve the aims of the project (e-participation) [17].
7. From afore mentioned results, a list of functional and non-functional requirements was extracted. The results were complemented by a desk research in order to

validate or discard the generality of the observed requirements and recommendations [18].

8. Analysis of the project implementation steps of VoicE and VoiceS was conducted in order to generalise a guideline for e-participation knowledge transfer [19].
9. The hands-on guideline for e-participation knowledge transfer was generalised and grounded on literature studies.

Related work and relevant literature the hands-on guideline grounds in

Kalampokis et al. present a model for the e-participation domain [20], which consists of the following layers: democratic processes, participation areas, participatory techniques, categories of tools and ICT technologies. The model is based on the e-participation framework put forward by Tambouris et al. [21]. The model for the e-participation domain summarizes the most important aspects and relations for e-participation in a conceptual model [20]. Thereby, the domain e-participation is divided into the three areas: actors, participation processes and information and communication tools (ICT tools). The areas are modeled separately and finally combined. The model put forward in [20] gives an overview of the complexity of the domain. It is not aimed at providing solutions how an e-participation initiative should proceed. This is where our approach digs into. The hands-on guideline conceptually builds on the aspects described in the domain model for e-participation and the underlying framework in its single steps.

Phang and Kankanhalli examine the suitability of various ICT tools for the achievement of e-participation objectives [8]. This work is based on Glass, who analysed offline participation techniques regarding the achievement of different objectives of citizen participation programs [22]. Phang and Kankanhalli transmit his results to ICT to technically support the participation techniques of Glass. A similar investigation was initiated in the DEMO-net project[6], where different categories of tools (e.g. forum) were analyzed for their characteristics und usage for e-participation [23]. Based on the chosen participation processes[7] according tools are selected. These results are considered in different steps of the hands-on guideline, too.

Phang and Kankanhalli also present a process for implementing e-participation initiatives, which consists of three steps: 1. Identification of the objective, 2. choosing the best participation techniques, and 3. choosing the electronic tools which support the participation techniques and thereof the achievement of the objectives. The hands-on guideline model bases on these steps, but focuses more on the design of participation techniques and tools. Beyond that, further steps are described in our hands-on guideline. Islam presents a process model with key phases of e-participation [24]. This model describes a meta-view of different phases of participation. Our approach focuses specifically on the design of such participation processes.

The guideline presented in the next section aims at supporting both, bottom-up and top-down e-participation initiatives thereby focussing on

- the e-participation processes and functionalities to be supported,
- the actors' needs regarding sustainable use of the application, and
- key aspects related to content and the topics to be discussed on the platform.

---

[6] Project title: Network of excellence for e-participation, see www.demo-net.org
[7] Phang and Kanhanhalli call them participation techniques [8].

3   Hands-On Guideline for e-Participation Initiatives

The hands-on guideline is structured along four phases for implementing an e-participation project: designing the initiative, preparation of ICT used and information material, realisation and evaluation of the initiative. Each phase consists of different implementation steps. Fig. 2 shows the guideline in a six-step iterative process.

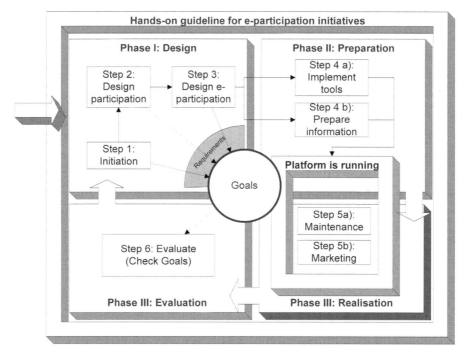

Fig. 2. Hands-on guideline for e-participation initiatives: a six-step iterative process

Step 1: Initiation of the e-participation project
When an e-participation initiative is initiated, the first step is to agree upon the objectives. This is also seen by Glass as an "important element of any participatory program" ([22], p. 180) and supported by Phang and Kankanhalli [8]. Therefore it is essential to focus on the first two of the three critical design factors around every engagement process [25]: Why are you doing it and who should be involved?[8] Consequently, the first guideline step aims on deciding the project objectives and (based on this decision) the stakeholders of the initiative. This step also includes the definition of project goals (expectations). In the following, the objectives of VoicE are described to give an example:

VoicE aims at enabling citizens to have a voice in EU legislation. In terms of content it focuses on the consumer protection policies. This fulfils the recommendation to choose an interesting and important topic [15], because consumer protection issues

---

[8] The third proposed factor (How to do it?) is decided in the subsequent steps of the guideline.

have an imminent effect on each citizen. VoicE is further based on the principles of a regional focus, i.e. making or keeping information as simple as possible, ensuring credibility, fostering personal opinions and making sure that the citizens' participation has a value [26].

Step 2: Design participation
Many e-participation projects failed and are still failing because participation processes are barely integrated into political processes (see e.g. [3, 22],). Results of participation should at least be forwarded to the political decision makers [27, 28]. Everything else leads to disappointment and disinterest in political participation in the end. Therefore, the aim of step two is to plan the participation processes and not to design the technical features (as also proposed by Phang and Kankanhalli with "select best-matching participatory techniques" ([8], p.131)). It is crucial in this step to plan the participation processes and the involvement of elected representatives in detail. The participation processes need to be integrated in and adapted to political processes. In order to fit the participation processes to the legislative/political processes and thereof to have the best possible impact of participation, a detailed analysis of processes and possible points of participation needs to be conducted in advance. Fig. 3 shows a model on how to integrate participation processes into political processes. The involvement of elected representatives needs to be organised from the beginning of the initiative. It is also an important objective of this step to formulate the expectations of the participation process. In this step, the use of multiple channels for participation – on and offline – needs to be investigated, too (cf. [10]).

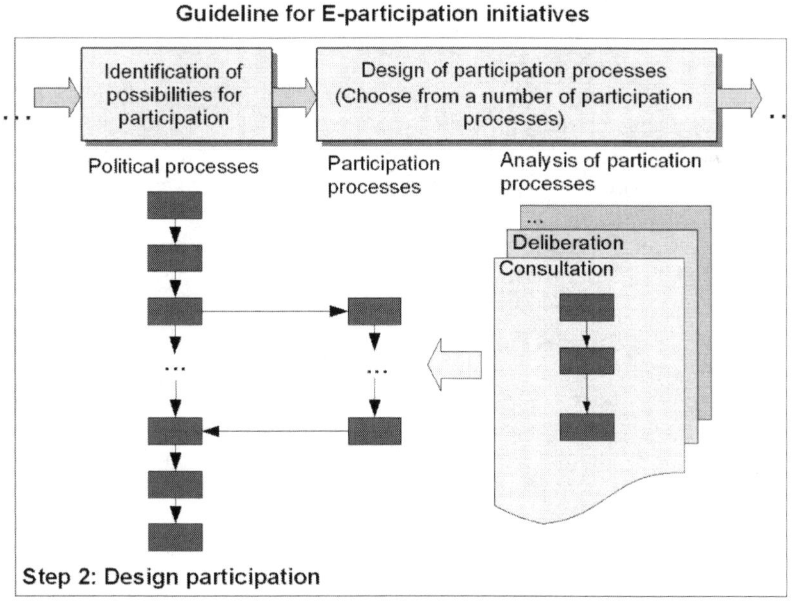

Fig. 3. Integration of participation processes into political processes (detailing step 2)

As a result from this step, the project team decides which of the e-participation areas[9] will be supported to achieve the objectives of the initiative. Besides that, decisions will be made on how these areas can be implemented, i.e. which activities are performed. The participation processes should only be decided with the involvement of (all/key) stakeholders. For this, requirements analysis focussing on the processes has to be conducted thoroughly. Finally, the goals of each activity have to be agreed with measurable values, e.g. the impact to be achieved.

In the beginning of the VoiceS project, a detailed analysis of processes and participation possibilities was conducted. We modelled the participation processes with the Business Process Modelling Notation (BPMN)[10]. The information and process models were useful and facilitated the analysis and design of political and participative processes [16].

Step 3: Design electronic participation
Based on the participation processes and user needs analysed in steps 1 and 2, the most appropriate media and channels have to be selected. If applicable, this includes as well deciding the choices of tools that are to be integrated into the platform to support the participation processes (cf. also [8]). The use of particular tools for e-participation cannot be recommended on a general level, because a) the usage should depend on the aims of the project and the processes established (see step 1, step 2 and [8]) and b) investigations did not unveil any preferred tools [14]. In terms of usability, the use of different participation features must be well-considered to not overload the users. Beyond that, participation features should only be provided in the case where the voice of participants is really heard by responsible authorities: An e-participation feature can only be used if the integration of the processes and results into the overall political process is ensured. It must be ensured that the users can see that their engagement will be recognized.

The design of the electronic participation means (i.e. ICT) should involve the real users in order to analyse requirements and design user-friendly services [14]. Respondents of the survey conducted for the requirements analysis of the VoiceS project [15] stressed that "electronic tools usually cannot replace face-to-face discussions". It is substantial for e-participation that communication by electronic means should not be more complicated than necessary. Hence, usability of e-participation platforms is of significant importance for the success of the project. E-participation features must base on easy-to-use tools in order to avoid usability flaws that could discourage people from online participation. Widely established tools and user paradigms ease the participation for users.

The usability of services is also of high relevance because usability evaluation plays a crucial role in e-participation evaluation methodologies [29, 30]. The usability and usefulness of the systems influence all e-participation evaluation perspectives, i.e. the socio-technical as well as the project and democratic perspectives. Small changes in the user interface of an e-participation application can result in completely different evaluation results. According to [31], bad usability in government web sites may even destroy the strategy of the whole website. This applies to e-participation platforms

---

[9] E-participation areas proposed by the network of excellence for e-participation DEMO-net are introduced e.g. in [23].

[10] The BPMN specification is available online at www.bpmn.org/

alike. Therefore systematic usability engineering is necessary – at least to detect minor design flaws that influence usability [32]. In this regard, the VoicE usability engineering lifecycle shaped up as usable to improve the system by iterative design of the systems' features, the interaction design and the user interface. In consequence, beyond the design of the platform, this step has to ensure usability of the e-participation means.

Step 4: Prepare information and implement the platform
The preparation of information should be organised in parallel with the setup of the platform functionalities and structure (implementation).

On the one hand, background information needs to be prepared. This task was based in VoicE on the selection of current European legislative proposals in the area of consumer protection and the review of content for the usage in the project [33]. The proposals should be easily accessible for consumers with little or no knowledge of European politics, so as to be a low-threshold starting point for participation. Furthermore, the legislative proposals should have a direct impact on citizens' everyday life. The careful preparation of information helped the project to be in time with the launch of the platform and to be able to easily update the contents for new developments. As a result from this experience, it is recommended to follow a well-structured process for information preparation in this step. This process should be related to the questions: What do you want to prepare, why and how do you want to prepare it? Another recommendation is to prepare questions for discussion in advance to stimulate discussions. This does not mean that all questions have to be posted at the outset, but can be thrown in at regular timeframes, e.g. one new question each week [33]. Such a preparation allows the fast reaction on developments as well as in case sparse discussions take place in the forum.

Besides the preparation of background information, it is of particular importance to prepare information about the participation process and the expectations to the participating parties. This information should answer the following questions:

- How does the participation process proceed (time frame, steps)?
- What can participants contribute to the process?
- What are the expectations and the goals of the participation process and how is it achieved?

This means that the users are informed about the results from step 1 and step 2 of the guideline in order to make the initiative transparent. When users are informed about how their contributions will be used, their willingness to participate may increase.

Step 5: Extensive marketing (involving stakeholders) and maintenance
Extensive marketing is an ongoing and important task. Yet, it needs to be seen in context with updating permanently the platform and publishing news (see maintenance). The marketing should already be initiated in advance and at least be active at the launch of the platform.

Maintaining the platform refers to activities necessary in order to keep the platform alive, to monitor the forum, to support the users, to publish news etc. The effort for doing so should not be underestimated and is an ongoing task through the whole project lifecycle. In order to support this step, the design phase of the electronic participation tools has to reflect the maintenance needs and has to plan the respective processes.

Maintenance should facilitate and support different instances with the same content in different languages in a multi-lingual context. Also the moderators and content administrators should be supported in summarising conclusions of discussions in simple and effective way.

Step 6: Evaluation
Millard recommends that e-participation initiatives should incorporate on-going evaluation [10]. Some evaluation frameworks are referenced in section 0. Evaluation of the e-participation platform, the processes and the actors' participation shall give insight into whether the goals of the e-participation initiatives are met and impact is reached with the electronic participation. This includes the assessment of the different perspectives (project, socio-technical and democratic) as well as the evaluation against the project goals formulated in earlier steps (see steps 1, 2, and 3). The evaluation results show whether the e-participation initiative is successful. Critical points, which need to be revised and improved in an iterative design cycle, are identified.

As indicated in Fig. 2, the guideline introduced in this section describes an iterative process to successfully plan and implement e-participation initiatives. Hence, the insights gained in the evaluation (step 6) feed back to revisions in earlier steps of the hands-on guideline.

4   Concluding Remarks

The guideline presented in this contribution sums up lessons and experiences from two e-participation projects: VoicE and VoiceS. The lessons and experiences from the projects are grounded and counterbalanced with insights from studying existing scientific works. The hands-on guideline helps projects and organisations to build up successful e-participation initiatives based on an iterative process. Case studies are necessary with projects in other e-participation areas in order to test the generality of the guideline.

Even though the guideline covers the whole e-participation project life-cycle, it may require further effort to give more specific guidance in certain respects to support e-participation decision makers, for example:

- Currently, no specific evaluation framework is recommended. Different evaluation strategies might be reviewed and updated in order to align them with the evaluation of goals as emphasized in steps 1-3 of the hands-on guideline. Subsequently, the guideline may require updates in order to streamline the goals definition (steps 1-3) with the evaluation (step 6).
- E-participation processes have so far not been extensively modelled and standardised. There is a lack of reference models for process patterns and process chains describing common processes in e-participation [34]. Further research is necessary to identify and model reference participation processes that support different e-participation areas. Such reference processes would be usable in step 2, where projects could easily choose and adapt reference processes for their objectives and needs.

- A toolbox of technical building blocks to support e-participation, and a reference architecture to combine these blocks efficiently, are needed. Such a toolbox should support the use of standardised reference processes (step 3) and the implementation step (step 4a). Requirements such as interoperability of services [34] need to be considered.
- Traditional project management is often used for software development, even though a variety of projects are suffering under this type of management. Implementation projects in e-participation often have to cope with constantly changing demands of citizens, governments and politicians, and they have to counterbalance technical and non-technical factors of electronic participation. Agile processes promise to integrate rapidly changing requirements and prioritizing better in the process (see e.g. [35]). The application of agile project management in e-participation with public administrations should be investigated. If agile methods shape up as useful, the guideline needs to be adapted.

Fine-tuning in the above aspects could improve the hands-on guideline and make it a key reference model for e-participation implementation. Subsequent research will focus on the development of the reference model.

The hands-on guideline presented in this contribution is a useful framework to support the effective and efficient implementation of e-participation projects.

Acknowledgement

VoicE and VoiceS are co-funded by the European Commission under the eParticipation Preparatory Action. This publication reflects the views only of the authors, and the Commission cannot be held responsible for any use, which may be made of the information contained therein.

References

1. Harth, T.: Internet und Demokratie - neue Wege politischer Partizipation: Überblick, Potential, Perspektiven. In: Woyke, W. (ed.) Internet und Demokratie. uni studien politik, pp. 8–24. Wochenschau Verlag, Schwalbach/Ts (1999)
2. Maier, J.: Web 2.0 - Moderatorenrechte für alle? Gibt es eine E-Partizipation 2.0 im Web 2.0? In: E-Partizipation: Beteiligungsprojekte im Internet. Beiträge zur Demokratieentwicklung, vol. 21, pp. 282–296. Stiftung Mitarbeit, Bonn (2007)
3. Albrecht, S., Kohlrausch, N., Kubicek, H., Lippa, B., Märker, O., Trénel, M., Vorwerk, V., Westholm, H., Wiedwald, C.: eParticipation - Electronic Participation of Citizens and the Business Community in eGovernment. In: Study on Behalf of the Federal Ministry of the Interior (Germany), Division IT 1 (January 2008)
4. Holzner, M., Schneider, C.: Consumer Protection, European Decision-Making and the Regions - the eParticipation Project VoicE. In: Cunningham, P., Cunningham, M. (eds.) Collaboration and the Knowledge Economy: Issues, Applications, Case Studies Part 1, pp. 351–356. IOS Press, Amsterdam (2008)
5. Scherer, S., Holzner, M., Karamagioli, E., Lorenz, M., Schepers, J., Wimmer, M.A.: Integrating Semantics, Social Software and Serious Games into eParticipation: The VoiceS Project. In: Macintosh, Tambouris (eds.) Electronic Participation: Proceedings of Ongoing Research and Projects of ePart 09, Schriftenreihe Informatik 31, pp. 151–158. Trauner Druck, Linz (2009)

6. Macintosh, A. (ed.): The Initial DEMO-net Landscape. Deliverable D4.1, DEMO-net Consortium (May 2006)
7. Frewer, L.J., Rowe, G.: Evaluating public participation exercises: Strategic and practical issues. In: Evaluating Public Participation in Policy Making, OECD, p. 85 (2005)
8. Phang, C.W., Kankanhalli, A.: A framework of ICT exploitation for e-participation initiatives. Communications of the ACM 51(12), 128–132 (2008)
9. Whyte, A., Macintosh, A.: Analysis and Evaluation of e-consultations. e-Service Journal 2(1 "e-democracy in Practice") (2003)
10. Millard, J.: eParticipation recommendations - focusing on the European level. In: Deliverable 5.1, Study and Supply Services on the Development of eParticipation in the EU (July 2009)
11. Commitee of Ministers: Recommendation CM/Rec (2009)1 of the Committee of Ministers to member states on electronic democracy (e-democracy). Recommendation, Committee of Ministers (February 2009)
12. Bicking, M., Wimmer, M.A.: Evaluation framework to assess eParticipation projects in Europe. In: Tambouris, E., Macintosh, A. (eds.) Electronic Participation: Proceedings of Ongoing Research, General Development Issues and Projects of ePart 2009. Schriftenreihe Informatik # 31, pp. 73–82. Trauner Druck, Linz (September 2009)
13. Karamagioli, E., Titorencu, M.: Deliverable D2.1. End-users' requirements report. VoicE Consortium (May 2008)
14. Scherer, S., Karamagioli, E., Titorencu, M., Schepers, J., Wimmer, M.A., Koulolias, V.: Usability Engineering in eParticipation. European Journal of ePractice (7) (2009)
15. Scherer, S., Wimmer, M.A. (eds.): VoiceS D 2.1 Requirements analysis report: Specification of (user) requirements for the VoiceS platform with focus on process models and user roles. Deliverable, VoiceS Consortium, pp. 78–91 (May 2009)
16. Scherer, S., Wimmer, M.A., Ventzke, S.: Modellierung von Prozessen für E-Partizipation in BPMN. In: Fischer, S., Maehle, E., Reischuk, R. (eds.) Informatik 2009, Im Focus das Leben. LNI, vol. 154, p. 205, pp. 1804–1813. Köllen Druck+Verlag GmbH, Bonn (September 2009)
17. Augustin, A.: Bedeutung und Gegenstand von Web 2.0 Technologien im Rahmen von bestehenden E-Partizipations-Projekten der Europäischen Kommission und besondere Analyse dieser Technologien im Bezug auf das Projekt VoicE/VoiceS. Project report, University of Koblenz-Landau (8 (2009)
18. Scherer, S., Wimmer, M.A., Ventzke, S.: Requirements and recommendations for eParticipation applications. In: Prosser, A., Parycek, P. (eds.) EDEM 2009 - Conference on Electronic Democracy 2009, books@ocg, vol. 251, pp. 187–197. Druckerei Riegelnik, Wien (September 2009)
19. Scherer, S., Wimmer, M.A., Ventzke, S.: VoicE D 6.4 Guideline for e-participation knowledge transfer. Deliverable, VoicE Consortium (October 2009)
20. Kalampokis, E., Tambouris, E., Tarabanis, K.A.: A Domain Model for eParticipation. In: Mellouk, A., Bi, J., Ortiz, G., Chiu, D.K.W., Popescu, M. (eds.) ICIW, pp. 25–30. IEEE Computer Society, Los Alamitos (2008)
21. Tambouris, E., Liotas, N., Kaliviotis, D., Tarabanis, K.: A framework for scoping eParticipation. In: dg.o 2007: Proceedings of the 8th Annual International Conference on Digital Government Research, Digital Government Society of North America, pp. 288–289 (2007)
22. Glass, J.J.: Citizen Participation in Planning: The Relationship Between Objectives and Techniques. Journal of the American Planning Association 45(2), 180–189 (1979)
23. Thorleifsdottir, A., Wimmer, M.A. (eds.): Deliverable 5.1: Report on current ICTs to enable Participation. DEMO-net Consortium (April 2006)

24. Islam, M.S.: Towards a sustainable e-Participation implementation model. European Journal of ePractice (5) (October 2008)
25. Acland, A. (ed.): Dialogue by Design: A Handbook of Public & Stakeholder Engagement. Dialogue by Design (March 2008)
26. Günes, L., Barahona, C.M., Setzen, F.: VoicE D4.1. Strategy for Marketing and Awarness-rasing Çampaign. Deliverable, VoicE Consortium (July 2008)
27. Coleman, S.: A Tale of Two Houses: the House of Commons, the Big Brother house and the people at home. Parliamentary Affairs 56(4), 733–758 (2003)
28. Coleman, S., Gøtze, J.: Bowling Together: Online Public Engagement in Policy Deliberation. Report (2002)
29. Lippa, B., Aichholzer, G., Allhutter, D., Freschi, A.C., Macintosh, A., Westholm, H.: Deliverable D 13.3: eParticipation Evaluation and Impact. DEMO-net Consortium (2008)
30. Macintosh, A., Whyte, A.: Towards an evaluation framework for eParticipation. Transforming Government: People. Process and Policy 2(1), 16–30 (2008)
31. Esteves, J.: A Semiotic Analysis of Spanish Local e-Government Websites. In: Proceedings of the 7th European Conference on E-Government 2007. ECEG, Academic Conferences Ltd (2007)
32. Nielsen, J.: Usability Engineering. Acad. Press, Boston (1993)
33. Fink, S., Holzner, M. (eds.): VoicE D 3.1 Editorial Report. Deliverable, VoicE Consortium (May 2008)
34. Scherer, S., Liotas, N., Wimmer, M.A., Tambouris, E., Tarabanis, K.: Interoperability Requirements, Recommendations and Standards in E-Participation. In: Charalabidis, Y. (ed.) Interoperability in Digital Public Services and Administration: Bridging E-Government and E-Business, ch. 6, IGI Global (to appear 2010)
35. Chin, G.: Agile project management: how to succeed in the face of changing project requirements. McGraw-Hill Professional, New York (2004)
36. Macintosh, A.: Characterizing e-participation in policy-making. In: Proceedings of the 37th Annual Hawaii International Conference on System Sciences (HICSS-37), Big Island, Hawaii, January 5-8, vol. 5, IEEE Computer Society, Los Alamitos (2004)

Virtual Communities as a Mechanism for Sustainable Coordination within the South African Public Sector

Godwin Thomas and Reinhardt A. Botha

School of ICT & Institute for ICT Advancement, Nelson Mandela Metropolitan University,
Port Elizabeth, 6031 South Africa
{Godwin.Thomas,ReinhardtA.Botha}@nmmu.ac.za

Abstract. Due to limited resources, organizations are constantly facing challenges. To take advantage of new opportunities and mitigate possible risks they look for new ways to collaborate with each other, sharing knowledge and competencies. Hence, coordination among partners is critical to achieve success. The segmented South African public sector is no different. Driven by the desire to ensure proper service delivery in the sector, various government bodies and service providers play different roles towards common goals.

As such, continuous coordination is required between the role players. This paper investigates Virtual Communities as a possible coordination artifact for supporting sustainable coordination within the South African public sector. The paper commences with a brief introduction. Thereafter, the paper carefully defines the notion of sustainable coordination. It continues then to show that Virtual Communities indeed support the requirements for sustainable coordination. Having argued this at a theoretical level, the paper moves to show how this may be applicable to the South African situation. The paper concludes by emphasizing on the value of virtual communities as separate entities to attain sustainable coordination service provision in the South African public sector.

Keywords: Sustainable coordination; Coordination mechanisms; Virtual Communities; South African public sector.

1 Introduction

Various types of Virtual Communities exist. These can be defined in terms of the subjects and tasks they deal with. However, they share similar characteristics. Virtual Communities can form, disband, and re-form to meet spontaneous and emerging situations. In addition, they transcend geographic location and time constraints enabling anywhere, anytime access.

Organizations are constantly faced with a dynamic and unstable environment that requires flexible and fast responses to changing and emerging business needs [1]. These requirements for agility and geographic independence are met by the properties of Virtual Communities. In addition to knowledge exchange between members, Virtual Communities may aid in coordinating work [2]. Well coordinated work processes are critical for organizational performance as they improve efficiency and produce high quality outcomes [3].

M. Janssen et al. (Eds.): EGES/GISP 2010, IFIP AICT 334, pp. 62–75, 2010.

Coordination among stakeholders is critical to ensure sustainable development and service delivery. The South African public service is no different than other organizations in that proper coordination between the various organizations (governmental or non-governmental) charged with delivering public policy/services will prevent both redundancy and gaps in service delivery.

However, this is easier said than done. South Africa has a complex governmental structure that involves a variety of provinces, local governments and municipalities with different authority and responsibility. The three spheres of government are distinct. However, they are also interdependent as they work together towards a common governmental goal. Therefore, all the spheres of government are required to observe the principles of cooperative government set out in chapter three of the Constitution. In summary, those principles call for a clear division of roles and responsibilities, a collective approach to policy, coordination of activities to avoid duplication and waste, effective use of resources, and constructive settlement of disputes. Hence, the need for a proper and sustainable coordination service provision.

Coordination according to Malone and Crowston [4] and Gittel [3] mostly depends on underlying processes of decision-making, communication, and sharing of objects. For instance most of the coordination mechanisms require that some decision be made and accepted by a group (for example, what goal will be selected or which actors will perform which activities). In turn, group decisions require members of the group to communicate in some form about the goals to be achieved, the alternatives being considered, the evaluations of these alternatives, and the choices that are made. This communication requires that some form of "messages" be transported from senders to receivers in a language that is understandable to both. Hence, communication can be seen as a coordination device for mutual understanding.

Virtual Communities promise new possibilities for people to create, communicate and share knowledge among each other, thus forming a network. In essence, it promises support for knowledge sharing in situations requiring mutual adjustment by individuals, groups or organizations. It can capture and diffuse through the network information relevant to sustainability outcomes.

The paper sets out to identify the prospects that Virtual Communities can offer for sustainable coordination. Specifically the paper argues for its appropriateness in the South African public service that requires such coordination form to enhance and ensure proper and continuous service delivery.

In order to argue the case, it is necessary to understand the goal, being sustainable coordination, better. The next section therefore looks to characterize the concept of sustainable coordination.

2 Characterizing Sustainable Coordination

In order to unpack the challenges of coordination this section firstly investigates what sustainable coordination entails. Thereafter, it delves into coordination mechanisms and their associated complexities. This section therefore sets off to identify from the literature on sustainability the properties that will characterize sustainable coordination. The characteristics identified will help in mapping and analyzing the advantages virtual communities can provide (section 3).

2.1 Sustainable Coordination

Underlying sustainability is the principle that we must meet the needs of the present without compromising the ability of future generations to meet their needs. Reflecting on the notion of sustainability, Fuch [5] and Rogers, Jalal and Boyd [6], based on a report by Brundtland "Our common future" [7], described sustainable development as a dynamic process of change consistent with future as well as present needs. In essence, sustainability is characterized by a continuous change process ensuring that current and future needs are met.

Attaining levels of sustainability requires the accumulation of core competences provided by individuals or organizations necessary to achieve a common purpose. Resource Dependence Theory stipulates that a single organization usually does not have all the necessary resources at its disposal [8]. Interdependency between organizations can lead to a network of organizations that collaborate, reorganizing themselves to adapt to situations quickly. According to Griffiths [9], networks are relevant to sustainability because they leverage the economies of scale and scope – they grow whilst keeping the constituent units small, flexible, responsive and innovative.

Having a common purpose is important for identifying/employing the right competencies to achieve desired outcomes. In addition, it serves as a reference point for monitoring progress and resource usage. Also characterizing sustainability is ensuring autonomy in decision making while linking relevant individualized work to meet a common purpose [8]. Hence, greater organizational commitment and employee satisfaction can be generated.

However, members forming alliances or partnerships must be willing to communicate to coordinate activities to achieve outcomes. Since a partnership means depending on each other to make decisions that will benefit all participating members a high degree of trust is required [10]. This usually entails sharing critical information between partners to achieve desired outcomes.

Furthermore, sustainability requires that limited resources are well utilized, hence the need to ensure that units of work are performed in line with a common goal. According to Jayatilaka [11] a meaningful and sustained development requires the concentrated efforts of a number of organizations managed effectively by skilled personnel. Hence, in line with Fuch, [5] projecting the need for governance. Any process in an organization needs an owner [12]; the coordination process should not be different.

While having autonomy allows freedom to act in accordance to specialized expertise, a governance framework ensuring alignment of work done to actual goal is critical. Hence, a balance between administrative control and autonomic decision making needs to be established to ensure success of an overall work process.

Drawing on the preceding discussion, Table 1 provides a summary of the properties described as characterizing sustainable coordination. We refer to the term "dynamic" in the table to represent adaptability, flexibility, agility, innovation and continuity properties mentioned in the discussion.

In order to understand the complexities associated with coordination, the next section discusses the coordination mechanisms that can be used to manage interdependencies between activities/actors.

Table 1. Properties of sustainable coordination

Properties	Authors
Dynamic	Fuch [5]; Pamkowska [8]; Rogers, et al. [6]; Griffith [9]; Gettel [3]
Control/steering	Fuch [5]; Jayatilaka [11]
Autonomy (decision making)	Griffith [9]; Ke & Wei [10]
Members/Partners	Griffith [9]; Pamkowska [8]
Trust	Pamkowska [8]; Gettel [3]
Communication	Griffith [9]; Malone and Crowston [4]; Brunland [7]
Common Purpose	Gettel [3]; Fuch [5]; Brunland, [7]

2.2 Coordination Mechanisms

Working together implies managing interdependencies among participants toward some common end [4]. Different types of interdependences and mechanisms to manage the dependencies have been identified in literature [13, 14]. Figure 1 shows coordination mechanisms to comprise two aspects: structure and process. The coordination structure provides the necessary connection to execute the process. The coordination process in a way builds the structure by facilitating communication and configuring decision making patterns. In addition, it complements modular-based structures by, for example optimally prioritizing or rearranging modules. Hence, the relationship between the mechanisms is reciprocal as they usually co-exist in an organizational setting.

Decision making, communication pattern [15] and modularization [16] constitute the three elements of coordination mechanism's structure. Modularization separates and groups system components in a variety of ways allowing much greater flexibility in end configurations [17]. Resources and capabilities need to be coordinated in adaptive ways to lead to a desired outcome, hence fostering a sustainable action of coordination. For example, a project can be divided to small manageable teams willing to collaborate to achieve a common outcome. There are a variety of coordination process mechanisms; however, they are classified in three major groups: mechanistic coordination, organic coordination and cognitive coordination. Yet, dependencies are very domain-specific, and the mechanisms to manage them must therefore be considered in a specific context as well.

In essence, there is no single blueprint or model for achieving coordination that will be adequate for all problem contexts. More likely, the coordination mechanisms or combination thereof will have to fit the type of the problem, work within the constraints and opportunities offered by the existing organizational landscape/capacity, take local political and social, economic and cultural context into consideration and adapt and innovate within space.

As shown in figure 1, new dependencies emerge through modularization, and a "shopping list" of coordination mechanisms can be selected from the catalog of controls (structure and process) to fit work context. At this level interdependent tasks are expanded, and then corresponding coordination mechanisms are inserted.

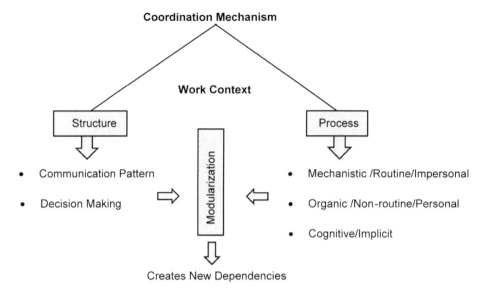

Fig. 1. Catalogue of coordination mechanisms

In order to help us attain a position of sustainable coordination the next section investigates the possible promise that the properties of virtual communities may provide.

3 Virtual Communities

Sustainable coordination does not happen by itself, so was the argument of this paper thus far. The previous section unpacked "sustainable coordination" and characterized it through enumerating specific requirements. This section sets out to argue that the properties exhibited by Virtual Communities promise to meet those requirements.

Virtual Communities can be described as self-organizing socio-technical systems as they exhibit both technological and social aspects [18]. They are strategic in that individuals through cooperative behaviour can be organized and focused towards actions to accomplish goals. In essence, they exhibit dynamic properties such as flexibility, adaptability, scalability and robustness. Fuch [18] describes Virtual Communities as dynamic systems based on ICT enabling communication that are regularized and structured by general rules of interaction, shared interest and general topics of interaction. Through continuous ICT-mediated communication feelings of togetherness and belonging, shared identity and common values can emerge. As such, Virtual Communities are dialectical systems in which the technological networks and social networks are interconnected and complement each other in a self-referential loop; they are self-organizing. As such, when establishing a Virtual Community, both the technological and social aspects (people and relationships) must be examined as they shape each other.

For example, while a virtual environment can provide interaction capability (e.g. email) the sophistication level of the interaction need (e.g. real time interaction via video conferencing) may arise with time, which can be supported by technology.

3.1 Virtual Communities for Sustainable Coordination

Virtual communities promise sustainability as they exhibit dynamic properties. They recognize that organizations will come together (form virtual teams), disband, and reform to solve or address important issues. Hence, they can form adaptive structures to suite any given context as need arises. For example, the Open Source Network community depends on volunteers across the globe for software creation and development. Virtual teams can transcend time and space boundaries and reduce costs by effectively using ICT [19]. In addition, they gather information, diffuse knowledge that provides the potential for innovation and enable rapid and effective response (e.g. Dell computers' reliance on business partners to fulfill major parts of their supply chains).

Furthermore, sustainable coordination as mentioned requires a "common purpose". By definition the formation of Virtual Communities depends on the members having a common purpose. For example, International Open Source Network (IOSN) is focused on promoting the strategic use of free/open source software solutions for sustainable human development.

The question "how do these members know about each other" begs. The motivation to participate in a community can be intrinsic or extrinsic [20]. These motivators are the drivers capable of evoking specific outcome behaviour. Common interests can lead to relationship building in both face-to-face and virtual communities. As such, having a common purpose provides a reason to participate and interact comfortably in a virtual community. Virtual communities can be formed around an infinite number of shared interests. Participants can be drawn together when they share projects (research or work) or through referrals or contracts for a common purpose. However, communication is needed to coordinate actions.

Communication is at the centre of a community to achieve a common purpose [21]. As noted in section 2.2, communication is important to attain sustainable coordination. Virtual communities provide interactive meeting places where people can add value to work-related practices thus, communication is attained. Communication is defined by the interactions among participants supported through ICT. Virtual communities enable concurrent conversation streams and can allow other electronic information to be integrated into an interaction.

Another essential for sustainable coordination is trust. Communication is an important trust building mechanism. Virtual Communities provide an interactive environment that facilitates trust building. Increased trust and commitment among partners can facilitate the processes of knowledge sharing, participative decision making and conflict resolution, which will further enhance trust and commitment of the participants and ultimately yields better joint performance [22]. According to De Moor and Weigand [21] trustworthiness grows out of iterative processes of interaction, observation, analysis and judgement.

Virtual communities consist of a network of competencies pulled together to achieve an outcome, hence, participants remain autonomous and independent [2].

Virtual communities promise autonomy as they allow people to work together independently and communicate via the internet. Members maintain the responsibility for decision making and control of information concerning their competencies in a virtual community.

Based on the characteristics exhibited by Virtual communities we argue that they can support sustainable coordination. However, they must be governed properly. Virtual communities as socio-technical entities need control and steering to maintain the common interest of the community [23]. Although virtual communities support decentralized and autonomic decision making, there is a need to monitor structures, control communication and information flow among members in accordance to the communities operation principles. To define rules and coordinate actions of a community different governance models exist. This is discussed in more detail in the next section.

3.2 Virtual Communities for Facilitating Coordination Processes

Virtual communities can facilitate the coordination of work processes. According to the theory of relational coordination, coordination that occurs through frequent, high quality communication supported by relationships of shared goals, shared knowledge and mutual respect enables organizations to better achieve their desired outcomes. As shown by Fuch [18], the self-organizing nature of Virtual Communities promises to support relationship building. With advancement in technology, there exist applications that can supplement the face to face interaction (e.g. Skype) to further strengthen relationships.

The underlying ICT infrastructure which hosts the community supports frequent and quality interactions for mutual adjustment especially in situation of uncertainty.

Also, structure-based mechanisms can be enabled as communication and decision making pattern can be reconfigured immediately to suite context (e.g multi-user virtual games). Therefore, Virtual Communities facilitate information exchange, thus communication takes place and quality decisions can be made. With support from a coordination process repository, coordination process mechanisms can be dynamically assigned to any given business process or workflow.

Virtual teams can be assigned to coordinate activities based on a business process or workflow that possibly spans across geographical boundaries. Coordination roles or referrals in Virtual Communities can serve as structural components to positively influence trust formation in the community [23]. According to Davidow and Malone [24] coordination and control of information are critical success factors for virtual communities.

However, since the traditional mechanisms of control, management, and steering are hardly applicable in Virtual Communities, different modes of governance in the virtual environment have emerged. The appropriateness or choice of governance structure or a combination thereof will depend on the context of a community's existence. According to Ahuja and Carley [25], although virtual communities may be non-hierarchical and decentralized from an authority standpoint they may still be hierarchical and somewhat centralized from a communication standpoint.

In a continuum of two extreme modes of centralized and decentralized governance structures as shown in figure 2 four basic modes of governance can be identified [26].

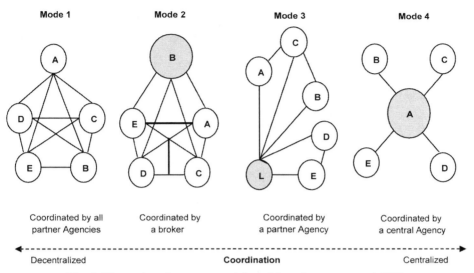

Fig. 2. The modes of governance. Adapted from Lattemann et al. [26].

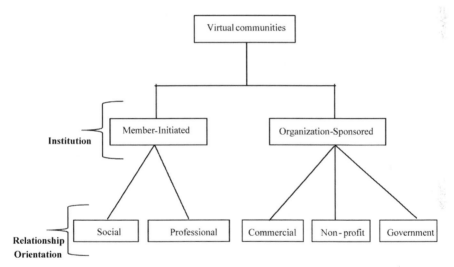

Fig. 3. A typology of virtual communities. Adapted from Porter [29].

Although Virtual communities promote autonomous decision making and encourages independent actions through modularization excessive decentralization has a strong potential to create inefficiencies, such as duplication of effort and resource wastage. To help avoid this, the management trend has shifted towards a governance structure that enables the best attributes of centralization and decentralization to be applied based on the needs of context [27]. Hence, it should not be assumed that non-hierarchical/decentralized communication structures are necessarily more effective than hierarchical/centralized structures. Rather, communication structure should be based on context characteristics.

Furthermore, the choice of a virtual community type can influence the governance structure. Figure 3 depicts a typology of virtual communities utilizing two main categories: Member-initiated and Organization-sponsored.

In order to enable optimal organization and management of functions and contents of virtual communities, the community type must be identified and defined [28, 29]. Also, a hybrid model can be adopted. However, to select a suitable model that will cater for the need of the community it is critical to characterize the domain or need context. In effort to identify a suitable model, the next section looks at the South African public sector to define the context of existence.

4   The South African Situation Analysis

The South African spheres of government are distinct, but interdependent as they collectively work toward common governmental goals. However, the size of the public sector, the number of role players, not to mention shortage of skilled personnel, affects the coordination of developmental activities. Hence, greater organization and coordination efforts are required. Each entity in the public sector contributes in its unique way to the success of the government. As such, each entity has specific needs. However, these entities also have several commonalities. Thus, well-coordinated programmes need to recognize the uniqueness of each entity, while exploring economies of scale for the commonalities. In order to understand the coordination challenges and requirements this section looks to provide an analysis of the South public sector situation with specifics in terms of the capacity building initiatives. It begins by looking at the South African public sector as-is in the next section.

4.1   The Case Status Quo

In effort to meet the challenge of cooperative government in the South African public sector, intergovernmental forums at national and provincial level dealing with issues of alignment, integration and coherence were developed. For instance, the Integrated Developing Planning (IDP), an intergovernmental planning instrument for the whole of government calls for dialogue between spheres. Thus, national priorities are influenced and shaped by the articulation by communities of their needs through the IDP process [30]. For instance, the need for training is guided by the integrated development plan (IDP). Hence, the need for cooperation as stipulated in the constitution across spheres.

As mentioned in section 2.1, no one single actor has all the resources (knowledge/information and competence) required to solve all problems. Thus, there is wide acceptance that a decentralized set of formal and informal agreements among diverse groups and organizations in the form of networks/partnerships hold the most promising institutional prospects to achieve sustainable development [31]. This form of interdependence is prominent in the South African public service as evident in the creation of agencies to carry out specific governmental tasks. For example there are numerous role players (internal/ external) involved in a variety of capacity building efforts in terms of training in the public service [30]. The development of interdependent relationships based on trust, loyalty and reciprocity enables collaborative activity to be developed and maintained.

However, as mentioned by Peter [32] one of the major problems facing contemporary governments is a lack of coordination and coherence across government departments or programs. This results in increased costs and reduced efficiency in the delivery of services to citizens. For instance, several training interventions in the South African public service are being made in all three spheres of government: national, provincial and local by numerous role players. However, these intervention programmes frequently illustrated misalignment with competency requirements and inappropriate content, duplication and fragmentation of efforts. In addition, there are conflicting schedules and an over-extension of staff who require the intervention. To help overcome these problems we discuss in the next section how the separation of coordination processes from work processes with Virtual Communities as the mediating artifact, can assist in meeting the coordination needs of the South African public sector.

4.2   The Separation of Coordination Processes from Work Processes

Considering the size and dynamic nature of the South African public service, the number of role players and communication pathways, we propose the separation of the coordination processes from the actual work processes to focus on the management of dependencies. This approach releases individuals who form nodes in the workflow from the task and worries of coordination to focus on core capabilities to provide the specialized services required in the workflow or business process. For instance, the task of consolidating and aligning training needs, scheduling, notifying and synchronizing appropriate stakeholders and monitoring should be handled as a primary task, not be imposed on employees as an extra background task.

Looking at the complexities involved in the coordination of the numerous programs/stakeholders in the South African public sector there is a need for a dedicated body to handle coordination activities hence, improve efficiency and performance. The institution should not necessarily be physical but virtual. Since work processes can span across organizational boundaries and may require high levels of flexibility we propose using virtual communities as the coordination artifact.

Virtual Communities, as mentioned in section 3.1, can serve as mechanism for sustainable coordination because the organizational model is fluid and flexible. They can provide access to skills/competencies and connect geographically dispersed members and resources.

Our proposed Virtual Community is aimed at providing a support service of coordinating work processes among stakeholders responsible for service delivery in the South African public service. The community is intended to coordinate a group of stakeholders with varying competencies, both internal (government bodies) and external partners (required competencies) pulled together to deliver value.

The Virtual Community will serve as an intermediate between partners without any self-interest. Its only objective is to improve the effectiveness of that particular community by quickly identifying the opportunities. For instance, from a holistic view of training activities, duplication and conflicts can be detected and resolved. Furthermore, groupings of training activities can help achieve economies of scale and scope.

Virtual Communities as self-organizing can maintain relationship with stakeholders, thus allowing the quick assignment of tasks to physical organizations based on the available information of stakeholder capabilities. All entities with potential to complete any component process can be identified. Therefore, the combination of processes to be performed, geographic location and potential prior experiences with different providers can be matched based on a given workflow. For instance, performance of training providers can be tracked and recorded for future decision making on subsequent training required.

Virtual Communities can provide tracking and aid assessment capability, hence increase service provision satisfaction. However, there must be appropriate feedback from cooperating agencies to the Coordinating Virtual community indicating process status to effectively manage an entire process. Thus, notification to relevant members can be established and if necessary allocate work to another when problems occur.

However, the type of services to be provided or the needs will determine the nature or type of community to be formed (e.g. for mentorship programmes or share experiences on training provided). As such questions about community types and appropriateness arise. The next section looks to answer the question on the type of community we deem appropriate for our case context.

4.3   The Virtual Community Formation

In forming a Virtual Community to attain sustainable coordination, considering the different types of existing communities as illustrated in section 3.2, we lean towards organization-sponsored communities. As primary stakeholders in the public service, the government should drive the process. As mandated by the constitution they have the primary objective of delivering service to the public through well coordinated collaborative means. The motivation here should be intrinsic since a higher commitment should be expected.

While commercial entities' participation in a community will probably be short lived (level of commitment), most often based on the duration of a project, government agencies as core members will be charged with the continual service provision. We recognise that in this case, the concern is not about sustaining the organization in terms of longevity, but rather recognising that in the search for sustainability there will be need for limited term or temporary projects. Hence, organizations will come together to solve the issues and disband once they have been addressed. Government agencies are required to look for opportunities to collaborate leveraging the economy of scale and scope. As such, government based agencies are in a position to serve as the member organization that can define the rules of the community and coordinate the actions of members respectively. For example, the Department of Provincial and Local Government (DPLG) a key role player with the responsibility of strengthening capacity to coordinate capacity building and service delivery can take the lead. However, the question on how to control or govern the behavior of members arises. The next section attempts to address the question.

4.4   The Virtual Community Governance

Overall, the complexity and nature of the public service can give rise to, conceptually, one large community consisting of all participants and composed of many smaller communities or sub-communities for different kinds of needs or context. Due to trust and control issues that might arise the role of "community coordinator" can be fulfilled by a group of individuals selected from different participating governmental agencies anchored by the process owner to form a central broker. For instance, when a certain business process is in action, a team to oversee the process can be generated dynamically. For example, dynamically generating teams based on classification of training types (e.g. training area, mentorship) or duration (short-term or long-term). As such representatives of contracted external bodies can be members until the project is completed. By establishing groups within the community that represent all the participants' interest, cooperative behaviours are likely to be induced and prevail. A neutral broker institution (possesses knowledge of the business process) can support the partners with coordination, without establishing any hierarchy.

A hybrid governance model that maintains both centralized and decentralized modes of coordination is desirable. While peer-to-peer communications might be very efficient in a situation where a project affects few individuals only; in a large community inefficiencies and duplications can be introduced. Hence, it is essential to form strategic partnerships, organize network activities and identify new collaboration opportunities to improve overall effectiveness. By increasing community coordination efficiency in an overall work process can be improved.

5 Conclusion

It has been established that there is a need for a mechanism that can aid in the achievement of a sustainable coordination of developmental activities within the South African public service. We propose that one strategic approach to attaining such a goal is through the separation of coordination processes from work processes supported by Virtual Community as the mediating artifact. Virtual Communities can unify the intent of organization(s) and focus members towards processes designed to accomplish a desired outcome. We maintain that because Virtual Communities provide an interactive environment that transcends location and time, provide flexibility and innovation, they can support suitable coordination. Rapid decision-making pertaining to tasks in a geographically distributed environment is possible. Separating coordination from actual physical work processes helps in avoiding duplication of effort and allows for reuse of knowledge gained by the coordinating team. The community can evolve through learning, and relationships strengthened through sharing, hence it is self-organizing.

Inspired by ICT, a virtual community provides a lot of advantages. However, understanding the technology is not enough, social aspects (people and relationships) need to be examined to achieve success. We suggest the use of a community coordinator (teams) to enhance relationships and trust in the community. Furthermore, established teams should be anchored by a coordination process owner, due to their knowledge and understanding of the domain. The selection of a governance structure depends on the context of the activity performed and can evolve as the context change. Thus Virtual Communities are capable of solving problems through varied adaptive partnership or structure reorganization. Hence, we believe Virtual Communities can serve as ideal mechanisms for coordinating work processes.

However, Communities typically make unstructured decisions under condition of uncertainty. Therefore an integrated knowledge management system that spans geographical boundaries is desirable. Such an infrastructure will enable and facilitate knowledge flows among participating organizations. Needed knowledge can then get to the relevant participants on a timely basis in a suitable and affordable manner to accomplish their common goal.

References

1. Keinänen, K., Oinas-Kukkonen, H.: Virtual organizing as a strategic approach to stay competitive–: a conceptual analysis and case study. IGI Publishing Hershey, Pensylvania (2001)
2. Sagers, G.W., Michael, D.H., Wasko, M.M.: Coordinating Efforts in Virtual Communities: Examining Network Governance in Open Source. In: Proceedings of the Tenth Americas Conference on Information Systems, New York, pp. 2697–2698 (2004)
3. Gittel, J.H.: Coordinating mechanisms in care provider groups; Relational coordination as a mediator and input uncertainty as a moderator of performance effects. Managment Science 48, 1408–1426 (2002)
4. Malone, T.W., Crowston, K.: The interdisciplinary study of coordination. ACM Computing Surveys, 87–119 (1994)
5. Fuch, C.: Towards a Global Sustainable Information Society (GSIS)? tripleC - Cognition. Communication, Co-operation 4(1) (2006)
6. Rogers, P.P., Jalal, K.F., Boyd, J.A.: An introduction to sustainable development. Earthscan Publications Ltd., London (2008)
7. Brundtland, G.H.: Our Common Future, The World Commission on Environment and Development. Oxford University Press, Oxford (1987)
8. Pamkowska, M.: Autopoiesis in Virtual Organizations. Advanced Information Technologies for Management – AITM 2007. Revista Informatica Economică 1, 33–39 (2008)
9. Griffiths, A.: Corporate architectures for sustainability. International Journal of Operations & Production Management 21, 1573–1585 (2001)
10. Ke, W., Wei, K.K.: Factors affecting trading partners' knowledge sharing: Using the lens of transaction cost economics and socio-political theoriesstar, open. Electronic Commerce Research and Applications 6, 297–308 (2007)
11. Jayatilaka, W.: Capacity Building for Sustainable Development. J. Natn. Sci. Foundation Sri Lanka 36, 81–97 (2003)
12. West, J., Cianfrani, C.A.: Unlocking the power of your QMS: keys to performance improvement. American Society for Quality, Milwaukee (2004)
13. Mintzberg, H.: The structuring of organizations. Prentice Hall, Engelwood Cliffs (1979)
14. Malone, T.W.: What is Co-ordination Theory? Working Paper. Sloan School of Management, Massachusetts Institute of Technology (1998)
15. Malone, T.W.: Modeling Coordination in Organizations and Markets. Management Science 33, 1317–1332 (1987)
16. Shen, S.Y., Shaw, M.J.: Managing Coordination in Emergency Response Systems with Information Technologies. In: Proceedings of the Tenth Americas Conference on Information Systems. Association for Information Systems, New York (2004)
17. Schilling, M.A.: Toward a General Modular Systems Theory and Its Application to Inter-firm Product Modularity. Academy of Management Review 25, 312–334 (2000)

18. Fuchs, C.: Towards a dynamic theory of virtual communities. International Journal of Knowledge and Learning 3, 372–403 (2007)
19. Lucca, J., Sharda, R., Weiser, M.: Coordinating Technologies for Virtual Organization. Mobile Computing 19, 31–51 (2002)
20. Ryan, R.M., Deci, E.L.: Self-determination theory and the facilitation of intrinsic motivation, social development and well-being. American Psychologist 55, 65–78 (2006)
21. de Moor, A., Weigand, H.: Effective Communication in Virtual Adversarial Collaborative Communities. The Journal of Community Informatics 32, 223–247 (2006)
22. Chi, L., Holsapple, C.W.: Understanding computer mediated interorganizational collaboration: a model and framework. Journal of Knowledge Management 9, 53–75 (2005)
23. Akram, A., Allan, R., Rana, O.: Virtual communities and community coordinator. In: 2005 International Conference on Semantics, Knowledge and Grid (SKG 2005), Beijing, China, November 27-29, p. 110. IEEE Computer Society, California (2005)
24. Davidow, W.H., Malone, M.S.: The Virtual Corporation - Structuring and Revitalizing the Corporation for the 21st Century. Harper Collins, New York (1992)
25. Ahuja, M., Carley, K.: Network Structure in Virtual Organizations. Organization Science 10, 741–747 (1999)
26. Lattemann, C., Kupke, S., Stieglitz, S.: The Governance of Virtual Corporations. Journal of E-Business 7, 53–64 (2007)
27. Ulrich, W.M.: IT Centralization versus Decentralization: The Trend Towards Collaborative Governance, System Transformation Portal,
    http://www.systemtransformation.com/
    Org_Transformation_Articles/org_decentralization.htm
    (retrieved October 25, 2009)
28. Markus, U.: Characterizing the virtual community, SAP Design Guild, 5th edn. (2002),
    http://www.sapdesignguild.org/editions/edition5/
    communities.asp (retrieved October 1, 2004)
29. Porter, C.: A typology of virtual communities: a multi-disciplinary foundation for future research. Journal of Computer Mediated Communication 10 (2004)
30. DPLG, & SALGA.: National Capacity Building Framework for Local Government. Pretoria: Department of Provincial and Local Government (2008)
31. Muller, K.: Sustainable Development: The Question of Integration and Coordination. Journal of Public Administration 39, 398–410 (2004)
32. Peter, B.G.: Managing Horizontal Government: The Politics of coordination. Public Adminstration 76, 295–311 (1998)

EGES Session 3: Adoption and Diffusion

Examining the Role of the Culture of Local Government on Adoption and Use of E-Government Services

Nurdin Nurdin[*], Rosemary Stockdale, and Helana Scheepers

Faculty of Information and Communication Technologies
Swinburne University of Technology
nnurdin@swin.edu.au, rstockdale@swin.edu.au,
hscheepers@swin.edu.au

Abstract. This paper describes research in progress to explore the role of culture in adoption of e-government at local government levels. The majority of research in electronic government highlighted cultural issues but they do not identify specific cultural traits influencing e-government adoption and use. From our literature review we identified four major cultural traits; adaptability, involvement, mission, and bureaucratic, that is explored in this research. Based on these cultural traits and other cultural issues surrounding the adoption of e-government, we develop a framework to explore the role of culture in adopting and using e-government systems at local government organizations. Evidences suggest that the adoption of e-government at local levels is either mandatory or voluntary which is followed by supportive policies from central governments. Our conclusion is that during the adoption process, the cultural traits contribute to the adoption and use of e-government systems.

Keywords: Organizational culture, e-government, adoption, local government.

1 Introduction

Research into the adoption of technology at organizational level has mainly focused on technological issues [1, 2], with fewer studies conducted on non-technical factors such as organizational culture and individuals within organizations [3]. The absence of considering cultural consequences in the adoption of technology at organizational level may lead to the failure of the adoption process as there are direct impacting influences between culture and information technology (IT) and between an organization's culture and its IT users [4]. Therefore adoption of technology by organizations should also focus on the organizational and cultural issues because culture plays a role as a significant success factor [5], and as a barrier to adoption [6].

The adoption of electronic government initiatives is no different from commercial information systems. Although some researchers have found that the success of e-government adoption is determined by technological factors [7], others have identified

---

[*] On leave from STAIN Datokarama Palu, Indonesia.

M. Janssen et al. (Eds.): EGES/GISP 2010, IFIP AICT 334, pp. 79–93, 2010.

cultural elements that contribute to electronic government adoption and use [8, 9]. Transferring technology from developed countries to developing countries or from private to public organizations has also caused cultural gaps that need to be addressed [10]. We thus recognize that culture exists in the context of e-government adoption and use, although few researchers or practitioners devote attention to the cultural issues during new technology adoption in government organizations at either central or local levels.

This research explores the role of cultural dimensions in adopting e-government at local government level. We examine how specific cultural dimensions have a role in local government technology adoption through a complex interweaving between technology and government. This leads us to form the research question as follows - *what cultural and sub-cultural dimensions play a role in local government technology initiatives, and how do they contribute to the adoption and use of local-e-government systems?* The contribution of this paper is the development of a deeper understanding of the role of cultural dimensions in the adoption and use of local electronic government.

The paper is organised as follows. First we define and discuss organizational culture before addressing the concept of e-government technology adoption at local level. We then examine four cultural dimensions and other sub cultural dimensions derived from organizational culture theories, which are operationalized in the context of e-government adoption. This is followed by a discussion of the cultural dimensions, which focus on external orientation and internal integration, as well as change and flexibility, and stability and direction. Finally the identified constructs are brought together to build a framework that will inform the next stage of the research into the role of culture in the adoption of local e-government initiatives.

2   Understanding Organizational Culture

The term culture has been widely used at national and organizational level. However, there is no single universal definition for culture. Hofstede [11] defines culture as *"programming of the mind which distinguishes the members of one human group from another"*. Sathe [12] said culture is *"the set of important understanding (often unstated) that members of a community share in common"*. Meanwhile, organizational culture is defined by Denison [13] as *"the underlying values, belief, and principles that serve as a foundation for an organization's management system as well as the set of management practices and behaviour that both exemplify and reinforce those basic principles"*.

An organization's culture forms the personality of the organization [14] through the socialization process of people in the workplace of the organization [15]. It becomes a beneficial asset for an organization if it supports the organization's mission, goals and strategies [16] and plays an important role in many aspects of the organization [17]; for example culture plays a role in the statement of mission and goals of the organization, and indirectly shapes behaviour [18]. Through organizational culture, individuals inside the organization obtain a common understanding of the core mission of their organization and that leads to consensus development on how to achieve organizational goals.

Organizational culture which is derived from individuals' experience and history is unique [19]. Certain organizations might have a strong culture while others might not, depending on how the culture is derived and established within the firm. A strong organizational culture, which is useful for organizations' development, is embedded in the long term interaction of its members in coping with external adaptation and internal integration [20]. This strong culture, then, can be used to counter internal and external problems [21] in maintaining the organization's survival in turbulent situations.

3 Electronic Local Government Adoption and Use

The adoption of technology in e-government has many similarities to that of an organization where decisions are made at a senior level and then assimilated into the organization [22]. The process of adoption may be mandated or voluntary [23, 24]. In certain contexts, voluntary adoption is more successful [23, 25, 26], while in another situation mandatory policy is the only way to induce technology usage because it can encourage the initial behaviour to adopt technology [27] . For example, a senior manager may drive primary adoption of innovation after identifying objectives to change some aspects of the business and then mandate the organization to adopt the technology [28]. In other words, both mandatory and voluntary adoption strategies offer the promise of successful technology adoption in the relevant context and situation.

This concept is no different from the adoption of technology in local government organizations where the use of technology is sometimes initiated by central governments through setting of certain goals or it is initiated at grassroots levels. A mandatory approach may exist in e-government adoption due to political nature and law-abiding citizens [29]. For example, the UK government launched a modernization agenda in 1997 to transform local authorities' performance across the UK. This new agenda has resulted in the implementation of electronic government at local level across the UK [30]. In a further step, the UK central government set "e-government targets" which mandated all government agencies to provide on-line interactions between government agencies and the public by 2005 [31]. Failure to conform to these policies and regulations can result in imposing of sanctions by central governments such as withdrawing funding that has been allocated to local governments [32]. Similarly, a mandatory approach was considered to have a significant impact on the success of the Smart Cards adoption in the medical sectors in Canada [33]. These examples show that a central government has the power to impose the adoption of e-government on local government bodies by delivering policies and regulations to improve governments' services.

A mandating policy to adopt e-government includes imposing processes, values, competencies and systems [34]. Heeks [34] argues that implementing e-government requires or imposes the formality of process and management, involves the role and skills of people, and is subjected to the rationality of organizational culture. In other words, central governments should contribute to e-government adoption at local level by supporting the change of management, empowering people to increase involvement, and adjustment of organizational culture to new technology.

However, in the US context, the adoption of e-government at local levels was initiated at grassroots levels in 2000 due to the demand of the citizens [35, 36] while the E-Government Act, which includes the planning of an e-government strategy and initiative implementation, was launched in 2002 [37]. This means the initiatives were developed on the basis of local government initiatives while in the next step the central government provided guidelines to support better implementation of the initiatives. For rapid adoption of e-government, the US government also provides incentives to encourage citizens to use the systems such as giving cost reductions for making online tax transactions through the federal portal [38].

In the developing countries context, the adoption of e-government can also be mandatory or voluntary. For example, the successful adoption of an e-government portal by government departments in Hong Kong was determined by voluntary decision and support from higher level of the government [39]. Similarly, in the case of electronic tax managed by Central Excise in India, the citizens are encouraged, rather than required, to adopt the system [40]. In both cases, the e-government initiatives are voluntarily adopted at lower levels but the initiatives are started at central level not at grassroots such as in the US. However, in contrast, in the case of Tanzanian's Integrated Tax Administration (ITAX) as a part of e-government implementation [41], adoption of the project was mandatory for all tax regions of the country by 2007. The initiative was under the control of and supported by a task force authority at central level.

E-government infrastructure, such as computer networks, communication systems and shared services are typically belong to various of entities at local and central levels which need a cohesiveness and dynamicity in its implementation [42]. This means both central and local government entities are involved in electronic local government development regardless whether the initiatives are mandatory or voluntary. Central government might provide ongoing supports because successful e-government projects may be abandoned or not sustained after years of adoption if supportive infrastructure, such as financial, political, technical, are terminated [32, 34, 43].

4   Culture Dimensions in E-Government Adoption

Researchers have identified many cultural value dimensions or traits; for example Leidner and Kayworth's [44] review of the literature on culture found 46 value dimensions of culture at national, organizational and sub-unit level. Out of those 46 cultural dimensions, four key traits, identified at the level of organizational culture, are indicated in major e-government research [10, 34, 45-48] and are therefore adopted as relevant to our study. These traits are those of adaptability, involvement and mission as identified by Denison and Mishra [17] and the trait of bureaucracy identified by Wallach [16].

Denison and Mishra's framework has been applied to empirical studies to examine cultural issues in a range of environments. Gateo and Wausi [49] applied the framework to understand organizational culture and the adaptation of technology in the Kenyan University system while Dasgupta and Gupta [8] used the framework together with Davis's TAM theory to explore the role of culture in internet adoption in India. Schaper and Pervan's [50] study examined some aspects of the framework in the context of e-government in Australia. However, these latter studies are broader in their examination of adoption beyond purely cultural influences, and the cultural traits from Denison and Mishra's framework have not been used in the specific understanding of cultural influences on local e-government adoption.

In examining the four organizational level cultural traits, the bureaucratic element from Wallach's [16] perspective is used to replace the cultural trait of consistency as proposed by Denison and Mishra [17]. Bureaucratic culture is concerned with explicit rules, regulations, and hierarchies in an organization, which is typical of government organizations where such explicit rules are implemented rather than implicit ones as proposed by Denison and Mishra [17] in the consistency cultural traits. The four organizational culture dimensions are discussed in the next sections.

4.1 Involvement

Involvement is a subjective psychological state of users which is practiced in forms of participation through behaviour and activities [51]. This cultural trait supports the members of an organization to gain a sense of responsibility, and commitment in the organization because they are highly involved in the organization's activities [17]. Denison and Mishra [17] add that when people in the organization have high involvement, the organization is more productive because they are more committed and responsible towards the organization's interest, but when the organization has low involvement, it experiences difficulties in responding to critical environmental change. However, in our study the concept of people involvement is defined not only by people inside the organization but also people outside the organization, such as citizens, that support the success of e-government adoption.

Low involvement of users influences user participation during the information system development because users' beliefs and attitude are not clearly formed [52]. This can affect the success of a system development adoption in a private or public organization. For example, the wide range of users' participation in e-stamping adoption in Hong Kong has contributed to its successful implementation [53]. This indicates that high participation of users in an organization's activities can determine the achievement of an organization's goals. Their participation is shown in the form of a high commitment to involvement in and support of the organization's projects.

A sense of commitment plays a role in many aspects of the involvement dimension such as in organizational change. This is identified in Rowlinson's [54] study of a public organization in Hong Kong, which experienced difficulties in changing its management when departments had a low level of commitment [54]. Government organizations that adopt new technologies often practice change that requires organizational integration and consolidation between their individuals and organization's interest. During the internal integration, government organizations need highly committed people because they will work hard to achieve organizational goals [55].

Building partnerships between stakeholders such as public, private and citizens [56] can support the success of collaboration in performing organizations' projects. The value of partnership is concerned with the relationship of individuals and organizations in fulfilling participants' shared goals [57]. Jae-Nam and Youne-Gul [57] argue that this partnership value positively affects people's willingness to participate, communicate, to share information, and support the management of organizations. Partners work together and take responsibility to achieve common goals of an organization.

A sense of responsibility can arise among individuals when they get benefit from the assigned tasks. For example, people get benefit from carrying out the tasks through the job learning that can empower their skill to improve productivity [58]. When individuals gain responsibility values from organizations, they tend to cooperate with each other in accomplishment of organizational tasks. Such cooperation increases the feeling of interdependence among them which results in a heightened sense of responsibilities towards helping others in achieving their goals [59].

In the context of e-government adoption and use, good participation of people through partnership building can enhance adoption as the high level of collaboration by multiple stakeholders will increase the level of acceptance and increase the quality as well as preventing conflict [60]. High levels of collaboration in the adoption of e-government results in establishing a high sense of responsibility and commitment to support the success of e-government projects, as seen in a study of e-government adoption in Singapore [61]. Stakeholders may include highly committed leaders with strong leadership who want to take real responsibility in facilitating a successful e-government adoption [53]. They show their commitment through their involvement by viewing information technology as a critical success factor for their organizations [62].

4.2 Adaptability

Adaptability is a value of an organization that focuses on external situation demand by developing norms and beliefs that support its capacity to respond to the need for change [17]. In other words, an organization's adaptability is driven by communities from outside of the organization [63]. Community expectations and demands often become a basis for governments in implementing new innovation in their organizations such as the demand of citizens for technology based services that enable them to access government services 24/7.

The development of technology has increased the demand for organizations' environments to be transparent. The transparency, which is driven by the technology, is practiced by organizations not only to their surroundings but also to themselves [64] and is their endeavour to adapt their environment through openness to all stakeholders. In government organizations, openness includes communicating details of systems and decision making to external observers [65]. The willingness of organizations to be transparent can enhance trust building between people inside an organization and external stakeholders and, as a result, contributes to organization responsiveness to their environment.

Trust can create and enhance positive conditions, such as positive interpretation of another's behaviour, which enhances cooperation at group level and raises an organization's performance [66]. Another positive impact is that the cohesion and collaboration between people is facilitated by the presence of the trust value [67]. As a result, collective action of people can be generated and maintained in performing organizational tasks. In addition, when the value of trust is perceived among stakeholders, the organizational risk toward innovative implementation is diminished as people are likely not to perceive the innovation as a risk to them.

Transparency and trust in organizations are driven by external factors. According to Markus external factors influence organizations and people to behave in certain ways [68]. This means organizations practice change in responding to external demand by behaving in the way of external factors expectations. Organizational change in certain areas such as in structure, job design, and rewards system are accompanied by cultural changes to avoid resistance from people [20]. The changes help organizations to adapt to new influences from the external environment in order to survive. In certain circumstances, organizational change might be problematic due to the lack of organizational learning or difficulty mobilizing internal support [69].

The lack of organizational learning can be addressed through the building of a learning culture. Organizations learn through individuals developing the capacity to identify and correct errors [70]. Government organizations can also learn from other failure [10, 34] to improve their adaptability toward environmental expectations. Local government can learn from the failures they make during the adoption and use of e-government initiative and improve their system through improvisation. Failure can be conceived as a value that provides opportunities to learn what is applicable and what is not applicable in a new system inside their organization. Looking at other local government organizations can also help a local government identify the best actions to be taken in delivering high performance of e-government. During the learning process, local governments can obtain positive values from other successful electronic local government adoptions and then implement them in their own environment.

4.3 Mission

Mission is a cultural trait that provides purpose and meaning to an organization and also gives direction and identifies goals that enable an organization to act in an acceptable way [17, 71]. The organization establishes the mission as an instrument of culture based in the managerial ethos and ideology of the organization and it therefore influences the development of the organization [72]. From the mission statement the organization acquires purpose and meaning as it defines social roles in the organization and designates the roles of employees as related to the organization's role [17]. Clarity in the mission of an organization may stimulate an organization's members to engage in organizational tasks which positively relate with the level of mission motivation and result in higher organizational performance. Clear mission statements also help organizations' members to understand why their organizations exist, what they do, for whom they do it, and what the benefits are.

Achieving the mission of an organization should be supported by stating a clear vision which depicts how their future organizations will look if they achieve their mission. In other words, *"vision refers to some idealized goal that the leader wants the organization to achieve in the future"* [73]. The vision will guide and determine the success of future organizational achievement and its employees by motivating stakeholders to accomplish their goals. This motivation arises as the consequence of a positive atmosphere created by the vision such as an increase in trust, and a good relationship between leaders and subordinates. Organizational vision positively affects the attribution of followers, trust in organizational leaders, and positive congruence between leader's and followers' beliefs and attitudes [74].

Mission and vision are transferred in the form of goal statements that enable organizations to operate them. The presence of operative goals in an organization is crucial because such goals depict the state of affairs which the organization tries to realize, the source of legitimation and existence, the source of standards for accessing the success of the organization, and an instrument to measure an organization's performance [75], although the goals must be measurable and achievable to enable organizations to accomplish them. The goals are not only stated in official terms but also embedded in a major organization's operating policies and in the daily decisions of employees that are reflected in the organization and employees' behaviour [76].

In e-government, the existence of clear mission, vision, and goals during the adoption and use process is important to maintain an organization's future directions. The mission and vision can be exhibited by top leaders who inspire a mindset change through government agencies to raise understanding of the importance of the transformation of government into e-government [77]. There is strong evidence that organizational visions can solve organizational cultural inertia during e-government adoption in government organizations such as the case of local government of Sragen [78]. Similarly, in the UK, local governments have a clear vision for "modernized" local government over a five year period where council and other services will be accessible through telephone or internet for 24 hours a day by their customers [46]. A further example is Singapore, which is held to have experienced success in e-government adoption through having a clear vision from the early implementation stage [79]. Success can also be achieved when the government organizations establish shared values through the setting of clear goals and priority agreements with communities when adopting e-government initiatives [46].

4.4 Bureaucratic

Bureaucratic culture refers to an organization's culture that has clear lines of responsibility and authority based on control and power [16]. Wallach argues that organizations are managed with strong explicit rules, are hierarchical, cautious, solid and procedural, and their people work in a systematic and an organized way in an environment where responsibility and authority are in clear lines. This appears to accord with organizations within a government environment and where those with a bureaucratic culture can achieve stability [80]. Since these organizations are well integrated through rules and hierarchies and are stable, their environment enhances the adoption of technology.

In bureaucratic organizational culture, explicit regulations are formalized which means rules, procedures, norms, standard of behaviour, and communication are written [81]. This provides an organization and its people with clarity in the regulations that enable them to perform their task and influence their behaviour according to organizational regulations. The behaviour of an organization and its members is practiced due to its conformity to the explicit regulations and the resulting formalization offers internal efficiencies. In addition, the explicit formal regulations can be an effective means for achieving coordination and integration inside organizations because the organizations and its members are bound to the regulations.

Furthermore, clear hierarchies are present in organizations in a bureaucratic culture that link people through vertical and horizontal line within the organization. In hierarchical organizations, people at higher levels set or ratify policies and objectives, and then communicate to lower level or subordinates who are charged with responsibility to take necessary actions [82]. In this way, the hierarchy provides legitimacy to senior people to direct subordinates to follow desired orders in performing organizational tasks. Coordination between people in horizontal levels is also well performed through the clear hierarchical relationship in organizations. In organizational social relationships, the hierarchical relationships are understood as an instrument to coordinate and determine the power and status among people [83]. As the result, organizations are solid and well structured because people have clear authorities, responsibilities, and job in the organizations.

Clear regulations and hierarchies help an organization and its members gain better coordination in accomplishing their tasks. Coordination integrates and links together different people at all levels and parts of the organizations to achieve a set of collective tasks [84]. Through the coordination people can work harmoniously to complete the subdivided tasks according their role. In the context of coordination, people are interdependent and work together in achieving organizational tasks which involves identifying goals, transferring goals to activities, assigning activities to people, and managing the relationships [85].

In the context of e-government, the presence of bureaucratic culture will benefit the process of the adoption because clear and explicit regulations and hierarchies support supervision to reduce the chance of errors, disobedience, and negligent behaviour among people. The equitable treatment of government clients is also guaranteed [47]. A bureaucratic culture underpins the effort a government organization and its people to achieve their goals to adopt e-government through a structure of conformity to the regulations. The solidity of government organizations, based on clear regulations and hierarchies, create a sense of responsibility to succeed in the adopting of e-government.

5   External and Internal Influences on Culture and Government Organization

The culture dimensions of an organization are related to both external adaptation and internal integration [14]. In studying the four cultural dimensions and identifying their sub-dimensions, we found that adaptability and mission appear to relate to the dynamics of external adaptation [17]. These external orientation cultural dimensions encourage organizations to develop their capacity to change in response to external conditions and expectations. External demands, such as global pressure on the prevention of corruption and public management reform [86], requires government organizations to change and adapt by implementing new technology. Another example, in the UK citizens' demands to interact with government agencies through electronic devices has led to local government implementing e-government initiatives [31].

On the other hand, the involvement and bureaucratic culture dimensions are influenced by internal integration. High levels of involvement by internal stakeholders in an organization will result in positive integration between the people and the organization's interest [17]. In addition, a bureaucratic culture creates a solid, well ordered, regulated, structured, and cautious organization [16]. This means government organizations are well governed and achieve better internal integration through implementing clear rules, regulations, hierarchies and structures.

A government organization's capacity to practice change and flexibility are determined by its culture of adaptability and involvement [17]. Meanwhile, the stability

and direction of government organizations are determined by their mission and bureaucratic cultural dimensions because government organizations are more solid and
governed by clear rules, regulations, hierarchies, structures and clear organizational
directions which are guided by clear mission statements [16, 17].

6   Theoretical Framework

The framework developed from the literature is depicted in Figure 1. The framework
shows the role of the four cultural traits and identified sub-cultural issues in e-
government adoption at local government levels. Cultural traits of adaptability and
mission have external orientation because they are driven by outside factors such as
citizens, while cultural traits of involvement and bureaucratic relate to internal integration because the need of government organizations to maintain their stability and
direction. All cultural dimensions influence the adoption and use of e-government
local government organizations, which is the focus of this study. Our framework depicts the adoption of e-governments as derived from either mandatory or voluntary
policy as found in the cases described in Section 3 and followed by supportive policies from both entities. This suggests that when e-government initiatives are adopted
at local levels across a country, both central and local governments are involved in a
dynamic and cohesive coordination to succeed the initiatives.

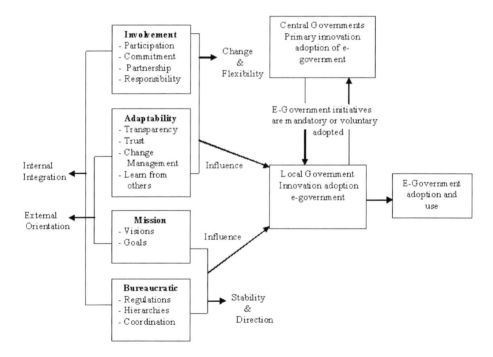

Fig. 1. The framework for exploring the role of culture in e-government adoption

7   Conclusions and Future Research

The framework in Figure 1 is derived from an extensive literature review into organizational culture, public administration, information systems and technology, and e-government literature. We have combined and modified cultural dimensions from Denison and Mishra [17], and Wallach [16] that are potentially relevant to government organizations. Further sub-cultural dimensions that support the organizational cultural dimensions have been drawn from the literature on public administration and management, IS and IT, and e-government to further inform the framework that will support exploration into local e-government adoption and use. The literature also supports the notion that adoption of e-government at local level can be mandated or voluntary both of which may be followed by supportive policies from central government through the provision of financial, political, and technical infrastructure.

Our framework represents a starting point for critical thinking in analysing cultural influences in local governments' adoption and use of electronic government. The framework is developed based on organizational culture theories that have evolved from the study of commercial organizations and may therefore have limitations in its applicability to an e-government environment. We intend to empirically test the framework to explore its validity for governmental environments and to examine for further cultural influences and interdependencies that have not yet been identified. A case study design is considered to be the appropriate method for conducting "how and why" enquiries into real world phenomena [87]. This methodology will allow for further, in-depth examination of the culture dimensions that influence and impact on local e-government adoption and use.

References

1. Dewett, T., Jones, G.R.: The Role of Information Technology in the Organization: A review, Model, and Assessment. Journal of Management 27, 313–346 (2001)
2. Iacovou, C.L., Benbasat, I., Dexter, A.S.: Electronic Data Interchange and Small Organizations: Adoption and Impact of Technology. MIS Quarterly 19(4), 465–485 (1995)
3. Cabrera, Á., Cabrera, E.F., Barajas, S.: The Key Role of Organizational Culture in a Multi-System View of Technology-Driven Change. International Journal of Information Management 21(3), 245–261 (2001)
4. Claver, E., et al.: The Performance of Information Systems Through Organizational Culture. Information Technology & People 14(3), 247–260 (2001)
5. Bagchi, K., Hart, P., Peterson, M.F.: National Culture and Information Technology Product Adoption. Journal of Global Information Technology Management 7(4), 29–46 (2004)
6. Romm, T., et al.: Identifying organizational culture clash in MIS implementation: When is it worth the effort? Information & Management 21(2), 99–109 (1991)
7. Ho, A.T.K., Ni, A.Y.: Explaining the Adoption of E-Government Features: A Case Study of IOWA County Treasurer's Offices. The American Review of Public Administration 34(2), 164–180 (2004)
8. Dasgupta, S., Gupta, B.: Role of Organizational Culture in Internet Technology Adoption: An Empirical Study. In: Proceedings of Americas Conference on Information Systems (AMCIS) 2008, pp. 1304–1311 (2005)

9. Heeks, R.: Most E-Government for Development Projects Fail: How can Risks be Reduced? (2003), `http://unpan1.un.org/intradoc/groups/public/documents/CAFRAD/UNPAN011226.pdf` (cited 2009 15 November)
10. Heeks, R.: E-Government in Africa Promise and Practice. Information Polity 7(3), 97–114 (2002)
11. Hofstede, G.: Identifying Organizational Subcultures: An Empirical Approach. Journal of Management Studies 35(1), 1–12 (1998)
12. Sathe, V.: Implications of corporate culture: A manager's guide to action. Organizational Dynamics 12(2), 5–23 (1983)
13. Denison, D.R.: Corporate Culture and Organizational Effectiveness. John Wiley & Sons, Toronto (1990)
14. Schein, E.H.: Organizational culture. American Psychologist 45(2), 109–119 (1990)
15. Denison, D.R.: What is Different Between Organizational Culture and Organizational Climate? A Native's Point of View on A Decade of Paradigm Wars. Academy of Management Review 21(3), 619–654 (1996)
16. Wallach, E.J.: Individuals and Organizations: The Cultural Match. Training & Development Journal 37(2), 28 (1983)
17. Denison, D.R., Mishra, A.K.: Toward a Theory of Organizational Culture and Effectiveness. Organizational Science 6(2), 204–223 (1995)
18. Martin, E.C., Terblance, F.: Building Organizational Culture That Stimulates Creativity and Innovation. European Journal of Innovation Management 6(1), 64–74 (2003)
19. Weber, Y., Pliskin, N.: The effect of Information System Integration and Organizational Culture on a Firm's Effectiveness. Information & Management 30(81-90), 81 (1996)
20. Cooper, R.B.: The Inertial Impact of Culture on IT Implementation. Information & Management 27(1), 17–31 (1994)
21. Sriramesh, K., Grunig, J.E., Dozier, D.M.: Observation and Measurement of Two Dimensions of Organizational Culture and Their Relationship to Public Relations. Journal of Public Relation Research 8(4), 229–261 (1996)
22. Fichman, R.G., Kemerer, C.F.: The Assimilation of Software Process Innovations. An Organizational Learning Perspective Management Science 43(10), 1345–1363 (1997)
23. Moore, G.C., Benbasat, I.: Development of Instrument to Measure the Perceptions of Adopting an Information Technology Innovation. Information Systems Research 2(3), 192–222 (1991)
24. Rogers, E.M.: Diffusion of Innovations, 5th edn. Free Press, New York (2003)
25. Agarwal, R., Prasad, J.: The Role of Innovation Characteristics and Perceived Voluntariness in the Acceptance of Information Technologies. Decision Sciences 28(3), 557–582 (1997)
26. Venkatesh, V., David, F.R.: A Theoretical Extension of the Technology Acceptance Model: Four Logitudinal Field Studies. Management Science 46(2), 186–204 (2000)
27. Agarwal, R.: Individual Acceptance of Information Technologies. In: Zmud, R.W. (ed.) Framing the Domains of IT Management, Pinnaflex Education Resources 2000, pp. 85–104 (2000)
28. Gallivan, M.J.: Organizational Adoption and assimilation of Complex Technological Innovations: Development and Application of a New Framework. The DATA BASE for Advances in Information Systems 32(3), 51–85 (2001)
29. Warkentin, M., et al.: Encouraging Citizen Adoption of E-Government by Building Trust. Electronic Markets 12(3), 157–162 (2002)
30. Beynon-Davies, P., Williams, M.D.: Evaluating Electronic Local Government in the UK. Journal of Information Technology 18(2), 137–149 (2003)

31. Baynon-Davies, P., Martin, S.: Electronic Local government and the Modernization Agenda: Progress and Prospects for Public Service Improvement. Local Government Studies 30(2), 214–229 (2004)
32. Griffin, D., Halpin, E.: An Exploratory Evaluation of UK Local e-Government From an Accountability Perspective. The Electronic Journal of e-Government 3(1), 13–28 (2005)
33. Aubert, B.A., Hamel, G.: Adoption of Smart Cards in the Medical Sector: the Canadian Experience. Social Science & Medicine 53(7), 879–894 (2001)
34. Heeks, R.: E-government as a Carrier of Context. Journal of Public Policy 25(1), 51–74 (2005)
35. Moon, M.J.: The Evolution of E-Government Among Municipalities: Rhetoric or Reality? Public Administration Review 62(4), 424–433 (2002)
36. Norris, D.F., Moon, M.J.: Advancing E-Government at the Grassroots: Tortoise or Hare? Public Administration Review 65(1), 64–75 (2005)
37. Lee, S.M., Tan, X., Trimi, S.: Current Practices of Leading E-Government Countries. Communication of the ACM 48(10), 99–104 (2005)
38. Eggers, W.D.: Boosting E-Government Adoption (2004),
    http://www.taxadmin.org/FTA/Meet/04am_pres/eggers.pdf
    (cited 2010 03 May)
39. Ho, S.Y., Ho, K.W.K.: Success of Electronic Government Information Portal: technological Issues or Manageria Issues? Journal of E-Government 3(2), 53–74 (2006)
40. Sahu, G.P., Gupta, M.P.: Users' Acceptance of E-Government: a Study of Indian Central Excise. International Journal of Electronic Government Research 2007 3(3), 1–21 (2007)
41. Schuppan, T.: E-Government in Developing Countries: Experiences from sub-Saharan Africa. Government Information Quarterly 26(1), 118–127 (2009)
42. Janssen, M., Chun, S.A., Gil-Garcia, J.R.: Building the next generation of digital government infrastructures. Government Information Quarterly 26(2), 233–237 (2009)
43. Rose, M.: Democratizing information and communication by implementing e-government in Indonesian regional government. The International Information & Library Review 36(3), 219–226 (2004)
44. Leidner, D.E., Kayworth, T.: Review: A Review of Culture in Information System Research: Toward a Theory of Information Technology Culture Conflict. MIS Quarterly 30(2), 357–399 (2006)
45. Dada, D.: The Failure of E-Government in developing countries: A Literature review. The Electronic Journal of Information Systems in Developing Countries 26(7), 1–10 (2006)
46. Ferguson, M.: Local E-Government in the United Kingdom. In: Local Electronic Government by Helmut Druke. Routledge, Hoboken (2004)
47. Ho, A.T.K.: Reinventing Local Governments and The E-Government Initiative. Public Administration Review 62(4), 434–444 (2002)
48. Pan, G., et al.: Escalation and De-Escalation of Commitment: A Commitment Transformation Analysis of an E-Government Project. Information Systems 2006 6, 3–21 (2006)
49. Getao, K.W., Wausi, A.N.: Organizational cultural dynamics and information and communication technology adaptation in a developing country: The case of the Kenyan joint university admission system. Information Technology for Development 2009 5(3), 224–232 (2009)
50. Schaper, K.L., Pervan, G.P.: Developing a Model Technology Acceptance Within the Australian Healthcare Sector. In: The Tenth Pacific Asia Conference on Information Systems (PACIS 2006), pp. 835–847 (2007)
51. Barki, H., Hartwick, J.: Rethinking the Concept of User Involvement. MIS Quarterly 13(1), 53–63 (1989)

52. Hartwick, J., Barki, H.: Explaining the Role of User Participation in Information System Use Management Science 40(4), 440–465 (1994)
53. Luk, S.C.Y.: The impact of leadership and stakeholders on the success/failure of e-government service: Using the case study of e-stamping service in Hong Kong. Government Information Quarterly 26(4), 594–604 (2009)
54. Rowlinson, S.: Matrix Organization Structure, Culture and Commitment: A Hong Kong Public Sector Case Study of Change. Construction Management and Economics 19(7), 669–673 (2001)
55. Boxx, W.R., Randi, Y.O., Dunn, M.G.: Organizational Values and Value Congruency and Their Impact on Satisfaction, Commitment, and Cohesion: an Empirical Examination Within the Public Sector. Public Personnel Management 20(2), 195 (1991)
56. Sethi, N., Sethi, V.: Public-Private-People Partnership in E-Government: A case Study of Singapure Tracks. In: Delivering E-Government by Sahu, G.P. (2006),
    http://www.iceg.net/iceg2006deg.pdf#page=188
    (cited 2009 24 November)
57. Jae-Nam, L., Young-Gul, K.: Effect of Partnership Quality on IS Outsourcing Success: Conceptual Framework and Empirical Validation. Journal of Management Information Systems 15(4), 29–61 (1999)
58. Prenclergast, C.J.: A Theory of Responsibility in Organizations. Journal of Labor Economics 13(3), 387–400 (1995)
59. Berkowitz, L., Daniels, L.R.: Responsibility and Dependency. Journal of Abnormal and Social Psychology 66(5), 429–436 (1963)
60. Scott, M., Golden, W., Hughes, M.: Implementation Strategies for E-Government: A Stakeholder Analysis Approach. In: Proceedings of 2004 European Conference on Information Systems (ECIS), pp. 1–14 (2004)
61. Tan, C.W., Pan, S.L., Lim, E.T.K.: Managing Stakeholder Interest in E-Government Implementation: Lesson Learned from a Singapore E-Government Project. Journal of Global Information Management 13(1), 31–53 (2005)
62. Jarvenpaa, S.L., Ives, B.: Executive Involvement and Participation in the Management of Information Technology. MIS Quarterly 15(2), 205–227 (1991)
63. Denison, D.R., Haaland, S., Goelzer, P.: Corporate Culture and Organizational Effectiveness: Is There a Similar Pattern Around the World? Advance in Global Leadership 3, 205–227 (2003)
64. Christensen, L.T.: Corporate Communication: The Challenge of Transparency. Corporate Communications: An International Journal 7(3), 162–168 (2002)
65. Mitchell, R.B.: Sources of Transparency: Information System in International Regimes. International Studies Quarterly 42, 109–130 (1998)
66. William, C.C.: Trust Diffusion: The Effect of Interpersonal Trust on Structure. Function and Organizational Transparency Business & Society 44(3), 357–368 (2005)
67. Mayer, R.C., Davis, J.H., Schoorman, F.D.: An Integrative Model of Organizational Trust Academy of Management Review 20(3), 709–734 (1995)
68. Markus, M.L., Robey, D.: Information Technology and Organizational Change: Causal Structural in Theory and research. Management Science 34(5), 583–598 (1988)
69. Greenwood, R., Hinings, C.R.: Understanding Radical Organizational Change: Bringing Together the Old and the New Institutionalism. Academy of Management Review 21(4), 1022–1054 (1996)
70. Argyris, C.: Organizational Learning and Management Information Systems. DataBase, 3–11 (Winter-Spring 1982)

71. Leuthesser, L., Kohli, C.: Corporate identity: The role of mission statements. Business Horizons 40(3), 59–66 (1997)
72. Fairhurst, G.T., Jordan, J.M.: Why are we here? Managing the meaning of an organizational mission statement. Journal of Applied Communication Research 25(4), 243 (1997)
73. Conger, J.A., Kangungo, R.N.: Toward a Behavioral Theory of Charismatic Leadership in Organizational Settings. Academy of Management Review 12(4), 637–647 (1987)
74. Awamleh, R., Gardner, W.L.: Perception of Leader Charisma and Effectiveness: The Effect of Vision Content. Delivery, and Organizational Performance Leadership Quarterly 10(3), 345–373 (1999)
75. Etzioni, A.: Two Approaches to Organizational Analysis: A Critique and a Suggestion. Administrative Science Quarterly 5(2), 257–278 (1960)
76. Perrow, C.: The Analysis of Goals in Complex Organizations. American Sociological Review 25(6), 854–866 (1961)
77. Kei, W., Wei, K.K.: Successful E-Goverment in Singapore. Communications of The ACM 47(6), 95–99 (2004)
78. Farholt, B., Wahid, F.: E-Government Challenge and The Role of Political Leadership in Indonesia: The Case of Sragen. In: Proceedings of the 41st Hawaii International Conference on System Sciences 2008, pp. 1–10 (2008)
79. Srivastava, S.C., Teo, T.S.H.: Electronic Government As A guided Evolution in Singapore: Vision For The World in The 21st Century. In: Academy of Management Best Conference paper 2005 PNP:EI, pp. 1–6 (2005)
80. Claver, E., et al.: Public Administration From Bureaucratic Culture to Citizen-Oriented Culture. The International Journal of Public Sector Management 12(5), 455–464 (1999)
81. Inkson, J.H.K., Pugh, D.S., Hickson, D.J.: Organization Context and Structure: An Abbreviated Replication. Administrative Science Quarterly 15(3), 318–329 (1970)
82. Ouchi, W.G.: The Transmission of Control Through Organizational Hierarchy. Academy of Management Journal 21(2), 173–192 (1978)
83. Mahoney, T.A.: Organizational Hierarchy and Position Worth. Academy of Management Journal 22(4), 726–737 (1979)
84. Van De Ven, A.H., Delbecq, A.L.: Determinants of Coordination Modes Within Organizations. American Sociological Review 41(2), 322–338 (1976)
85. Malone, T.W., Crowston, K.: What is Coordination Theory and How can It Help Design Cooperative Work System. In: Proceedings of the Conference on Computer Supported Cooperative Work, Los Angeles, California, October 1990, pp. 357–370 (1990)
86. Wong, W., Welch, E.: Does E-Government Promote Accountability? A Comparative Analysis of Website Openness and Government Accountability. Governance: An International Journal of Policy, Administration, and Institutions 17(2), 23 (2004)
87. Yin, R.K.: Case Study Research - Design and Method, 3rd edn. Sage, Thousand Oaks (2003)

Diffusing the Ubuntu Philosophy into E-Government: A South African Perspective

Hossana Twinomurinzi[1], Jackie Phahlamohlaka[2], and Elaine Byrne[1,3]

[1] Department of Informatics, University of Pretoria
Pretoria, South Africa
twinoh@up.ac.za

[2] Defence, Peace, Safety and Security, Council for Scientific and Industrial Research
Pretoria, South Africa
jphahlamohlaka@csir.co.za

[3] Department of Epidemiology & Public Health Medicine, The Royal College of Surgeons in Ireland, Dublin, Ireland
elainebyrne2@rcsi.ie

Abstract. Information Systems (IS) researchers are increasingly calling for contextual approaches to Information and Communication Technologies (ICT) innovations [1]. The call proceeds from the realization that ICT and e-government policies are often adopted and developed with a blind focus on the ICT artifact, and with little reflection on the contribution of ICT to the context [2]. This paper emanates from an ethnographic study that investigated how ICT can facilitate government policy implementation in a development context. The study found it necessary to understand the role of tradition and its potential influence on ICT implementations in South Africa. The paper reviews the context of the South African government and its conspicuous inclination to the way of life, Ubuntu. Ubuntu is growing in popularity and is increasingly being applied as an African solution to African problems such as poverty, political strife and trade. Using Grounded Theory analysis, the findings revealed the critical importance of ICT not threatening tradition but rather complementing it, the role that ICT could play in enabling or enhancing community assemblies, and the marginalized role of women citing how ICT might be used as a means to empower rather than marginalize women even further. We conclude that e-government needs to be re-conceptualized in South Africa for a more culturally acceptable and relevant approach to the use of ICT innovations for development.

Keywords: Keywords: Policy Implementation, e-Government, ICT for Development.

1 Introduction

South Africa has one of the highest socio-economic income inequalities in the world having more than 43% living below the poverty line [3] and 23.6% unemployed [4]. Human development consequently underlies most of the government initiatives. Among the principal avenues identified towards achieving the development is through

M. Janssen et al. (Eds.): EGES/GISP 2010, IFIP AICT 334, pp. 94–107, 2010.
© IFIP International Federation for Information Processing 2010

e-government [5]. South Africa's e-government policy identifies its four critical features as: interoperability (cross-functionality across different departments); ICT security (dealing with the security of government electronic systems and information); economies of scale (achieving this includes investments in research and development to developing local skills with the ability to produce internally), and: elimination of duplication (abolish unnecessary duplication of similar IT functions, projects and resources) [5]. South Africa has however been bold enough to admit that despite the open and active sponsorship and support for e-government, the expected benefits and development outcomes are yet to be fully realised [6].

IS researchers argue that such outcome challenges are often because the ICT initiatives fail to take into account the important contextual aspects of the implementation environment, and in many instances adopt overly deterministic business models [1]. The same conflict is seen in South Africa. The focus of the e-government policy, illustrated through the success factors, reflects this critique. The criteria indicate a technical and deterministic approach to e-government with an inadequate emphasis on the social and contextual nature of ICT.

This paper reports on findings from a project centred on creating an awareness of the Promotion of Administration Justice Act 3 of 2000 (PAJA) through the use of Group Support Systems (GSS). A GSS is a specialised type of ICT system designed to facilitate people working together towards a goal [7]. The PAJA seeks to overcome the historical apartheid injustices by empowering the public to expect from government a reasonable opportunity to make representations before receiving a negative decision (an administrative action), and to ask for written reasons and/or challenge the government.

1.1 South African Government: Batho Pele

With the fall of apartheid, South Africa enacted a new Constitution as the supreme law in 1996. The founding provisions of the new constitution are grounded in the values of "dignity, the achievement of equality and the advancement of human rights and freedoms, non-racialism and non-sexism, supremacy of the constitution and the rule of law and in universal adult suffrage" [8]. The new constitution called for a radical transformation in government from the previous apartheid style where government administrators made decisions without consultation to a more democratic style where decisions must be made in a more consultative manner. The government through the new constitution of 1996 has since brought into effect a number of policy reforms in an effort to "heal the divisions of the past and establish a society based on democratic values, social justice and fundamental human rights" [8].

Transformation formally began in 1995 with the White Paper on the Transformation of Public Service [9] hereafter abbreviated to WPTPS. The WPTPS established the institutional framework that would guide the introduction of new policies and the implementation of the new constitutional mandates. It was shortly followed in 1997 by the White Paper on Transforming Public Service Delivery, labeled as the Batho Pele White Paper [10]. The Batho Pele White Paper specifically aimed at creating a participative model of governance. The Batho Pele White Paper was adopted into policy in 2002 and branded Batho Pele. Batho Pele literally means "People First" and the resultant adage 'We belong, we care, we serve' became the belief set to guide the government. Batho Pele formally redefined the outlook of government to correspond more to the harmonious South African way of life, Ubuntu.

1.2 South African Way of Life: Ubuntu

Ubuntu is an indigenous South African philosophy that comprehends individual existence as being inseparable from the collective through warm and filial relationships. Ubuntu is short for the Nguni proverb 'Umuntu ngumuntu ngabantu' which literally translated means "a person is a person through their relationship to others" [11]. The notion of Ubuntu subsumes an individual's personality, place and provision as having everything to do with the collective – we are who we are because we come from and belong to a certain collective. Any attempt to define Ubuntu in an English sentence reduces its deep indigenous meaning [12]. Ubuntu is an African awareness of being. The Ubuntu way of life is clearly an African collectivist philosophy which lies in sharp contrast to the more individualistic and self-centered Western way of life. The core values of Ubuntu are communalism, interdependence, humanness, sharing and compassion. Ubuntu does not imply that individual choice is lost and resigned to traditional leaders but means that traditional leaders carry the burden to express the choice of the individuals as a collective interest.

Batho Pele is an embodiment of the values of Ubuntu. The adage Batho Pele itself expresses the Ubuntu way of life in prioritizing the interests of the citizen according to the quality of life rather than on the neo-liberal basis of traditional economics.

1.3 Linking ICT and Ubuntu

During the PAJA project the social and contextual nature of ICT emerged as fundamental to understanding how e-government could support the emancipation of people from different forms of deprivation such as poverty, disease and oppression. The principle finding which facilitated this understanding was that citizens could easily understand the philosophical underpinnings of the government's over-arching policy of Batho Pele as it strongly correlates to the South African way of life, Ubuntu. However, the difficulty arose with linking the provision of multi-purpose centres or any other technologically enabled initiative to this policy. Once these ICT innovations were linked or an association was made with local traditions and culture the communities recognised the potential of ICT to their development and enthusiastically embraced these opportunities. Consequently this paper reflects on the question: Can e-government in South Africa support human-development by connecting ICT innovations to the South African philosophy of life, Ubuntu?

To provide the context to these findings this paper is structured accordingly. Section 2 reviews the literature on e-government and the diverse discourse about what human development means. Section 3 presents the research approach used to conduct the research, Grounded Theory. Section 4 presents the findings and the analysis. As required in Grounded Theory, we compare the findings with contemporary theory used in ICT for Development (ICT4D) discourse, Amartya Sen's Capabilities Approach, which argues for creating opportunities for development based on what people are able to do and to be. Section 5 presents the conclusions from the paper and the contributions to knowledge.

2 Literature Review

2.1 E-Government

E-government is a popular field of research within IS without a commonly agreed upon definition but broadly understood as "the use of information technology to enable and improve the efficiency with which government services are provided to citizens, employees, businesses and agencies" [13]. In striving for the perceived benefits of e-government almost all governments around the world are enthusiastically embracing, or having e-government pressed upon them. High on the list of these perceived benefits are the promises of better governance, cost reduction and improved efficiency of government services [14]. E-government literature suggests that the transition from government to e-government exposes governments to opportunities to improve government practices through process redesigns [15]. The literature generally posits five stages of e-government evolution;

- One way communication where information flows from government in a single direction – out. An example would be the static information provided by a government website
- Two-way communication where information also flows back to government but no immediate response should be expected. An example is the typical contact us form on government websites
- Exchange where government has an active presence on the internet and is able to actively communicate back and forth with its clients as well as carry out online transactions. An example is filing tax returns and making the payments online.
- Portal is where the government establishes a single point of contact for all government offerings regardless of the services that may be required by its constituents. An example may be a citizens paying taxes and traffic bills from a single portal without realizing that the two payments are for two different government entities
- Political participation is where citizens may be able to vote online using the e-government portal.

Many governments in adopting the utopian view have overlooked the fact that the strategies used in the private sector for customer satisfaction, retention and adoption cannot be directly applied to citizens. They quickly fall into the trap of treating citizens as business clients. There is a fundamental difference in that citizens have rights from government and duties to government while business clients have a choice [16]. Governments have a legal and moral responsibility to serve all the citizens and the different constituents within the country [15].

2.2 Development and ICT4D

One of the driving forces in government is 'development'. The nature of development is a subject of continuing theoretical debate [1] ranging from something that happens in the third world [17] to a structured and linearly staged process of enabling developing countries to catch up with developed countries [18]. There is, however, one underlying theme in the discourse on development; there is an urgent need to lift people (especially women and children) out of deprivation. Deprivation is more prominent in developing countries where many are dying of preventable illnesses, hunger and the like, not only because of any lack of knowledge but also because of the lack of means to deal with these problems [18].

A range of reasons have been offered as to why certain countries experience development and why others remain mired in poverty, unable to raise the standards of living, despite following the same prescripts: colonialism, globalisation, unequal trade agreements, the lack of democracy and religion [19].

Strategies on how to achieve development became a subject area of interest soon after the end of the Second World War and the subsequent creation of independent states. The discourse on development since that time gradually transformed in three significant periods: the 1950s, the 1960s, and the 1980s. The 1950's called for aggregative analytical frameworks proposing investment in modern activities and an emphasis on good planning, e.g. the big push [20] and the take-off sustained growth [21]. Those approaches did not yield much success. The 1960's saw the flawed argument that developing countries needed to emulate the key characteristics and stages of growth that developed countries had passed through to get to where they are [18]. From the 1980s to date the development discourse has gradually expanded to include individual information from household surveys such as the impact and role of health and education on development. Considering that South Africa was in a state of apartheid before 1994, all its development efforts have been based on the current approaches to development since the 1980's wave.

The discourse on ICT4D has followed closely behind development in a supporting and enabling role and is traced back to the 1950s where ICT was viewed as something that could automate government administrative functions. The main concern in ICT4D today, similar to development, is how to innovate ICT towards socioeconomic development amongst the billions of underprivileged people in the world. Avgerou [1] summarised the current discourse on ICT4D as falling along two continuums; how development occurs, and how ICT is innovated to contribute to the process of development.

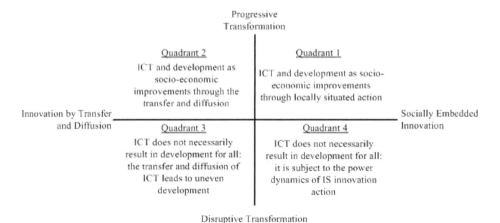

Fig. 1. Discourse on ICT4D [1]

On one continuum, development ranges from occurring progressively at one end and disruptively at the other. Progressive development happens when development is accepted uncritically. Disruptive development happens when the development is accompanied by fundamentally different norms from existing ones and may require substantial changes in social and individual behaviour. On the second continuum, on the one hand ICT is innovated to contribute to the process of development where it is transferred and diffused from developed to developing countries. On the other hand, ICT is adapted from within the social context of the developing country. Avgerou (2009) combined the two influences to result in four quadrants (Fig. 1).

In quadrant 1, ICT is innovated with a view to improve life conditions from within the local context, taking into account the embedded historical, cultural and social meaning. Quadrant 2 adherents suggest that it is possible to create an ICT tool which is modeled using best-practices. It is argued that such a model is then able to work across all situations and bring about development as seen in the 'best-practice' literature. In quadrant 3, ICT is at times implemented but only benefits a select few. The discourse here questions the power relations that exist in society and how these powers may be carried over when new ICT is implemented. Quadrant 4 demonstrates how ICT is accepted as a force of socio-economic change, but one that brings with it power relations. ICT in this sense in fact leads to greater levels of domination and inequality hence extending the socio-economic and digital divide.

South Africa's approach to e-government fits in quadrant 2 in its prescriptive approach that assumes an ICT model derived from technical business best-practice can quickly be diffused across the diverse segments of government. That model does not take into account the context of South African government with its very strong inclination to Ubuntu. Based on the Ubuntu inclination, South Africa's e-government approach should position itself in quadrant 1. This paper argues that for a fit with quadrant 1 a fundamentally different approach to ICT is needed in e-Government in South Africa.

3   Research Approach

This paper emanates from one of the author's ethnographic immersion in a research project entitled 'Enabling access to human rights through thought processes and web-based Group Support Systems (GSS) tools'. As the author progressed through the PAJA project and reviewed literature on Development, ICT4D and e-government, four issues stood out:

- Development is dependent upon the perspective which is adopted e.g. traditional economists consider development as an indicator of Gross Domestic Product while others consider it as the freedom to make choices [1, 22]
- There is a rapidly growing demand for ICT4D theory and inquiry, as evidenced by the rise in academic and practitioner conferences and/or journals with either a special track or entire publication dedicated to ICT4D [23]
- Consistent with ICT4D, there are dangers and problems that have resulted from developing countries blindly adopting IS approaches which have worked in developed countries [24, 25].

- African developing contexts are characterized by the collectivist nature of society [12]. The collectivist culture is largely ignored when researching African environments yet is critical to understanding the contextual process of ICT implementations towards human development [26]. The collectivist nature, called Ubuntu, surfaces strongly in South Africa's approach to government Batho Pele.

The thoughts culminated into seeking to develop an explanatory theory or framework that could account for how e-government could be harnessed contextually in the spirit of Ubuntu to lead to improvements in human development. Ethnographers refer to such thoughts as the 'grand' research question because it is deliberately wide and not hedged in with firm hypotheses, research designs, sub-questions and instruments [27]. As the PAJA project progressed the researcher clarified the grand research question delimiting its scope and internal structure into the finer primary research question: How could ICT be used to facilitate policy implementation in a human development context?

Three field locations were enrolled as research sites for the PAJA project in 2005 and over three years generally maintained the same 46 research participants. Lebotloane is in the North West Province and the research was hosted by Lerethlabetse Multi Purpose Community Centre (now called the Lerethlabetse Thusong Service Centre); Siyabuswa is in the Mpumalanga Province and the research was hosted by the Siyabuswa Education Improvement and Development Trust (SEIDET); and the University of Pretoria is in the Gauteng Province and the research was hosted by Department of Informatics. The common denominator in selecting the research sites was a solid institutional base and the availability of computers. Since the PAJA project was a longitudinal research project, cross-institutional linkages could provide better grounds for long term sustainability and such institutions are usually already established within their communities. Since the limited research funding did not include for the provision of computers it meant that the host institutions needed to have an existing computer infrastructure.

The research at each site was carried out in a workshop setting. The purpose of the workshops was to raise awareness about the process involved in the implementation of the PAJA. The workshops were designed to demonstrate the possibilities for the use of ICT (particularly GSS) to support the PAJA process simulated using case scenarios. Over the period 2005 to 2008, one workshop was held at each site every year, making a total of nine workshops over the three years. The workshops each year were always planned so that we completed the three sites within a month. Data was collected at every workshop activity using different data collection instruments.

The rich ethnographic data from the observations, electronic logs, videos, questionnaires, interviews and field visits during the project were analysed using Grounded Theory to develop a substantive theory that could explain how ICT could be used to facilitate policy implementation in the spirit of Ubuntu. Additional information on the influence of Ubuntu on daily life was obtained from structured interviews conducted with six research participants from three different regions of South Africa, four of who were from rural areas and two from urban areas. Two of the people from the rural areas are community leaders while one of those from the urban area is from a royal family. The interview questions were derived from Whitacre's [28] literature on customs and tradition which seeks to understand the role of tradition as a set of customs, beliefs and practices, and the influences that tradition wields.

Grounded Theory (GT) techniques have been shown to be helpful when attempting to create theory from data, rather than data emerging from theory [29]. Kelle [30] refers to the divergent approaches on how to conduct Grounded Theory as a conflict between whether categories emerge or are forced out from empirical data. The paper adopts Strauss and Corbin's approach [31] since we were already guided by the context. Their approach starts with open coding where concepts that fit the data are produced. It is followed by axial coding where the derived concepts are investigated for causal relationships. Analytical memos are created during axial coding which form the basis of selective coding. The memos are the researcher's record of analysis and perceptions for further data collection. It ends with selective coding where an assumed core category is selected and related to the other categories systematically into a substantive theory. The obligation of Grounded Theory to engage the substantive theory that emerges from the findings with formal theory [31] is done in Section 4 using Amartya Sen's Capabilities Approach.

Grounded Theory emerges from the symbolic interactionist view of human behaviour [32] which posits that people assign meaning based on social interactions, which meaning is handed down and modified from generation to generation. Generalization in qualitative studies such as this is made against theory and not against populations making qualitative generalizations more analytical than statistical as may be the case in quantitative studies [33]. Hence data obtained from structured interviews from six research participants who are positioned to comment on their customs and traditions is sufficient for analysis if the bias of the researcher can be made explicit.

4   Analysis and Findings

The findings from the PAJA project that were significant in terms of the need to diffuse the Ubuntu philosophy as part of an e-government approach in South Africa were:

- The importance of entry into research sites through local leadership in terms of acceptability and sustainability of ICT projects. If local leaders (traditional and/or community leaders) introduce a group favourably, it almost guarantees acceptance and support by the community members
- The use of mediators on the computers in the communities is acceptable and appreciated. For example, one person used the computer for others who did not have the computer skills and that this was replicated outside the workshop as well
- Women were very active and felt comfortable in sharing opinions and views. Due to anonymity (and maybe the context) there did not seem to be any discrimination between comments from men or women. Though this could be because these were simulated scenarios, it still shows potential
- There was fairly good rapport between government administrators who were present and others. This showed that most service delivery problems are probably not due to any personal animosity but rather communication and understanding processes and procedures.

4.1 Traditional Practices

Tradition plays a very important role in all South African cultures in relation to Ubuntu. The research participants all expressed great respect and reverence for their traditions and cultures. The comments below typify the sentiment:

— "They highly respect their traditional leaders as they remind and help them to practice and respect their tradition."
— "They highly honour their culture, for example boys and girls still go to initiation school where they are taught about their culture in both communities (Sotho & Ndebele)."

Children grow up hearing about their traditional cultures and beliefs and how they are played out in daily life. An upbringing in cultural values applies both to the people who live in the urban areas and those who live in rural areas. The strong respect people have for culture and tradition is reflected in the popularity of initiation schools and shows the tensions that exist between modernization and development. For example, attendance at initiation schools, though optional, is considered of such great importance that if a person, male or female, has not gone to initiation school, the person will be despised within the community and be seen as a social misfit.

— "We grow up seeing these beliefs done and talked about that when we grow up we make it a point that we do the same that was done and then pass them on to other people. Initiation school for example is a strong belief in the Siyabuswa community that when a person has not gone to the school he/she would be discriminated on until he/she goes to the school."

At initiation school, the youth are ushered into their traditional customs and are taught some of the 'secrets' of their culture. Initiation school creates a very strong rite of passage into adulthood. Many youths choose to attend initiation schools even when a number of young adults lose their lives each year due to harsh conditions, such as spending days in cold weather, or through unsanitary practices, such as sharing knives for circumcision. However, many of the older traditions have been modernised, such as circumcision increasingly being conducted in hospital, whilst maintaining the initiation schools in terms of the cultural importance of such a rite of passage and the ceremonies around it. During the initiation school's rite of passage one of the most important cultures that is handed down is the spirit of oneness among people - the spirit of Ubuntu.

4.2 Tensions between Modernization and Tradition

As described in the popular African literature Things Fall Apart [34] and Heart of Redness [35] modernization raises tensions between traditions handed down over many generations and new modernized culture driven by ICT or different forms of authority. For example, some of the research participants noted that they hold dear their allegiance to the traditional leaders and their authority but are more cognizant of the greater government authority.

— "…there are also those who do not have respect."
— "They have a little respect to traditional leadership as most of them respect modern or local council."

Traditionally, decisions that affect the community at large are taken collectively. Community meetings (Imbizos) are called and the case for and against the issue are made. Through traditional structures, community members can air their opinions and concerns. This is in keeping with the spirit of Ubuntu or collective personhood and collective morality [12] which is a fundamental concept in most African societies. Principles of continuous consultation and consensus, the use of ceremonies to express meaning and the need for spiritual and individual reflection are all principles on which the concept of Ubuntu is based. There are also other reasons why people choose to come together within communities, such as social reasons, such as funerals and marriages; religious reasons, mainly church; community meetings, e.g. concerning rising cases of thefts, unemployment; and political reasons, the African National Congress (ANC) as the biggest party in South Africa holds regular meetings and draws big crowds. The choice to attend meetings is usually optional or may be on invitation only, such as political or traditional meetings.

Community meetings are usually dominated by a few people, such as the elders or leaders, at times leaving the ordinary people feeling that the decisions that are adopted do not reflect their individual and collective preferences. At other times, the ordinary people feel that their leaders to whom they have given the responsibility for carrying out the groups decisions either distort them or are corrupted along the way. Minority groups such as women and youths very rarely have a direct voice in these meetings and if they desire to express themselves usually must resort to using the medium of men they know. In the traditional meetings, women generally only play an advisory role.

— "They feel that information is being distorted from them and the service is not delivered."
— "We the sisters will always play an advisory role at the back."

Regardless of the nature of meeting, the means of communicating at such an assembly is through loud speakers booming from a car driving through the streets of the community, word of mouth, the use of flyers and posters in streets, community radio stations, phones and through school outlets. More recently mobile phones are increasingly becoming a preferred method of communication.

4.3 Discussion

Traditional practices are strong and any ICT innovation needs to embrace the role of leaders and their inclusion in a communal approach. E-government in South Africa needs to adopt a more embracive approach that addresses the technical aspects of ICT innovations as evidenced in the e-government policy, but in a contextualised socio-technical manner. Collaborative ICT has the potential to address previous inequities and enable all voices to be heard, as well as provide a means for leaders and government administrators to hear these voices. The approach to e-government needs to consider a holistic approach where all the people, including the women, are able to express themselves through their own traditional means in a spirit of Ubuntu, rather than through means imposed by external agents [18].

ICT needs to be viewed as tools than enhance the collective spirit and not simply for use by individuals with skills. Those with skills can acceptably act as mediators. Such an approach to e-government is similar to Amartya Sen's [36] views on development which centres on choice and the freedoms for people to make the choices they desire. Sen's [36] views on development have significantly influenced the United Nations approach to development and echo many of the features of Ubuntu and this is reflected in his Capabilities Approach to development. Sen [36], contends that the assessment of well-being should be concerned with an individual's capability to function, which he regards as "what a person can do or can be", and the real opportunities that the person has especially compared with others. The Capabilities Approach (CA) assesses individual well-being and social arrangements based on what individuals are able to do and to be. The basic premise is that by enlarging the choices available to individuals they can live the life they choose. In CA it is not enough to only remove obstacles that inhibit individuals from living the life they value; individuals should be provided with the means to achieve such a life.

In relation to e-government, CA illustrates that for development the existence of opportunities does not necessarily mean they can be drawn upon and utilised. For example, the South African government is in the process of rolling out ICT facilities in what are known as Thusong Service Centres (TSC) (formerly called multi-purpose community centres) where individuals have the opportunity to collaboratively interact with the government through channels such as the Internet and e-mail. In reality, these opportunities cannot be drawn upon because both the government administrators and the citizens do not know how to use the Internet or e-mail. As such, the real value of the ICT facilities as a development commodity within the TSCs does not exist. Sen [36] further advocates that commodities are desired for their characteristics rather than for their intrinsic value. Using the example of the Internet facilities within the TSCs, the Internet facilities can be used for different purposes such as interacting with government, self-help improvement programmes, for business or even as a social communicator. Owning or having a commodity does not necessarily mean that the owner will use all the features or abilities of the commodity or use them for a certain purpose. For example, as shown above, the internet facilities in the TSCs are not used to interact with government and yet are designed to be "one-stop centres providing integrated services and information from government, to communities close to where they live as part of a comprehensive strategy to better their lives" [37]. The success criteria outlined in the e-government policy assumes that ICT is desired for its intrinsic value. Government should reflect and be explicit about how ICTs can be used to achieve its development outcomes. It would mean changing the e-government policy to reflect the same development inclinations as government or making explicit how the suggested technical criteria will lead to development.

Additionally, the well being of a person is determined by what the individual succeeds in doing with the commodities and the characteristics of the commodities - a notion Sen [36] terms as functionings. A functioning is defined as "an achievement of a person: what he or she manages to do or be". A functioning must be distinguished from owning the good and the characteristics of the good as well or having utility in the form of happiness from that functioning. Functionings can hence be seen as features of a commodity and not the commodity. Consequently, for e-government to meaningfully contribute to development, government must assist people to use the facilities which are available. Collaborative ICT in its ability to facilitate groups of people to work together is able to play such a role between groups of people on one end and government administrators on the other end. In areas and instances where computer skills are limited, it is possible for the groups to use one mediator acting on behalf of the group.

Examining e-government as the development of people's capabilities, through providing the means to achieve (ICT innovations), but also the freedom to achieve (the skills, resources and environment), entails re-conceptualising e-government. Freedom to achieve is contextual and in South Africa involves a communal, rather than an individualistic, view of development. Collaborative ICT has the potential of addressing some of the cultural inequities through facilitating a more inclusive spirit in community assemblies and in enabling all voices to be heard.

5 Conclusions

E-government can be re-conceptualized to provide a more contextualized approach which will be more culturally relevant. The implications of this re-conceptualization are:

- A focus more on what can be done with the ICT, rather than the intrinsic value of ICT
- The use of mediators and collaborative ICT to expand capabilities of the collective
- Ability to address inequities persistent in traditional practices in a culturally sensitive way
- Revising the 'success factors' of e-government to alternatively use 'the means to achieve', 'the freedom to achieve' and 'achievement'

Batho Pele is an embodiment of the values of Ubuntu. The evident misalignment between the deterministic South African approach to e-government and the living reality of a government inclined towards development can be overcome by adopting an approach which is consistent with the spirit of Ubuntu.

References

1. Avgerou, C.: Discourses on Innovation and Development in Information Systems in Developing Countries' Research. In: Byrne, E., Nicholson, B., Salem, F. (eds.) Proceedings of the 10th International Conference on Social Implications of Computers in Developing Countries. Dubai School of Government, International Federation for Information Processing, Dubai, United Arab Emirates, p. 510 (2009)
2. Heeks, R., Bailur, S.: Analyzing e-government research: Perspectives, philosophies, theories, methods, and practice. Government Information Quarterly 24, 243–265 (2007)
3. The Presidency: Development Indicators: Mid-Term Review. The Presidency, South Africa, Pretoria (2007)
4. Statistics South Africa: Latest Key Indicators, Statistics South Africa, Pretoria, vol. 2009 (2009) (StatsOnline)
5. Republic of South Africa: Electronic Government: The Digital Future - A Public Service IT Policy Framework. In: Administration, D.o.P.S.a. (ed.) Department of Public Service and Administration, pp. 1–25 (2001)
6. Harris, L.: SITA calls on private sector for help. Computing SA, 10–11 (November 2006)

7. Dennis, A.R., Wixom, B.H., Vandenberg, R.J.: Understanding Fit and Appropriation Effects in Group Support Systems via Meta-Analysis. MIS Quarterly 25, 167–193 (2001)
8. Republic of South Africa: Constitution of the Republic of South Africa, 1996. vol. 2008. South African Government Information (2008)
9. Republic of South Africa: White Paper on the Transformation of Public Service. In: South African Government Information (ed.). Government Printers (1995)
10. Republic of South Africa: White Paper on Transforming Public Service Delivery (Batho Pele White Paper). In: Administration, D.o.P.S.a. (ed.), vol. 388, p. 34. South African Government Gazette (1997)
11. Swanson, D.M.: Ubuntu: An African contribution to (re)search for/with a 'humble togetherness'. Journal of Contemporary Issues in Education 2, 53–67 (2007)
12. Mbigi, L.: Ubuntu. The African Dream in Management. Knowledge Resources (Pty) Ltd. (1997)
13. Carter, L., Belanger, F.: The utilization of e-government services: citizen trust, innovation and acceptance factors. Information Systems Journal 2005, 5–25 (2005)
14. UNCTAD: Using ICTs to Achieve Growth and Development. Trade and Development Board: Commission on Enterprise, Business Facilitation and Development. Expert Meeting in Support of the Implementation and Follow-up of WSIS: United Nations, Geneva, Switzerland (2006)
15. Davison, R.M., Wagner, C., Ma, L.C.K.: From government to e-government: a transition model. Information Technology & People 18, 280–299 (2005)
16. Belanger, F., Hiller, J.S.: A framework for e-government: privacy implications. Business Process Management Journal 12, 48–60 (2006)
17. Chari, S., Corbridge, S.: The development reader. Routledge, London (2008)
18. Cypher, J.M., Dietz, J.L.: The process of economic development. Routledge, London (2009)
19. Secondi, G.: Economic Growth, Economic Development, and Human Development. In: Secondi, G. (ed.) The Development Economics Reader, xxiv, 555 p. Routledge, London (2008)
20. Rosenstein-Rodan, P.: Problems of Industrialization of Eastern and South-Eastern Europe. Economic Journal 53, 202–211 (1943)
21. Rostow, W.W.: The Take-Off Into Sustained Growth. Economic Journal 66, 25–48 (1956)
22. Byrne, E., Jolliffe, B.: Free and Open Source Software - Development as Freedom? In: Silva, L., Westrup, C., Reinhard, N. (eds.) Proceedings of the 9th International Conference on Social Implications of Computers in Developing Countries. IFIP TC 9 - WG 9.4, Sao Paolo, Brazil (2007)
23. Avgerou, C.: Information systems in Developing Countries: a Critical Research Review. Journal of Information Technology 23, 133–146 (2008)
24. Kanungo, S.: On the emancipatory role of rural information systems. Information Technology & People 17, 407–422 (2004)
25. Wade, R.H.: Bridging the Digital Divide: New Route to Development or New Form of Dependency? Global Governance 8, 443–466 (2002)
26. Hofstede, G.: Culture's Consequences. Sage, Beverly Hills (1980)
27. Atkinson, P., Coffey, A., Delamont, S., Lofland, J., Lofland, L.: Editorial Introduction. In: Atkinson, P., Coffey, A., Delamont, S., Lofland, J., Lofland, L. (eds.) Handbook of Ethnography, xviii, 507 p. Sage, London (2001)
28. Whitacre, R.A.: Johannine polemic: the role of tradition and theology. Scholars Press, Chico Ca (1982)

29. Willis, J.: Foundations of qualitative research: interpretive and critical approaches. Sage Publications, Thousand Oaks (2007)
30. Kelle, U.: "Emergence" vs. "Forcing" of Empirical Data? A Crucial Problem of "Grounded Theory" Reconsidered. Forum: Qualitative Social Research 6 (2005)
31. Strauss, A.: Qualitative Analysis for Social Scientists. Cambridge University Press, New York (1987)
32. Coyne, I.: Grounded Theory. School of Nursing & Midwifery, pp. 1–27. Trinity College Dublin, Dublin (2009)
33. Lee, A.S., Baskerville, R.L.: Generalizing Generalizability in Information Systems Research. Information Systems Research 14, 221–243 (2003)
34. Achebe, C.: Things fall apart. Heinemann, London (1962)
35. Mda, Z.: The heart of redness. Oxford University Press, Oxford (2000)
36. Sen, A.K.: Development as freedom. Oxford University Press, Oxford (1999)
37. Republic of South Africa: Thusong Service Centre: Business Plan 2006 - 2014. vol. 2007. Government Communication and Information System (2007)

EGES Session 4:
Back-End Transformation

Transformative and Innovative E-Gov for the Next Generation: Linkages of Back Offices for One-Stop Portal

Osamu Sudoh[1,3] and Yumiko Kinoshita[2,3]

[1] Professor, [2] Assistant Professor,
[3] Graduate School of Interdisciplinary Informatics, the University of Tokyo
7-3-1 Hongo Bunkyo-ku Tokyo 113-0033
{Sudoh,kinoshita.yumiko}@iii.u-tokyo.ac.jp

Abstract. It is imperative that e-Gov platform for the next generation achieves integrative administrative services via citizen's one-stop portal and back-office linkages among ministries and external organizations. This objective aims to make further advancement in system integration and coordination by employing cloud computing and service-oriented architecture (SOA). To achieve these goals, expertise knowledge must be provided as well-organized citizen services, for which e-Gov platform should be built upon loose-coupling of databases. Japan's e-Gov policy has addressed these needs and designed its national service platform using master registry for standardized metadata, which is the first attempt in the world. This paper discusses the objectives of Japan's e-Gov policy, the architecture of one-stop service platform, and its evolutionary process of back-office linkages using common registry. It is proposed to manage metadata in labor saving manners according to a matrix of operation and disclosure classes via pre/post-process filters assigned.

Keywords: e-Gov, one-stop service, loose coupling, public innovation, XML.

1 Next-Generation e-Gov Platform for Japan

One of critical tasks in establishing e-Gov platform for the next generation is to achieve integrative administrative services via citizen's one-stop portal and back-office linkages among ministries, agencies and external organizations. This objective is pursued by further advancement in inter-governmental and inter-organizational coordination by employing cloud computing and service-oriented architecture (SOA), for strategic challenges i.e. the support of private enterprises including smaller firms [1], the facilitation of labor market to face employment issues of today [2], the reform of policies for the aging society [3] and the promotion and utilization of environmental protection technologies [4]. To achieve these goals, expertise knowledge must be provided as well-organized services to citizens with advanced information technologies (IT). For these purposes, e-Gov platform should be built upon loose-coupling of data, which are currently owned by individual institutions. Japanese government has addressed the

M. Janssen et al. (Eds.): EGES/GISP 2010, IFIP AICT 334, pp. 111–124, 2010.
© IFIP International Federation for Information Processing 2010

need of database linkages in e-Gov and designed its national service platform using service hub regulating registry, directory and operation processes.

Strategic Headquarters for the Promotion of an Advanced Information and Telecommunications Network Society, established in Japan's Cabinet Office, presented a report entitled '*i-Japan Strategy 2015* ' in July 2009 [4]. The report elaborated on priority areas for Japan's e-Gov initiative such as further utilization of IT in healthcare, revitalization of industry and local communities and nurturing of new industries, and improvement of digital infrastructure. These efforts are imperative so that Japanese industries continue to innovate e-Commerce and management system, implement Business Process Reengineering (BPR), for all sizes of enterprises, and gain competitiveness in global markets, strengthening safety measures, and integrating digital technologies in production and delivery of services for enhanced value-added products. According to these directions, the government supports the digitization of public and administrative information as well as the reform and optimization of administrative processes and systems by designing e-Gov and e-Municipality platform based on cloud computing system to integrate servers and databases owned by administrative agencies. National and local governments are also encouraged to implement BPR, and as a part of their optimization efforts, the use of National e-Post Office (P.O.) Box, a type of repository for citizens, is emphasized to reduce administrative costs substantially[1]. They will allow for the facilitation of social security reform and the provision of a wide range of services.

In October 2007, Project Team for the Next Generation e-Gov and Public Services, chaired by Osamu Sudoh (the author), was launched in Japan's Cabinet Office to discuss technical directions to implement full-fledged one-stop service for citizens. In October 2009, a report on the next generation e-Gov system and one-stop service published was summarized [5]. This report specified design, methodology, and technical specifications for back-office linkages with several attempts leading to the first-ever common registry and directory across organizations. In line with this report, this paper discusses the objectives of Japan's e-Gov policy for the next generation, the architecture of one-stop service platform, and the process of back-office linkages. As for the incorporation of the registry, also to be prepared for virtualization technology of future enhanced networks and security, it is proposed to manage information in cost and labor saving manners according to a matrix of operation and disclosure class via pre- and post-process filters and XML schemes.

2   Needs for Integration and Linkages of Back Offices in e-Gov

Sudoh, Inoue, and Nakashima [6] articulate the issue of aging society, and is developing preventive healthcare system utilizing IT as a part of Japan's e-Gov initiative. Various research projects for preventive medicine utilizing IT are currently underway in the world. Pfizer and Grameen Health (GH) announced a partnership for healthcare

---

[1] The report expects for a reduction of costs by 30% by the introduction of e-PO Box.

delivery and financing for the exchange of expertise knowledge, and the provision of micro-health insurance, telemedicine and mobile healthcare[2]. These developments can be called service innovation as they represent a new combination [7] of technologies, new services, means of delivery, and social infrastructure.

In line with urgent social and economic needs for the next generation, European Union, for instance, released a report on e-Gov strategy [2][3] focusing on 'a single information market enabling cohesion and growth.' An important aspect of this direction is that enterprises and institutions, when they are capable of accumulating high-level expertise and produce enhanced value added, may maintain a closed environment to generate expertise knowledge while they can choose to open themselves for partnership and outsourcing to access external sources for information services. Is the next generation e-Gov platform designed to standardize knowledge, or to generate capacity to allow for the diversification of knowledge through the implementation of cloud computing and SOA in and through public domains?

An immediate challenge for the e-Gov initiatives is cost sharing with business sectors and external organizations, which have grown substantially through the implementation of IT and investment into human capital. Furthermore, it is important to provide education and secure skilled human resources in service sectors, which share a large part of employment in today's economy. The idea of using knowledge-intensive services for providing high-quality public services is being presented for the development of skilled human capital and acquisition of external knowledge. Inter-overnmental e-Gov initiative is also promoted to share information on employment for higher mobility of workers [8].

To provide citizens with high-quality services to achieve service innovation in society and economy, administrative agencies may face challenges in building cooperation and partnerships with private firms because of knowledge and technological intensity inherited in such services. Therefore, it is important to incorporate loose-oupling of databases owned by multiple organizations based on advanced service technologies. Furthermore, cloud computing is currently recognized as 'information utility,' and the balance of public cloud and private cloud must be considered carefully in terms of Hardware-as-a-Service (HaaS), Platform-as-a-Service (PaaS), and Software-as-a-Service (SaaS) so that differentiation and competitiveness of services are achieved in data specifications and database linkages. (Please refer to Rimal, Choi, and Lumb [9] and Zhang and Zhou [10] for a good survey and description of cloud computing system).

Information utility means that customer interacts directly with a central computer and information files from a remote terminal [11]. Therefore, network-based services are offered to both small and large companies. For instance, Google's Bigtable is de-

---

[2] Micro-health is a low cost health insurance for i.e. one dollar per person a year. Bellinghen, D.V.: Grameen Health and Pfizer Announce Novel Partnership To Explore Sustainable Healthcare Delivery Models for The Developing World, Corporate news (September 24, 2008), http://www.pfizer.be/Media/Press+bulletins/Philantropy/Grameen+Health+and+Pfizer+Partnership.htm

[3] The report mentions that 'key issues are addressed as the realization by Member States of the value of a single market in information and communication technologies (ICT).' http://ec.europa.eu/information_society/eeurope/i2010/greenknowledgesociety.pdf

signed to handle a mixture of structured data and unstructured data [12] for the use of home networking and a variety of terminals [11]. Therefore, Bigtable currently allows clients to set up 'lazy replication between their tables (cross-data-center replication)' [12]. In the future, it is likely and possible to name information by itself, achieving object-to-object connectivity, object storage and retrieval through name resolution and routing by bringing a new abstraction technique [13]. Such a large scale database is adopting expressive queries to describe server-side filtering of data [12]. On the other hand, specifications of data are an important area for us to elaborate when cloud computing is introduced in private and public domains while some of current cloud systems may not employ SOA yet. In this case, cloud computing should deploy novel data management approaches, such as analytical data management tasks, multi-tenant databases for SaaS, and hybrid designs among database management systems (DBMSs) [14].

To achieve one-stop services for citizens, SOA-based system and other types of systems must be coordinated, and deployed over new architectures. Denmark summarized a report in 2004, in which 2500 examples of e-Gov projects in EU were surveyed to find what constitutes better e-Service in public administrations. Good public service requires database linkages by establishing a system for coordinating multiple and simultaneous service requests [4], one-stop portals, proactive and self services, and agent-based services [15]. To do so, it says that workflows of administrative operations and processes must be aligned well, and common service modules must be increased. It is also important to help users to cope with complex legislation and procedures requiring expertise rarely possessed by the average citizens. e-Gov strategy for the next generation must meet these technological, socio-economic, and democratic challenges in the delivery of one-stop services [4, 5]. The following sections deal with e-Gov initiative in Japan to discuss its objectives, challenges, approaches, and advantages.

3   Providing Full-Fledged One-Stop Portal

Project Team for the Next Generation e-Gov and Public Services in Japan's Cabinet Office presented technological approaches for one-stop portal in October, 2009 [5]. One-stop portal is a front-end of all public services for citizens, and is an integrative part of administrative service platform. Administrative services and applications will be coordinated in this one-stop portal. As Fig. 1 shows, Japan's one-stop portal provides easy to understand information for citizens, and agent-based services. The one-stop portal also responds to user's request for information through proactive service on website, provides customizing functions of webpage[5], and helps intelligent search so that citizens can find information on administrative procedures and documents easily.

To link databases among multiple organizations, it is important to visualize current operation, process, and data. It is technically possible to achieve back-office linkages as long as databases are structured, metadata schemas are standardized, and the

---

4 Back-office clearing house corresponds to 'service hub' in Japan's e-Gov system, which is
  explained in detail in later sections.
5 The customization of webpage is the function to create so called 'My Page.'

specifications of interface and conversion rules of codes and XML schemas are fixed. Then, cross reference of administrative information, location, access protocols, and data format is achieved for existing systems employing different technological specifications. To do so, however, it is not necessary to consolidate all administrative information in one location, but only metadata schemas should be processed at the central service hub in registry, directory, and process control. Therefore, back offices are to be loosely-coupled, which provides extensibility to designs.

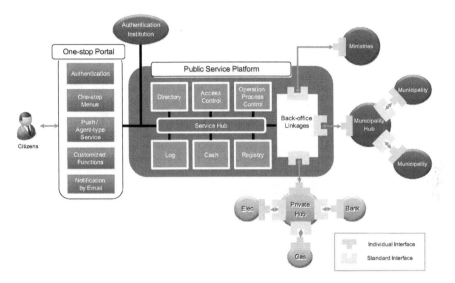

Fig. 1. Next-generation One-stop Portal for Japan's e-Gov [5]

Japan's e-Gov systems are categorized into legacy system[6], local information platform[7], and SOA-based system. The public service platform must respond to distinct technologies employed for these different types of systems in e-Gov infrastructure. Therefore, as Fig. 2 shows, each external system must be filtered through a type of adopter (filter) for back-office linkages to minimize reconstruction efforts of existing systems and maximize the potential of service integration. Currently, the service hub has directory, registry, and operation process control functions. The directory designates a list of services and representative agencies, location IDs, and citizen's log-in IDs. The registry controls specifications of metadata and services. Operation process control function navigates citizen's request for services.

Administrative agencies and external organizations access to a collection of metadata, which is to be controlled in public service platform. For example, a local

---

[6] Legacy system refers to all systems that are difficult to get connected or coordinated with external systems. A large part of Japan's e-Gov systems are legacy enterprise system.

[7] Local information platform refers to operational and technical standard for municipalities' system. It governs specifications for multi-agency systems to facilitate inter-linkages of systems operated by national government, local governments, and private sectors.

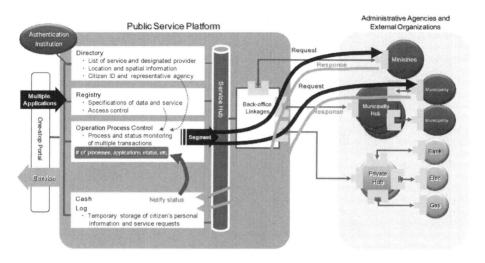

Fig. 2. Public Service Platform with Service Hub [5]

municipality's system is granted an access to a central server to reference metadata schemas in directory and registry, so that multiple applications from citizens are handled by operation and process control functions in coordination with several public and private systems, and authentication is granted in one process. Data format and access protocols are managed in the public service platform via the service hub. The server reduces information passed into a service to key data stored by national and local governments' enterprise systems. This mechanism of database linkages is gathering attention, not only from government agencies, but also as a collaboration platform for public, private and academic institutions.

When a citizen accesses the one-stop portal, the operation process control finds a list of services to be processed. The directory provides addresses of representative agencies while the registry defines service specifications. Other citizen's information is obtained from the log. All procedures go through the filter to get to the external systems. Corresponding external systems return services to be stored temporarily in cash, and the operation process control function notifies the citizen of the result of his or her requests at one time. Therefore the process control function handles a story space i.e. story, actor, scenario, and context in this web information system.

4   Achieving Back-Office Linkages

4.1   Goals and Challenges

To achieve the consolidated one-stop service and back-office linkages, metadata characterization should be defined in the registry and directory to retrieve data from multiple locations. Then, public information must be digitized and disclosed according to pre-specified protocols and mechanisms to make them available for citizens. Data are currently controlled by each administrative agency and external organization, but in principle they should be accessible for citizens according to a unified standard procedure. In Switzerland, Document Management System (DMS) started in 2007 in an organizational unit called Competence Center (CC) to manage all government documents on web-based collaboration platform, and avoid distributing documents in print or email [16]. Chinese e-Gov, for example, designed data storage utilizing ETL (extraction, transformation and loading) technique by using dimensional data in a star structure [17]. It is also proposed to create metadata table and subscribe information of users [18].

The standardization of all metadata schemas in XML may give huge burdens on public agencies and private organizations to restructure databases particularly when several distinct systems are being employed. In addition, the configurations of XML schemas to link existing relational and object-based databases would require constant updates of themselves as new services are added to the central service hub[8]. Besides, the disclosure of personal information and the standardization of all service processes and operations are currently not realized. In such a situation, standardized term tables and data definitions need to be revised and updated constantly by each agency and organization as their meaning and usage are under unintermittent pressure for change so that the quality of public services is maintained and improved. In addition, to provide customization functionality for the portal i.e. mash-up and access to external contents, information extraction techniques[9] are necessary, for example, the use of hidden tables in web pages to induce entity relationships [12], statistical entity extraction [19], entity disambiguation using Markov Logic Networks, and semantic web with cloud computing [20].

It should be noted that the server will be capable of extracting XML schemas and entity relationships, or interpret entities from unstructured data. It is also supposed that the public service platform becomes open to the adoption of third-party applications for the promotion of BPR. Virtualized networks would access public information directly through the filter[10]. With these challenges behind, the service platform is designed to have conversion libraries[11] for Japanese letters and characters as well as pivot tables for

---

[8] According to Ma et al. [21] who surveyed more than 8,500 database schemata, even developers would feel hard to work with 20 or more relationships. SAP/R3's relational schema contains more than 21,000 tables.

[9] Information extraction techniques are used at entity-level, sentence-level, and page or corpus-level. Statistical method can be embedded into the filter after the linkage of back offices would reach a certain level of coordination; however, existing technologies for information extraction normally require machine learning or human annotation to achieve a good analysis of dependencies. It is possible that the current public websites, user's request history, and help files are used to extract important entity or object metadata, and use them as metadata characterization.

[10] The filter handles constraints for the registry such as component construction (based on existence and inclusion of components), identification (the constructor of a set), equality generation (for a set of objects from one class or from several classes), object generation, and representation of constraints through structures [21].

[11] Legacy systems need extra systems for database linkages such as datastore, a conversion filter, and directory for ID conversion. Systems based on local information platform do not necessarily need these systems. SOA-based advanced systems are capable of achieving semi-automatic linkages. Therefore, it is supposed that SOA-based systems are suitable for operation and process optimization.

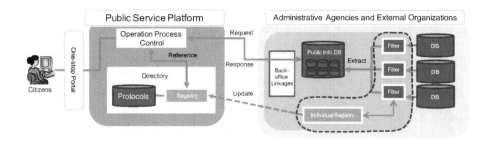

Fig. 3. Prerequisite Set-up for Back-office Clearing [5]

XML schemas to a certain degree (see Fig. 3). These conversion libraries are prepared as a set of standardized templates for all public services for the one-stop portal.

4.2 Public Service Platform

Common Registry and Directory

As previously mentioned, the loose-coupling of databases is proposed so that only the metadata is defined by datatype, attribute and character associated with public information, service processes, in which services of representative agencies are extracted into the public server and controlled by the public service platform. To enable these procedures, the registry and directory are designed as follows.

First of all, ministries and external organizations go through the filter to create a list of core terms in a table (See Fig. 4). Terms can be extracted from existing public websites, help files, and menu bars so that most commonly used terms and key terms are registered in the initial term table. The interface has a matching and pop-up function. A designated personnel in administrative agencies and external organizations uses the filter to feed information to the public service platform. The functionalities of the filter are to analyze documents and data provided against the term table and information that has already been supplied by the other agencies and organizations, prompt the personnel to apply necessary changes and modifications to data definitions according to a preset style guide (a set of rules on the use of character codes and letter sets, and grammatical guidelines at sentence and term levels), and assign ministry ID, department ID, personnel ID, original term ID, timestamp, multi-lingual ID, and other discretionary IDs. It also returns information quality analysis[12] to the personnel for later changes and updates.

In this pre-process procedure, agencies and organizations specify operational and disclosure classes[13] so that information and data are controlled according to a matrix of operation and disclosure protocols. The operation class refers to a stage of processes in

---

[12] The quality of feeding information can be scored by accessibility, security, representational quality i.e. ease of understanding, contextual quality, and concrete representation [21].

[13] Class-wise representation based on Entity-Relationship models uses classes, and object-wise representation do not use classes [22]; however, the registry and directory need these classes to direct multiple processes to multiple locations securely.

a service i.e. life stages and workflow, lifespan of objects, loop and networked data, phases in the life cycle, recording of the development, enhancement, and ageing of objects [21]. Disclosure class is defined in standardized protocols regarding the level of disclosure of information for each service request. Each agency and organization does not reconstruct XML schemas for their databases, but the filter attaches XML, automatically or semi-automatically, with some inputs from the personnel which are prompted by the filter, and update history is logged so that the log can be used later to direct multiple service requests to multiple locations.

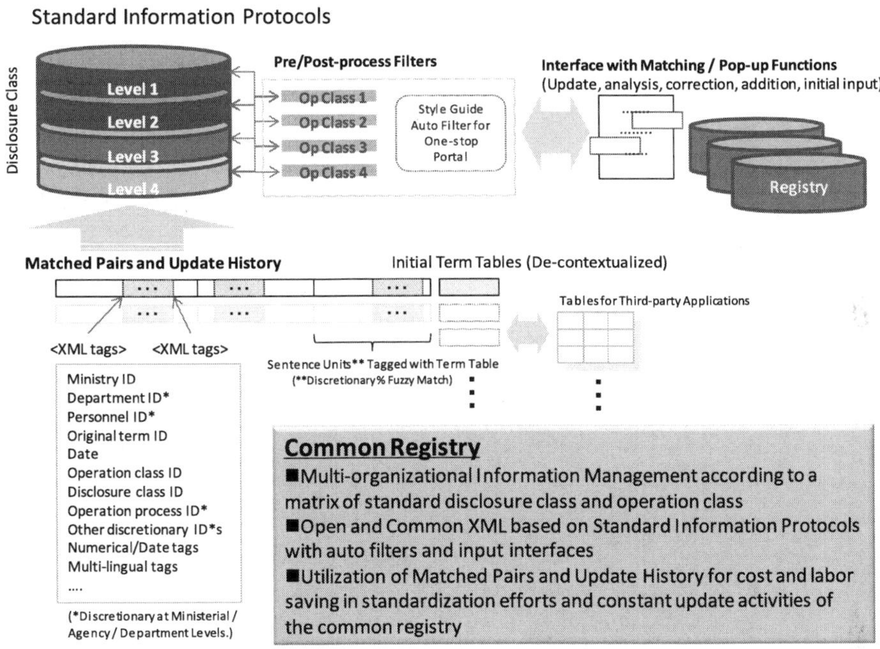

Fig. 4. Schematics of Registry and Directory

Term tables and XML

As previously described, the term table is the initial step to construct the registry and directory. The table works as a reference for agencies and organizations to feed data as a prerequisite step to launch the one-stop portal. The table should be a collection of common terms and key terms are registered without relational or object attributes i.e. utilization recording meta-structures, and quality meta-structures. Index, external keys, and object names and instances can be added to the term table when they are supplied from existing structured databases. The character conversion table is utilized in this process.

Once the list of core terms is created, the designated personnel access to the list and supply data from own databases. The interface requests automatically for necessary information, and the provided data is associated with a term or multiple terms to be stored at a sentence level[14]. Sentences are stored in matched pairs[15]. These data, then, represent meta-characterization in terms of insertion, update, deletion time, keyword characterization, utilization pattern, format descriptions, utilization restrictions, rights i.e. disclosure, obligations and costs, and technical restrictions. These data, when XML are inserted, represent temporal, spatial, ownership, representation, and context data [21]. The filter return an analysis report to the personnel according to these criteria so that the agency or organization can improve the information for later updates and changes[16].

The data of matched sentences supplements the representation of associations of objects and entities, which are lack of in the information and data stored in the central registry and directory. (Please refer to Franceschet, Gubiani, Montanari, and Piazza [22] for more information on entity relationship and XML schema.) It is suggestive that the sentences should not be nested or linked in a star structure to avoid inconsistencies of meta structures. The directory references multiple sentence units for requesting multiple agencies and organizations to process a service request[17]. In such a case, the log obtained during the pre process procedure is also utilized. As the matched pairs are used more in the provision of one-stop services, meta-properties i.e. category, source, and quality information can be used to update the filter functionality so that the filter is able to give an analysis on usage, meta characterization, log dimension, etc. Simultaneously, the analyzed information should be used to update the term table so that terms, which are no longer used or not frequently used, are eliminated. It is also preferred that third-party applications are allowed to reference both the initial term table and matched pair histories according to a discretionary disclosure class assigned.

Pre- and Post-process Filters

When the citizen requests for a service, the operation process control references XML in the registry and calls for services from multiple locations according to the directory. In this process, the disclosure class ID and operation class ID are used to give multiple service requests to different systems. These processes go through the filter to get to

---

[14] The filter searches for a term to be associated with the supplied data at a sentence level. In this process, the sentence should contain an exact matched term, and in a 60-80% matching range (or another discretionary matching percentage) at a sentence level. The minimum unit of association is 100% matched character sets. It gives easiness for the personnel, even when the personnel is not a technician, to review the information and add necessary updates. The maintenance of the matched pairs is extremely easy when there is a chance only in document version number, numerical expressions in a sentence, proper nouns, etc.

[15] XML, sentence pairs, and their update histories should be open to the other agencies and organizations for consistency and quality improvement across all agencies and organizations.

[16] It is possible to add steps later such as aims, purposes, and subjects i.e. actors involved, method and heuristics (i.e. specification language, and simplification approach), developed documents results (i.e. results, deliverables), enabling condition for step (i.e. gathering, dependencies, participation, etc), and termination condition for step (i.e. completeness, correctness, sign-off, contracts, quality, and obligation for the step fulfilled) [21].

[17] Circulation meta-structures for documents, for instance to display objects in different phases for legal documents, should be stored in databases controlled by agencies and organizations.

individual registry or external systems (See Fig. 5). The filter applies post process according to the terms and style guide so that the log of pre process procedure is used to make a backward induction and feedback to external systems. This post process procedure maintains consistency in data quality and process control.

The designation of IDs in the registry enables secured information management and access control according to the disclosure class. Agencies and organizations can save time and costs for restructuring each database, and have more flexibility in its design. These functions allow for the coexistence of open protocols and closed schemata designed by each ministry, agency and organization. The frequency of reference to the initial term table should be reduced gradually as new sentences are associated and sentence pairs are accumulated. The standardization efforts and constant maintenance of libraries will be saved. An inquiry made by the citizen will be responded in a consistent manner across agencies due to the existence of style guide and pre- and post-process functions in the filter, and the quality of the presentation of services via the one-stop portal will be improved.

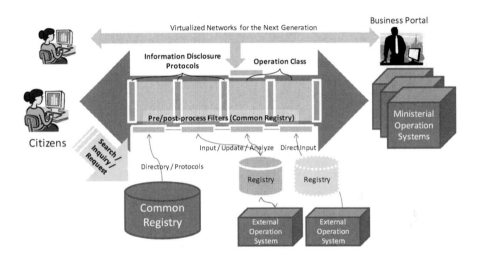

Fig. 5. Pre- and Post-process Filters

5   Organizational Aspects for the One-Stop Portal

Japanese government has focused on the optimization of public organizations and the improvement of public services in the e-Gov initiatives. Known and anticipated bottlenecks, as described in [23], exist particularly in the assignment of control and progress monitoring roles in the achievement of loose-coupling of databases. For example, the government has been facing a serious issue with matching personal information for the provision of public pension due to the lack of coordinated databases. To provide citizens with appropriate public pension services, the government should coordinate multiple kinds of personal information such as individuals' past occupational history, income, and insurance record. The contribution of this paper is to have proposed a technical solution to break down the organizational silos and introduce the concept of loose-coupling of databases via the registry and directory. Another known issue is related to personal information disclosure. The government is currently discussing institutional issues and possible organizational solutions. One solution will be the establishment of third-party organizations to monitor the use of personal information, and to handle claims so that confidentiality is protected appropriately. In many ways Japan has learned from the case of EU.

Meanwhile, Japanese government has presented a roadmap to implement the one-stop portal starting from central ministries, and then local governments. The portal is going to be implemented into quasi-public sectors, such as utility companies, in which e-Gov system must be able to handle transactions for financial settlements, and tax return. To overcome the known and potential organizational issues, real-life instances should be incorporated thoroughly. In this regard, this paper emphasizes on using standardized XML and enhancing 'reasoning' capability to structure meta-data sets and relationships of service scenarios, in which 'data integrity' is more focused in each business operation system owned by ministries and agencies. It is important to note that, whether or not a pre-defined ontology is prepared i.e. an event-driven service-oriented architecture (EDSOA) [24], which affects the entire government systems, its implementation timing and the balance of XML-based schema sets should be carefully decided when we deal with diversified services. At this point, some features based on ontology and natural language processing functionality, which are to call from relational databases or XML-based databases, are conceptualized in the process filter to supplement the standardized XML schema and handle complex real-life scenarios. As use cases will be collected and studied, then, the varying meaning of data elements and their ambiguity should be assessed to reorganize the meta-data sets based on probability and statistics features to be built in the filters.

6 Conclusion

This paper discusses the objectives of Japan's e-Gov policy for the next generation, the architecture of one-stop service platform, and the process of back-office linkages as an evolutionary model. The establishment of networks is an imperative component of e-Gov strategy, and represents the importance of the transition to innovative and transformative e-Gov. To provide citizens with expertise knowledge through e-Gov infrastructure to achieve service innovation, administrative agencies may face challenges in building cooperation and partnerships with private firms because of knowledge and technological intensity inherited in such services. Therefore, it is important to loosely couple databases based on cloud computing, SOA, and virtualization technologies. To do so, cross reference of administrative information, location, access protocols, and data format should be achieved for existing systems employing different technological specifications. Back offices must be connected with the public service platform consisted of the operation process control, the registry, and the directory. As for the incorporation of the registry, it is proposed to manage information in cost and labor saving manners according to a matrix of operation and disclosure class via the pre/post-process filters, which is going to be the world first scenario for the one-stop portal system. These developments can be called service innovation in that they represent a new combination of distinct technological fields, new services, means of delivery, and new social infrastructure. Meanwhile, the proposed architecture has not been fully deployed yet, and we should anticipate organizational issues to arise in the future implementation stage. It is essential to build up use cases in real world situations and device appropriate countermeasures.

Acknowledgements

This research is supported by 'Development of the Fastest Database Engine for the Era of Very Large Database and Experiment and Evaluation of Strategic Social Services Enabled by the Database Engine' as a part of 'Funding Program for World-Leading Innovative R&D on Science and Technology (FIRST),' Japan's Cabinet Office and Council for Science and Technology Policy. This work is also a part of 'Info-plosion: Cyber Infrastructure for the Information-explosion Era,' Grant-in-Aid for Scientific Research on Priority Areas, MEXT.

References

1. Brun, M.H., Lanng, C.: Reducing barriers for e-business in SME's through an open service oriented infrastructure. In: International Conference on Electronic Commerce, pp. 403–410. ACM, New York (2006)
2. Forge, S., Colin, B., Bohlin, E., Cave, M.: A Green Knowledge Society -An ICT policy agenda to 2015 for Europe's future knowledge society. A Study for the Ministry of Enterprise, Energy and Communications, Government Offices of Sweden (2009),
   http://ec.europa.eu/information_society/eeurope/i2010/greenknowledgesociety.pdf
3. Niehaves, B., Ortbach, K., Becker, J.: The Demographic Challenge: Aging and Depopulation and their Consequences for E-Gov - A Case Study. In: Hawaii International Conference on System Sciences, pp. 1–8. IEEE Press, Los Alamitos (2009)
4. Strategic Headquarters for the Promotion of an Advanced Information and Telecommunications Network Society: i-Japan Strategy 2015 -Striving to Create a Citizen-Driven, Reassuring & Vibrant Digital Society, Towards Digital inclusion & innovation. Report released on July 6, 2009 for Japan Cabinet Office (2009),
   http://www.kantei.go.jp/foreign/policy/it/i-JapanStrategy2015_full.pdf
5. Project Team for the Next Generation e-Gov and Public Services: Mid-term Report. Document prepared for the 9th meeting (October 26), IT Strategic Headquarters, Japan Cabinet Office (2009), http://www.kantei.go.jp/jp/singi/it2/nextg/meeting/dai9/siryou4.pdf
6. Sudoh, O., Inoue, S., Nakashima, N.: eService Innovation and Sensor Based Healthcare. In: Oya, M., Uda, R., Yasunobu, C. (eds.) Towards Sustainable Society on Ubiquitous Networks, pp. 1–14. Springer, Boston (2008)
7. Schumpeter, J.A.: The Theory of Economic Development. Translation Publishers (1934)

8. Forge, S., Blackman, C., Bohlin, E., Cave, M.: A Green Knowledge Society -An ICT policy agenda to 2015 for Europe's future knowledge society. Study for the Ministry of Enterprise, Government Offices of Sweden (2009)
9. Rimal, B.P., Eunmi, C., Lumb, I.: A Taxonomy and Survey of Cloud Computing Systems. In: International Joint Conference on INC, IMS and IDC, pp. 44–51. IEEE Press, Los Alamitos (2009)
10. Liang-Jie, Z., Qun, Z.: CCOA: Cloud Computing Open Architecture. In: International Conference on Web Services, pp. 607–616. IEEE Press, Los Alamitos (2009)
11. Chen, R.: Google: The World's First Information Utility? Business & Information Systems Engineering 1, 53–61 (2009)
12. Cafarella, M.J.: Web-scale extraction of structured data. ACM SIGMOD Record 37, 55–61 (2009)
13. Ohlman, B., Eriksson, A., Rembarz, R.: What Networking of Information Can Do for Cloud Computing. In: International Workshops on Enabling Technologies: Infrastructures for Collaborative Enterprises, pp. 78–83. IEEE Press, Los Alamitos (2009)
14. Katsaros, D., Mehra, P., Pallis, G., Vakali, A.: Cloud Computing: Distributed Internet Computing for IT and Scientific Research. Internet Computing 13(5), 10–13 (2009)
15. Millard, J., Iversen, J.S.: Reorganisation of Government Back-Offices for Better Electronic Public Services -European good practices (back-office reorganisation). European good practice case studies, Final report to the European Commission 3(6), 363–370 (2004)
16. Fraefel, M., Neuroni, A.C., Riedl, R.: Reflecting the relevance of communication in e-government-projects: two case studies in the field of knowledge management in the Swiss public administration. In: Chun, S.A., Sandoval, R., Regan, P. (eds.) Annual International Conference on Digital Government Research, pp. 180–189. ACM, New York (2009)
17. Hu, X., Wang, K.: Application of Data Warehouse Technology in Data Center Design. In: International Conference on Computational Intelligence and Security, pp. 484–488. IEEE Press, Los Alamitos (2008)
18. Guo, Q., Zheng, H., Li, J., Wang, X.: Design and Implementation of Data Management Center Based on Web Services. In: International Conference on Hybrid Intelligent Systems, vol. 2, pp. 322–326. IEEE Press, Los Alamitos (2009)
19. Zhu, J., Nie, Z., Liu, X., Zhang, B., Wen, J.R.: StatSnowball: a Statistical Approach to Extracting Entity Relationships. In: International World Wide Web Conference, pp. 101–110. ACM, New York (2009)
20. Sheu, P.C.Y., Wang, S., Wang, Q., Hao, K., Paul, R.: Semantic Computing, Cloud Computing, and Semantic Search Engine. In: International Conference on Semantic Computing, pp. 654–657. IEEE Press, Los Alamitos (2009)
21. Ma, H., Schewe, K.D., Thalheim, B.: Modelling and Maintenance of Very Large Database Schemata Using Meta-structures. In: van der Aalst, W., Mylopoulos, J., Sadeh, N.M., Shaw, M.J., Szyperski, C. (eds.) Information Systems: Modeling, Development, and Integration, pp. 17–28. Springer, Heidelberg (2009)
22. Franceschet, M., Gubiani, D., Montanari, A., Piazza, C.: From Entity Relationship to XML Schema: A Graph-Theoretic Approach. In: Hunt, Z.B.E., Unland, M.R.R. (eds.) Database and XML Technologies, pp. 165–179 (2009)
23. Janssen, M., Gortmaker, J., Wagenaar, R.W.: Web Service Orchestration in Public Administration: Challenges, Roles and Growth Stages. Information Systems Management 23(2), 44–55 (2006)
24. Overbeek, S.J., Klievink, B., Janssen, M.: A Flexible, Event-Driven, Service-Oriented Architecture for Orchestrating Service Delivery. IEEE Intelligent Systems 24(5), 31–41 (2009)

The Influence of Resource Dependency Tolerance on Inter-organisational Alliance Governance

Mark Borman

The University of Sydney
mark.borman@sydney.edu.au

Abstract. The potential of inter-organisational alliances is well recognised but not always realised. An appropriate governance structure has been identified as an important contributor to success. However governance research has typically not examined influences on the *coverage* of an alliance and how they are reflected in the governance structure put in place. Based on resource dependency theory it is suggested that organisations have a resource dependency tolerance level and that this will manifest itself in the scope and depth of an alliance. Given the extent of any dependency is determined by a combination of the importance of a resource, the degree of control by another and the availability of alternatives these factors are key considerations when organisations are constructing an alliance governance structure. An exploratory case study of a local government alliance in Australia is presented to illustrate the proposed connection between resource dependency tolerance and alliance governance structure. The case also highlights that not all participants in an alliance will necessarily have the same resource dependency tolerance level and that this can make it difficult to agree upon the coverage of an alliance and its associated governance structure.

Keywords: Governance, resource dependency theory, shared services partnership, local government, alliance.

1 Introduction

The benefits of inter-organisational alliances and the contribution of information systems to those alliances have long been promoted in the literature [30], [11], [1]. Such alliances are seen as leading to increased efficiency and improved service delivery [20] and are increasingly prevalent in the public as well as the private sector [18] [29]. Many inter-organisational alliances though fall short of meeting their expectations [2]. In particular alliances are seen as difficult to manage [9], [38] with partners often being heterogeneous and with a diversity of interests and priorities [33]. Provan and Kenis [34] emphasised the importance of governance to the effective operation of interorganisational alliances yet also suggested that there is a paucity of academic research in the area. With the governance aspect of particular interest here being the *coverage* of an alliance – its scope and depth – it is proposed here that adopting a resource dependency perspective will provide improved understanding of why particular choices are made.

M. Janssen et al. (Eds.): EGES/GISP 2010, IFIP AICT 334, pp. 125–137, 2010.
© IFIP International Federation for Information Processing 2010

Resource dependency theory typically focuses on how organisations manage *existing* dependencies within their operating environment through the development of relationships with other organisations [31]. Where organisations are creating alliances to perform activities that were previously performed internally the emphasis shifts to the creation of new dependencies [6]. At the point of formation organisations have an opportunity to determine the *degree of dependency* they are prepared to accept. It is argued here that organisations will have a specific dependency tolerance which will be reflected in the governance structure put in place – in particular as it relates to the *coverage* of the alliance.

Shared Services Partnerships (SSPs) are the inter-organisational alliance form of specific interest here. At a broad level the concept of shared services is the aggregated provision of back-office services [35], [42], [26] typically underpinned by ICTs [16]. Shared services have been promoted as an area offering enormous potential with authors such as Schulman et al [36], Kagelmann [22] and Ulbrich [42] suggesting they provide an effective mechanism to deliver improvements in support processes. In the public sector, they are seen as a core element of reform efforts [3] and a key plank of eGovernment initiatives [37]. The potential to extend the benefits of shared services by aggregating activities across small government agencies and departments has led to the formation of multiple SSPs [3], [21], [42]. As with other forms of interorgansiational alliances such initiatives have often failed to realise their potential [41] with the SSP's governance structure being seen as an important influence on success [21]. As such it would appear to be of value to improve understanding of SSP governance structures and why specific choices are made.

The remainder of the paper comprises two sections. The first provides a brief introduction to governance and highlights the need to extend research beyond examining the *mechanics* of governance *within* an organisation to consider the governance of alliances *between* organisations – and in particular governance choices related to the coverage of a relationship. Resource dependency theory is proposed as a potential way of explaining why the coverage of inter-organisational relationships differ. It is suggested that the *resource dependency tolerance level* of the parties to an alliance will be a key influence on governance choices related to the *scope* and *depth* of that alliance. The second section presents the results of an exploratory case study designed to show how the proposed approach can be used to understand the choices made by one SSP.

2   Governance, Resource Dependency Theory and the Relationship between the two

2.1   Governance

A useful overarching view of corporate governance is provided by Keasey and Wright [23] who consider it to be a framework for the effective regulation, monitoring and control of companies which allows for alternative internal and external mechanisms for achieving the underlying objectives. The Cadbury Committtee [8] similarly considers corporate governance to be "the system by which companies are directed and controlled" (p15).

Organisations such as the IT Governance Institute [ITGI] [19] though have increasingly recognised that governance matters are not necessarily constrained to the boundaries of a single organisation while also suggesting that governance becomes more complex and challenging when one moves beyond those boundaries – "In the extended enterprise environment there is no standard pre-existing governance structure" (ITGI, 2005, p67). Where research has investigated inter-organisational governance it has typically focused on the construction and operation of rules i.e. direction and control [5], [24]. Yet, and in contrast to traditional company level governance the entity being defined is not a well accepted, pre-defined given. As such issues surrounding the choice of activities to be provided by an alliance i.e. its coverage should also be examined. Authors such as Heide [17] and Frazier [14], for example, suggest that the initial *choices* regarding an alliance and associated governance structure – in particular those concerning the extent of the relationship – have profound implications for subsequent performance. Provan and Kenis [34] have identified a number of influences on the emergence and effectiveness of inter-organisational governance structures – specifically trust, number of participants, goal consensus and the nature of the task. They note however that while their selection explains some of the variance in the choice of one structure over another it is neither comprehensive nor systematic. Resource dependency theory offers the potential to provide the basis for a more comprehensive analysis.

2.2 Resource Dependency Theory

Building upon work in social exchange theory [12], [40] the central proposition of resource dependency theory is that an organisation's survival is influenced by its surrounding social, political and task environment and hinges on its ability to procure critical resources from that environment. Such resources can be tangible or intangible and include capital resources, information, leadership, guidance and institutional legitimacy [28]. To secure the flow of needed resources, organisations try to restructure their dependencies and exchange relationships by establishing links with other organisations [43] that seek to deliberately increase the extent of coordination [17], [10].

Pfeffer and Salancik [31] argue that for any specific resource the degree of dependency of an organisation is a function of the importance of it to the organisation and the available sourcing options. Specifically it is determined by:

- The *importance* of the resource to the survival of the organisation
- The extent to which the resource is *controlled* by another
- The extent to which there are *alternative* sources of supply

While the bulk of research focused on resource dependency has examined the management of *existing* dependencies it has been recognised that it is important to also consider the establishment of *new* dependencies where internal activities are moved outside the boundaries of an organisation with the formation of outsourcing arrangements or the creation of collaborative alliances. Provan [32] suggested that a cost of developing collaborative activities is the loss of operating autonomy and Gray and Wood [15] argued that it was therefore necessary to maintain a balance between collaborative dependency and organisational autonomy. Kumar and van Dissel [25] argue that a combination of the activities shared and the coordination mechanism put in place determines the degree of dependency.

2.3   Resource Dependency Tolerance and Governance

Blending a consideration of governance and research dependency it is suggested that
when organisations enter into a collaborative alliance they need, at the outset, to specify a governance structure that not only considers how the venture will be directed
and controlled but also, and more fundamentally, what resources will be *included* and
the *depth* of collaboration sought. It is felt that the determinants of dependency identified by Pfeffer and Salancik [31] – importance, control and alternatives – effectively
capture the essential aspects of both the scope and depth of the relationship. Considering them within a context of establishing an alliance should assist organisations in
identifying appropriate points of focus when deciding upon the coverage of that alliance and constructing the governance structure that will regulate that coverage – see
Figure 1. Specifically given a particular tolerance an organisation will seek to construct an alliance that creates the matching resource dependency.

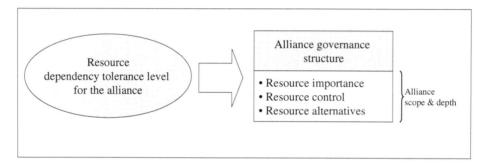

Fig. 1. Resource dependency tolerance and governance structure

A brief outline of each dependency determinant is given below:

- Resource importance

Pfeffer and Salancik [31] suggest that there are two aspects to the importance of a
resource, the proportion of an organisation's inputs it represents and its criticality – or
the ability of an organisation to function without it. With regard to the latter, a nar-
rower focus is provided by Wernerfelt [44] who differentiates between non-core and
core resources – the latter being the source of an organisations competitive advantage.

- Resource control

Pfeffer and Salancik [31] suggest control relates to the ability to impose restraints on the
possession, allocation and use of a resource. Brennan and Buchanan (1985) argue
the importance of carefully constructing the rules that relate to a relationship – and hence
the control of resources – while Willcocks et al [45] have examined and classified different types of relationship contract on the basis of how comprehensive and rigid they are.

- Resource alternatives

Pfeffer and Salancik [31] suggest dependency is influenced by the availability of
alternative sources of a resource – and whether an organisation has the ability to

transfer its business to them. A key concept from transaction cost theory – asset specificity – assists in understanding the determination of transferability. Asset specificity is where an asset is highly specialised and of value only in relation to a particular transaction or relationship [46]. Its existence thus limits the ability of an organisation to move between business partners.

3 Methodology

Having outlined the proposed relationship between dependency and governance[1] empirical research was conducted to determine whether it helped to enhance understanding of why and how inter-organisational alliances – in particular SSPs – are constituted the way they are.

Given the exploratory nature of the research a case study based approach was determined to be appropriate [4], [39]. Australia was chosen as the location for the case since it has been recognised as an early adopter of shared services in the public sector [26].While the specific locus of study was the New England Strategic Alliance of Councils (NESAC) the perspective from which dependency was assessed was that of each of the four councils participating in the alliance. As such interviews were conducted with the General Manager of each council, each being between one and two hours in duration. Between one and three follow up interviews were subsequently conducted with each interviewee. A semi-structured interview protocol was followed to introduce a degree of commonality while minimising the potential for overlooking any unique aspects [13]. Interviews were also supplemented by a review of publicly available, and interviewee provided, documentation to enhance the ability to triangulate data and corroborate the perspectives provided [47]. With regard to analysis, data was coded in terms of its relationship to the governance and resource dependency related concepts identified[2] – an approach in accord with the recommendations of Miles and Huberman [27] and Yin [48] who suggest organising data "around the substantial topics of the case study" (Yin, 1981, p60).

4 Results

4.1 History

In 2004 the Department of Local Government (DLG) moved to amalgamate the councils of Armidale-Dumaresq, Uralla, Guyra and Walcha in the Australian State of New South Wales. In response the councils proposed a strategic alliance – NESAC – to develop and provide shared services as an alternative. Based on the principles of efficiency, performance and autonomy it was proposed that NESAC would:

- Identify one-off savings of $1.3m and subsequent annual savings and benefits of at least $1.7m across fourteen identified functional areas of focus.

---

[1] As it relates to establishing the scope and depth of an inter-organisational relationship.

[2] Specifically resource dependency tolerance, resource importance, resource control and resource alternatives.

Those areas were: community services, customer service, finance and budgets, human resources, information technology, land information and GIS, loans and investments, internal audit and risk management, plant and fleet operations, records, regulatory and planning functions, review, supply and procurement, works operations.

- Implement a performance management system to measure increased service levels, new services provision and implement a sustainable approach to asset management.
- Protect local employment and economic activity.
- Retain local autonomy and representation.

After strong lobbying by the councils and the local parliamentary representative the DLG agreed to defer amalgamation with the condition that NESAC was implemented successfully[3].

NESAC was established under an initial four year period and structured such that the General Manager of each council had a portfolio responsibility for the delivery of specific shared services. Those services were to be supplied by the host council and sold to the other councils. In addition each General Manager would retain responsibility for the delivery of services outside the remit of NESAC to their local council. At the outset shared service provision was proposed for fourteen functional areas and a business case was prepared for each one. After realising benefits from the initial reorganization, recurrent benefits were expected to be realised principally through reduced duplication, increased productivity and streamlined council functions. An advisory committee comprised of the Mayor and Deputy Mayor of each council was also established with each member having equal voting rights. Resolutions passed by the advisory committee also need to be ratified by the individual councils.

Combined the four councils serve a population of over 40,000 across an area of 18,140 sq km with a budget of $75 million. Out of a total of 649 staff approximately 90 work in shared service teams. From the outset it was specified that there would be no forced redundancies and no forced relocations of staff.

In February 2009 Walcha council withdrew from NESAC. Subsequently two of the remaining councils determined not to extend their involvement beyond the renewal date of October 2009.

4.2 Resource Dependency Tolerance

The resource dependency tolerance level of each council was subjectively assessed at a holistic level following discussion with interviewees regarding their attitudes towards collaborating with one another. Table 1 illustrates the levels and differences. In particular there was an overarching desire in some instances to preserve autonomy.

> *"I think mainly because they could see an erosion of their power and influence to go any further than that and certainly wasn't supported at a political level because they wanted to keep autonomy."* Council A

> *"They wanted to actually create business units within the individual councils to deliver shared services and we didn't want a bar of that because obviously we didn't want services centralised any way, shape or form"* Council D

---

[3] The New England Weeds Authority was also included as a member of NESAC.

Table 1. Resource dependency tolerance levels with respect to NESAC

Council	Resource dependency tolerance level
Council A	Very High
Council B	Low
Council C	High
Council D	Very Low

The construction of NESAC's governance structure along the dimensions of *resource importance*, *resource control* and *resource alternatives*, as outlined below, can therefore perhaps best be understood as an attempt to accommodate the differences rather than a reflection of a particular, consistent level of resource dependency tolerance. Indeed the positions of the individual councils with regard to their preferred position along each dimension varied significantly.

4.3 Resource Importance

While NESAC supplies a number of services there was considerable disagreement regarding what its focus should be.

> *"they wished everything to be shared services right across the board. They wanted everything and we said we didn't want everything. Some services we wanted to be delivered locally"* Council D

> *"Each service has a different footprint"* Council B

Some interviewees suggested NESAC should only provide back office services

> *"I think there's some services that don't add value to the ratepayer. They don't care where they get their rate notices from. I think a lot of those types of things lend themselves to shared services .. those back office type functions. I have a little bit of a different opinion when it comes to the engineering services, all those types of things. I think the ratepayer would notice a difference if he couldn't come in here and talk to an engineer I think it makes a difference to the ratepayer then if he loses that local part of those services."* Council B

While others disagreed

> *"if we can get together and do a road in 2 weeks not nine months they are going to be happy"* Council C

Interviewees also highlighted that for a particular activity there can be variations with regard to the extent to which it is included – it is not an all or nothing prospect. The consensus however was that NESAC did not really contribute to the main activities of the councils.

"In engineering we came together to develop policies and share ideas but everyone wanted to keep control of their assets" Council A

"While IT and admin are costly they are nothing compared to engineering which NESAC scarcely touched. I mean engineering is phenomenal. We spend 70% of our money on engineering" Council C

4.4 Resource Control

NESAC's control of resources was universally seen to be weak. Decisions could not be imposed. Councils could retain services and even maintained a degree of "influence" over those that were transferred to NESAC.

The formal NESAC charter sought to accommodate the varying perspectives of the four councils and was seen as being ineffective and open to interpretation.

"Every time somebody said I don't like that their, I don't know, desires were accommodated...which makes everything weaker because you try and do everything for everyone and you do nothing for no-one." Council A

Any decision taken by NESAC's advisory board required approval by all the individual councils.

"we had decisions .. that had been sitting on the table for some 12 months, 14 months, Two years because the general managers couldn't come to an agreement because their councils couldn't come to an agreement" Council C

There was also no requirement to take up many of the services with the level of involvement left with each council.

"effectively for many things something of an opt in basis; there's no kind of compulsion that we're in this together and we'll do everything together, more that initiatives get raised and then councils if they're interested can opt into it" Council A

The reluctance to cede control by the councils was further reflected in the operating structure put in place.

"we had a very unique management arrangement around these functions – see we might have IT but we had the IT reporting to four general managers all of which had a bearing on how the IT system operated and all had different ideas about what IT meant or what it should have achieved.. what happened is everybody then retained control of everything." Council A

4.5 Resource Alternatives

Alternatives to NESAC existed for the supply of a service and in some cases appear to have been actively maintained or nurtured.

"[Council D] *always kept things in reserve. They were never going to stay. They were always going to go. They kept their business as it was running.*" Council B

"*I still had all the staff that I had before I went in. So I just had to retrain them slightly and just go back the way we were before wasn't too difficult*" Council B

"*members of other resource sharing initiatives .. not a problem*" Council D

There were also not perceived to be significant issues in moving activities from NE-SAC to another supplier even with IT which might a priori be considered difficult to disentangle.

"*It's a fully managed service. We just hook in through an Internet connection. So it's basically exactly what we were getting before and rather than all the service, etcetera, housed in Armidale, they're actually housed in Mascot*" Council B

The charter of the alliance itself had no clauses hindering the ability to withdraw.

"*we just passed a council resolution and we were out basically*" Council D

Given the varied resource dependency tolerance levels of the councils *with regard to NESAC*, and based upon the governance structure dimensions identified, it appears possible to identify distinctive coverage related governance preferences associated with low and high dependency tolerance levels – see Figure 2.

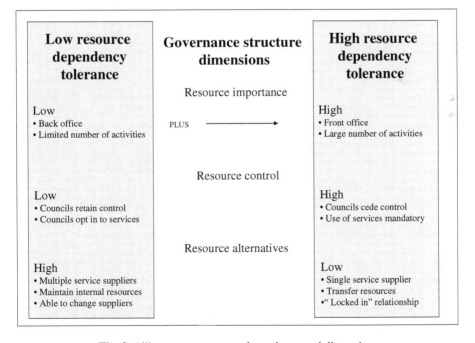

Fig. 2. Alliance governance – dependency and dimensions

Figure 2 suggests that councils with a low tolerance sought a very different alliance compared to those with a high tolerance. For example from a resource importance perspective they wanted the activities included to be restricted in number and low impact. High tolerance councils by contrast wanted a much broader range of activities included including their front office – which they considered core to their operations. Interviewees suggested that NESAC never managed to reconcile the differences.

5 Conclusion

The NESAC case suggests that it is useful to examine the construction of an alliance's governance structure – and in particular its coverage aspects – from the perspective of the participants' resource dependency tolerance levels. Furthermore when considering a governance structure the dimensions of resource importance, resource control and resource alternatives appear to capture key levers through which dependency can be managed. The case also however makes it clear that there will not always be a common resource dependency tolerance level across participants to an alliance and that where this is the case there may be significant difficulties in constructing an acceptable governance structure that will subsequently function to meet the varied expectations. It would therefore appear important to surface the dependency tolerance levels of all potential partners prior to entering into an alliance to ensure that there is congruency. This could be done quite simply through discussions centred on their desires regarding the three resource dependency dimensions.

The research contributes to the literature primarily through extending governance and resource dependency research into new areas and combining the two. In particular it highlights the need for governance research to look beyond the boundaries of an individual organisation. Furthermore once in the realm of inter-organisational alliances such research needs to consider the *coverage* of the alliance as well as its direction and control. From a resource dependency perspective the need to study the *creation* and management of new dependencies as organisations enter into alliances is highlighted, extending the historical research focus beyond the moderation of pre-existing dependencies. Combining the two perspectives, the research suggest that the governance structure of an alliance will be constructed such that it reflects the resource dependency tolerance limits of its participants.

In terms of future research a major limitation of the current paper is that it examined only a single case. Further case studies are required. Do alliance governance structures typically reflect the resource dependency tolerance limits of their participants? Are the dimensions identified here the key ones? Why do organisations have differing tolerance levels? More fundamentally, a shortcoming of the current case is that there was not a consensus view of the coverage of NESAC and the alliance ultimately collapsed. As such it is not possible to provide any insight regarding *how* to ensure that the desired coverage is effectively captured by an alliances governance structure. Case studies of successful alliances are required for this.

It might also be interesting to look beyond a single alliance to consider the complete portfolio of alliances an organization maintains to see if there is any interplay between them – for example the tolerance level of an organization toward a specific alliance might be influenced by the other alliances it has in place. Finally it would be valuable to examine the relationship between the benefits of an alliance and the dependency level – is it the case that the greater the dependency the greater the benefits? Are there disadvantages associated with high dependency alliances?

References

1. Aoki, M., Gustafsson, B., Williamson, O.E.: The firm as a nexus of Treaties. Sage, London (1990)
2. Barringer, B.R., Harrison, J.S.: Walking a tightrope: Creating Value Through Interorganizational Relationships. Journal of Management 26(3), 367–403 (2000)
3. Becker, J., Niehaves, B., Krause, A.: Shared Services Strategies and their Determinants: A Multiple Case Study Analysis in the Public Sector. In: Proceedings of the Fifteenth Americas Conference on Information Systems, San Francisco, California, August 6-9 (2009)
4. Benbasat, I., Goldstein, D.K., Mead, M.: The Case Study Research Strategy in Studies of Information Systems. MIS Quarterly 11(3), 369–386 (1987)
5. Borman, M.: Identifying Appropriate Governance Principles for Different Types of Sourcing Arrangement. In: Proceedings of the Fifteenth Americas Conference on Information Systems, San Francisco, California, August 6-9 (2009)
6. Borman, M.: Recognising The Need For A Context Sensitive Decision Making Framework For Cosourcing – A Case Study In The Financial Service Sector. In: Proceedings of the 15th European Conference on Information Systems, St. Gallen, Switzerland, June 7-9 (2007)
7. Brennan, G., Buchanan, J.M.: The Reason of Rules: Constitutional Political Economy. Cambridge University Press, Cambridge (1985)
8. Cadbury Committee: The Financial Aspects of Corporate Governance, Gee, London (1992)
9. Culpan, R.: Multinational Competition and Cooperation: Theory and Practice. In: Culpan, R. (ed.) Multinational Strategic Alliances. Haworth Press, New York (1993)
10. Cyert, R.M., March, J.G.: A Behavioural Theory of the Firm. Prentice Hall, Englewood Cliffs (1963)
11. Dosi, G., Freeman, C., Nelson, R., Silverberg, G., Soete, L. (eds.): Technical Change and Economic Theory. Frances Pinter, London (1988)
12. Emerson, R.M.: Power Dependence Relations. American Sociological Review 27(1), 31–41 (1962)
13. Firestone, W.A., Herriott, R.E.: The Formalization of Qualitative Research: An Adaptation of "Soft" Science to the Policy World. In: Herriott, R.E., Firestone, W.A. (eds.) Multisite Qualitative Policy Research in Education: A Study of Recent Federal Experience, Authors, Concord, Report No. NIE-400-80-0019 (1982)
14. Frazier, G.L.: Interorganizational Exchange Behaviour in Marketing Channels: A Broadened Perspective. Journal of Marketing 47, 68–178 (Fall 1983)
15. Gray, B., Wood, D.J.: Collaborative Alliances: Moving from Practice to Theory. Journal of Applied Behavioural Science 27(1), 3–21 (1991)
16. Hagel III, J., Seely Brown, J.: Your Next IT Strategy. Harvard Business Review 79(9), 105–113 (2001)
17. Heide, J.B.: Interorganizational Governance in Marketing Channels. Journal of Marketing 58, 71–85 (1994)
18. Huxham, C.: Collaboration and Collaborative Effort. In: Huxham, C. (ed.) Creating Collaborative Advantage. Sage, Thousand Oaks (1996)

19. IT Governance Institute: Governance of the Extended Enterprise. Wiley, Hoboken (2005)
20. Janssen, M., Joha, A.: Motives for Establishing Shared Service Centres in Public Administrations. International Journal of Information Management 26(2), 102–115 (2006)
21. Janssen, M., Joha, A.: Understanding IT Governance for the Operation of Shared Services in Public Service Networks. International Journal of Networking and Virtual Organisations 4(1), 20–34 (2007)
22. Kagelmann, U.: Shared Services als Alternative Organisationsform: Am Beispiel der Finananzfunktion in Multinationalen Konzern. Deutscher Universitäts-Verlag, Wiesbaden (2001)
23. Keasey, K., Wright, M.: Issues in Corporate Accountability and Governance. Accounting and Business Research 23(91A), 291–303 (1993)
24. Kendrick, R.: Outsourcing IT: A Governance Guide. IT Governance Publishing, Ely (2009)
25. Kumar, K., van Dissel, H.G.: Sustainable Collaboration: Managing Conflict and Cooperation in Interorganisational Systems. MIS Quarterly 20(3), 279–300 (1996)
26. Longwood, J., Harris, R.G.: Leverage Business Process Outsourcing Lessons to Build a Successful Shared Business Service Organisation, Report G00144283, Gartner, Stamford (2007)
27. Miles, M.B., Huberman, A.M.: Qualitative Data Analysis: An Expanded Sourcebook, 2nd edn. Sage, Thousand Oaks (1994)
28. Oliver, C.: Network Relations and Loss of Organizational Autonomy. Human Relations 44(9), 943–962 (1991)
29. O'Toole, L.: Taking Networks Seriously. Public Administration Review 57(1), 45–52 (1997)
30. Piore, M.J., Sabel, C.F.: The Second Industrial Divide: Possibilities for Prosperity. Basic Books, New York (1984)
31. Pfeffer, J., Salancik, G.R.: The External Control of Organizations: A Resource Dependency Perspective. Harper and Row, New York (1978)
32. Provan, K.G.: Interorganizational Cooperation and Decision-making Autonomy in a Consortium Multihospital System. Academy of Management Review 9(3), 494–504 (1984)
33. Provan, K.G., Milward, H.B.: Do Networks Really Work? A Framework for Evaluating Public-Sector Organizational Networks. Public Administration Review 61(4), 414–423 (2001)
34. Provan, K.G., Kenis, P.: Modes of Network Governance: Structure, Management and Effectiveness. Journal of Public Administration Research and Theory 18(2), 229–252 (2008)
35. Quinn, B., Cooke, R., Kris, A.: Shared Services: Mining for Corporate Gold. Prentice-Hall, Harlow (2000)
36. Schulman, D.S., Dunleavy, J.R., Harmer, M.J., Lusk, J.S.: Shared Services: adding value to the business Units. Wiley, New York (1999)
37. Sorrentino, M., Ferro, E.: Does the Answer to eGovernment lie in Intermunicipal Collaboration? An Exploratory Italian Case Study. In: Wimmer, M.A., Scholl, H.J., Ferro, E. (eds.) Electronic Government, pp. 1–12. Springer, Berlin (2008)
38. Spekman, R.E., Forbes, T.M., Isabella, L.A., MacAvoy, T.C.: Alliance Management: A View from the Past and Look to the future. Journal of Management Studies 35(6), 747–772 (1998)
39. Strauss, A., Corbin, J.: Basics of Qualitative Research: Grounded Theory Procedures and Techniques. Sage, Newbury Park (1990)
40. Thibaut, J.W., Kelley, H.H.: The Social Psychology of Groups. John Wiley and Sons, New York (1959)

41. Ulbrich, F.: Implementing Centers of Excellence: A Case Study. In: Proceedings of the Fifteenth Americas Conference on Information Systems, San Francisco, California, August 6-9 (2009)
42. Ulbrich, F.: Improving Shared Service Implementation: Adopting Lessons from the BPR Movement. Business Process Management Journal 12(2), 191–205 (2006)
43. Ulrich, D., Barney, J.B.: Perspectives in Organizations: Resource Dependence, Efficiency and Population. Academy of Management Review 9(3), 471–481 (1984)
44. Wernerfelt, B.: A Resource-Based View of the firm. Strategic Management Journal 5(2), 171–180 (1984)
45. Willcocks, L.P., Lacity, M., Cullen, S.: Outsourcing: Fifteen Years of Learning. In: Mansell, R., Averou, C., Quah, D., Silverstone, R. (eds.) The Oxford Handbook of Information and Communication Technologies. Oxford University Press, Oxford (2007)
46. Williamson, O.E.: The Economic Institutions of Capitalism. Free Press, New York (1985)
47. Yin, R.: Case Study Research: Design and Methods, 3rd edn. Sage, Thousand Oaks (2003)
48. Yin, R.: The Case Study Crisis: Some Answers. Administrative Science Quarterly 26, 58–65 (1981)

Content Management Implemented as Shared Service: A Public Sector Case Study

Anton Joha[1] and Marijn Janssen[2]

[1] EquaTerra, 150 Minories, London, EC3N 1LS, United Kingdom,
Tel.: +44 (0)845 8387500
anton.joha@equaterra.com
[2] Delft University of Technology, Faculty of Technology, Policy & Management
Jaffalaan 5, 2600 GA Delft, The Netherlands
Tel.: +31 (0)15 2781140
m.f.w.h.a.janssen@tudelft.nl

Abstract. Sharing services has gained the interest of governments to reduce costs. The basic idea is that services provided by one department can be provided to others with relatively few efforts. A new emerging trend is the implementation of content management (CM) shared services. As a new phenomenon, there is little understanding of this concept. This paper addresses this knowledge gap by investigating a public sector case study and analyzing the decision process concerning the introduction of a CM for Shared Service Centers (SSCs). The case is analyzed using a decision framework based on a multi-theory approach found in outsourcing literature. The differences with other types of SSCs are highlighted. The complexity of this arrangement originates from the need to manage content in the many parts of the organization and the involvement of many different roles. A CM SSC requires a holistic decision-making approach by balancing the management, technology and content dimensions carefully, as these dimensions influence the resulting arrangement and potential benefits.

Keywords: Content Management, Public Sector, Shared Services, Sourcing.

1 Introduction

There has been an explosion of information created and used by governments internally, but also provided by governments via the Internet to inform or facilitate citizens. As such, governments are looking for ways to manage the myriad of content in an efficient and effective manner. In a report, Doculabs identifies the use of shared services for content management as a new frontier for governments to reduce costs, and improve quality, alignment, compliance and control [1]. Shared services have been hailed as a solution to reduce costs and improve services, although the promises might be relatively difficult to realize [e.g. 2]. By unbundling services and then concentrating them within a shared services center, the basic premise for shared services is that services provided by one department or organization can be provided to others with relatively few efforts [e.g. 2, 3, 4]. This should result in both cost

M. Janssen et al. (Eds.): EGES/GISP 2010, IFIP AICT 334, pp. 138–151, 2010.

savings and service quality improvements. The choice for sharing services is a major decision that has a long-term and strategic impact [2]. Governments are under increasing pressure to be transparent by sharing and making their information publicly available [5, 6]. New technological advances allow organizations with data-intensive processes and ever increasing amounts of content like reports, forms, e-mails, spreadsheets, images and other digital content that is used for internal or external purposes, to deliver content management functionality as a shared service. This approach should result in economies of scale and scope by centralizing and standardizing the content on the one hand, and in the effective creation and use of decentralized content by its users on the other hand [7, 8].

In this paper, we use a decision framework to explore a content management (CM) SSC. The aim of this paper is to identify and understand the decision choices that need to be made when introducing and implementing such a novel shared services arrangement. The research described in the paper has an explorative-descriptive nature and a retrospective view of the decision process of the introduction of a SSC was created. The structure of the paper is as follows. In the following section, we discuss the theoretical background and the decision framework for analyzing the CM SSC case study. This is followed by a section with an outline of the research approach used to gather and analyze the data. The following section then describes the case study of a shared service arrangement in the Commonwealth of Virginia in detail, while in the next section the empirical findings are further analyzed and discussed. In the final section, the key research findings are highlighted and conclusions are drawn.

2 Background

2.1 Content Management

Content management is the set of processes and technologies that support the collection, managing, and publishing of information in any form or medium. Much of the content is stored in information silos and not serving the user base of the whole organization [1]. Goodwin and Vidgen [9] view content management as a process instead of a product and define it as "*an organizational process, aided by software tools, for the management of heterogeneous content on the web, encompassing a life cycle that runs from creation to destruction*". Content management is a collaborative process. Different roles are involved in this process, e.g. the creator of the content, the editor and quality manager, the administrator and the user who wants to read or use the content [10-12]. Goodwin and Vidgen [9] describe the content life-cycle by the main processes of create, review, store, publish/exchange, archive and destroy. They found that despite all efforts CM is a difficult endeavor and challenges include content revision, consistency, navigation, data duplication, content audit and control, track, authorize and reconstruct changes.

2.2 Shared Services

SSCs are a particular type of sourcing arrangement, where resources and services are retained in-house. There are many definitions of SSCs in literature [13]. Generally, a SSC is a separate and accountable semi-autonomous unit within an (inter) organizational entity, used to bundle activities and provide specific pre-defined services to the operational units within that (inter)organizational entity, on the basis of agreed conditions [3]. SSCs seem to be especially suitable for public administrations, as in current practice each agency often develops and maintains its own systems and services [14, 15]. By bundling the development, maintenance and use of services, the costs can be shared among the agencies, innovations out of reach might become feasible, and the money freed can be used to improve service levels without any of the agencies having to give up their autonomy.

2.3 Decision Framework

There are many theories underpinning sourcing theory and its decision-making process. Lee et al. [16] and Jayatilaka, Schwarz, and Hirschheim [17] provide an overview of sourcing theories and the strategic determinants influencing these decisions. We adopt a process-driven, multi-theory decision approach and use four major decision categories for implementing shared services: (a) make-or-buy decision, (b) scope and type of shared-service arrangement, (c) cost benefits and risks assessment, and (d) implementation choice and change management strategy. This framework was used in previous research to analyze SSCs in other areas [18]. The categories are shown in the left column of Table 1. In general, the process starts when politicians and/or public managers make the sourcing decision. Next, the scope and type of the shared-service arrangement should be decided on, which will result in the identification of various options available to share services. Thereafter, the cost benefits and risks of the identified options should be assessed and the decision to implement one arrangement should be taken. Finally, the shared-service arrangement should be implemented using a change management strategy.

Table 1. Decision categories when introducing SSCs and their driving theories and motto (based on [16])

Decision categories	Driving theories	Driving motto
1. Make-or-buy decision	- Core competencies theory - Resource-based theory	Performing activities either in-house or by external suppliers.
2. Scope and type of shared services arrangement	- Coordination theory - Resource dependency theory - Transaction cost theory	Determining the potential scope and options for sharing services, including the objectives that should be met.
3. Cost benefits and risks assessment	- Power-political theory - Principal-agent theory - Transaction cost theory	Assessing the financial feasibility of the shared services options, also taking into account the risks involved.
4. Implementation choice and change management strategy	- Power-political theory - Organizational theories	Defining the optimal way to implement the shared services concept within the organization.

The make-or-buy decision for sourcing is largely explained by *resource-based theory* and *core competency theory*, which state that organizations should retain core capabilities in-house and that non-core capabilities do not have to be owned. Choices about the scope of services and the type of shared-service arrangement are driven by coordination, transaction costs, and resource dependency theory. *Coordination theory* looks at the management of interdependencies between organizational business processes [19]. The basic idea behind *resource dependency theory* is that organizations are dependent on external resources to function [20]. The problem that resource dependency theory emphasizes is that the environment changes and resources become more or less scarce, resulting in power differences between organizations and providing an explanation of how independent organizations come to depend on and dominate each other. Cost benefits and risks assessment of the selected sourcing options are often based on the power-political, principal-agent, and transaction cost theories. The basic idea of outsourcing is based on the *transaction cost theory* [21]. Transaction costs result from the transfer of property rights between parties and exist because of friction in economic systems. The idea is that an organization will tend to expand until the cost of organizing an extra transaction internally becomes equal to or higher than the costs of carrying out the same transaction on the open market. The use of a communication network and integration technology will decrease the transaction costs, enabling organizations to source functions and to focus on their core competencies. Finally, *principal-agent theory* deals with the relationship between the principal and agent based on the division of labor, information asymmetry and environment, and partner behavior [22]. Both the transaction cost and principal-agent theories are based on rationality, an efficiency criterion used for explaining outsourcing structures. Political organizational theories are used for explaining organizational arrangements and include social, coordination, risk, and strategic management theories. These view actors as political entities having different degrees of power. The way shared services will be implemented and how changes are managed depend on power political and organizational theories, which are interdisciplinary and based on knowledge from the fields of psychology, political science, economics, anthropology, and sociology. They seek to explain behavior and dynamics in both individual and group contexts.

3   Research Methodology

The objective of this study is to analyze and improve our understanding of a content management SSC in practice by identifying the issues involved during the decision-making phase. This analysis should increase our knowledge of a CM SSC and can be used by practitioners to support the change process. Theory concerning a Content Management SSC is scarce and owing to the complex nature of shared service arrangements, a qualitative approach based on a case study research was adopted for this research [23]. In the shared services both technology and organizational issues play a role. Case study research is one of the most common qualitative method used in information systems (IS) [24]. The case study research methodology is particularly well-suited to IS research, since the object of the discipline is the study of IS in organizations, and the "interest is shifted to organizational rather than technical issues" [25]. This research was based primarily on secondary data collection and evaluation in a qualitative setting. Documents, presentations, internal reports relating to the set up of a SSC were gathered and examined in order to acquire a good understanding of the decision-making processes and aspects. The analysis of documents allowed creating a retrospective view of the decision processes that contribute to the understanding of content management shared service arrangements.

4   Case Study

The Commonwealth of Virginia is a U.S. state on the Atlantic Coast of the Southern United States which is well known for its innovative capacity. The capital of the Commonwealth is Richmond and the state population is nearly eight million [26]. The modern government is ranked by the Pew Center on the States with an A– in terms of its efficiency, effectiveness, and infrastructure. This is the second time Virginia received the highest grade in the nation, which it shares with two others [27]. The Content Management (CM) initiative is focused on promoting the adoption of CM throughout the Commonwealth. Prior to a Commonwealth-wide focus on CM, several agencies had implemented their own agency-specific CM systems based on a variety of platform solutions. In 2008, a feasibility study was done to create a shared service offering and based on the results of this study, it was determined that demand did exist for a CM shared service [28]. To allow agencies and localities to benefit from content management in a cost effective manner, a working group comprising representatives from 12 agencies and localities collaboratively designed a content management shared services offering that would have to be operational at the end of 2009. The CM Shared Service is realized by a single solution platform that is utilized by multiple agencies and localities. Agency content is stored in a consolidated CM repository with appropriate security to control retrieval access. Each participating agency or locality shares in the use and corresponding costs of the hardware, software, and support resources that comprise the offering and agencies pay on a per user basis for use of the service.

While agencies will still be responsible for their mission-specific applications, an increasingly greater number of application functions can be provided and maintained centrally [29]. Shared services can improve service delivery and potentially free agency resources. This goes beyond the area of CM and touches other areas. In combination with other areas improved economies of scope and scale might be accomplished [29].

4.1   Make-or-Buy Decision

Content management is primarily an internal core function, where internal, confidential documents are shared between employees and external documents are shared with citizens. The question whether to outsource this function or to keep it in-house was not an issue as CM was viewed as a core function because of its direct impact on daily operations and risk regulation requirements. This follows the suggestion by *resource-based* and *core competency theory*. An important issue at this stage is to determine which CM activities such as the implementation and testing, can be outsourced and if the organization is already using certain third parties that deliver the technology and software to support content management, in order to be sure that the future solution is consistent and compatible with the already existing technology.

4.2 Scope and Type of Shared-Service Arrangement

The goals for introducing the CM shared services offering are [30]:

- Cost reduction and operational efficiencies by more customer-oriented business processes, reduce manual inputting, faster and easier information finding, more efficient use of resources, eliminate having redundant copies of documents and reduce the volume of paper resulting in less physical storage requirements and costs related to space, printing, copying, filing and distribution.
- Resolve retention issues by having a searchable document repository, and appropriate destruction of documents reduces the cost and time required to respond to the Freedom of Information Act (FOIA), eDiscovery and audit requests, automated linkage to records management retention policies allows appropriate retention and destruction of documents, automated approval routings and document holds prevent improper destruction of documents.
- Increased security and risk reduction by having a secure repository ensuring confidentiality of information, facilitating disaster recovery options, supporting accountability and agile decision-making, increasing compliance with legislation, regulation and potential litigation.
- Customer improvement by providing customer-centric services to citizens, businesses, and government entities making the services easier to use, more accessible, more cost efficient and by managing enterprise information by making all appropriate state-managed data available to all levels of government, citizens and businesses.

The above shows that the goal was to realize a variety of objectives in different areas. The CM Shared Service was intended to provide the following core functions:

- *"Scan Interface: The ability to accept scanned documents and metadata from industry standard scanning and document capture software to index and provide long-term storage in the content repository.*
- *Store: The ability to accept, index, and provide long-term storage of content.*
- *Search: The ability to perform content searches based on a set of stored metadata and full-text search.*
- *Retrieve: The ability to view selected content, typically as a result of a performed search.*
- *Records Management: The application of Library of Virginia-approved retention and disposition schedules to facilitate appropriate retention and timely destruction of records protected by the Code of Virginia.*
- *Basic Security: The use of security provisions to require appropriate authentication and authorization to search, retrieve, view, add, and modify content.*
- *Email Management (Manual): The ability to manually capture, index, and store emails (e.g. drag & drop to folder in Outlook) into the content repository.*

- *Simple Workflows: The use of simple workflow capabilities including acceptance of scanned image content and simple linear step processes (e.g., three-step approval workflow)."* [31]

Following Malone [32], *coordination* is defined as *"the additional information processing performed when multiple, connected actors pursue goals that a single actor pursuing the same goals would not perform"*. This both affects which services can be shared as well as the way these services need to be shared in terms of its governance. There are 4 organizational entities and roles involved in the Commonwealth's CM SSC governance [28]:

- The CM SSC is responsible for the provision of CM services. There is a core staff with ECM architect, system administrator, business analyst, and project manager roles who have to ensure a good performance of the CM system, and also are involved in program management for those agencies that also want to use the CM platform. Internal users can get support or training regarding the CM system via the CM SSC.
- The Chief Applications Officer (CAO) and the office of the CAO, responsible for demand governance in terms of setting business strategy and application standards.
- The Chief Information Officer (CIO) and the office of the CIO, responsible for supply governance in terms of setting the IT strategy, policy and delivering the technology underlying the business services.
- The internal and external users using the CM SSC by creating content as input for the CM system and using its documents.

The CAO is ultimately responsible for the CM SSC and the program management required to extending the scope of the CM shared service to other agencies, but strategic and tactical decisions that have to be made regarding the CM SSC will be discussed in a board with representatives from the offices of the CAO, CIO and the internal user organization.

4.3 Cost Benefits and Risks Assessment

Before Commonwealth started to introduce the CM SSC offering, they assessed the potential cost savings. Commonwealth had to sort through and determine in which activities sharing was possible (see 4.2), where their mission-specific and data privacy boundaries lay, and what they hold in common. This data was used to calculate the cost savings that could be achieved by sharing services. Also the costs for software, hardware, storage, licenses and supporting staff had to be determined. In this analysis the alternative without SSC was also calculated by determining the total recoveries. In table 2, the business case is presented that was created for implementing the CM SSC.

Table 3 shows what investments need to be made for implementing the CM SSC over the coming 5 years, where the number of users is assumed to increase each year. The total investment costs can be compared with the costs that can be saved. The breakeven point occurs between month 42 and 45 [33]. It should be noted that realizing cost reduction is often more complicated than initially thought [2]. Central procurement is possible for licenses, software, hardware, etc, and therefore an appropriate procurement process needs to be put in place. This refers to the principles of the *transaction cost theory* [21]. A governmental agency will tend to organize its own transactions until the cost of organizing an extra transaction internally becomes equal to or higher than the costs of carrying out the same transaction by or with other governmental agencies. In case an agency would implement a content management operation themselves they would need to have minimally 4 servers. Suppose that 7 agencies would do this, 28 servers would be required for each individual agency. By sharing services for these 7 agencies, and bundling the activities, 12 servers are necessary for production and 4 for delivery and testing, which adds up to only 16 servers. The content management shared services would require 5 core staff members, while each agency would need to have on average 1.5 core staff members, which would be 10.5 in total, twice as much as the content management SSC [34]. Participating agencies pay for use of the service through a flat monthly per user fee. This price is estimated to be $55 per user per month, but the price can be subject to change as the overall cost of the offering and number of participants is refined.

Table 2. Business case for the CM Shared Service Center [33]

	Year 1	Year 2	Year 3	Year 4	Year 5	TOTAL
Software	916K	668K	221K - 632K	632K - 1.11M	700K - 1.25K	3.14M - 4.58M
Hardware	565K	569K	622K - 726K	726K - 934K	830K - 1.14M	3.21M - 3.83M
Support Resources	302K	556K	605K	605K	605K - 970K	2.67M - 3.04M
Implementation	250K - 500K	0	0	0	0	250K - 500K
Total Costs	1.93M – 2.18M	1.79M	1.45M - 1.96M	1.96M - 2.65M	2.14M - 3.36M	9.27M - 11.95M
Total Recoveries	884K - 922K	1.77M - 1.84M	2.12M - 2.95M	2.83M - 4.42M	3.54M - 5.9M	11.14M - 16.03M
Number of Users	1.000 – 1.500	2.000 - 3.000	3.000 - 4.000	4.000 - 6.000	5.000 - 8.000	

4.4 Implementation Choice and Change Management Strategy

A change readiness assessment was designed to determine the organization's capability of, and receptivity toward, a planned change [35]. Such an assessment was conducted and the results of the assessments formed a baseline and may be re-administered to measure change over time. Moreover, the results were used to inform the change management strategy and plan and to help reduce project risks. The introduction of a CM SSC was perceived by the respondents as positive [35]. They came up with various suggestions including:

- Use the data to shape change management and PMO activities
- Continue involvement of agencies in system design

- Engage agencies in developing implementation strategies
- Provide post-implementation training for management on "how" to use the system information to manage better
- Actively pursue funding and leadership engagement

Another outcome was that the more personal the impact of the implementation, the more personal the communication method desired [35]. *Organizational theories* pay attention to how a change strategy needs to be implemented. Three main strategies exist, the big-bang strategy, an incremental strategy, or a combination of these two strategies [36]. Commonwealth used the incremental strategy by first doing a pilot and then gradually trying to connect as many agencies as possible to use the shared service. However, the technology and platform to support all potential agencies was already anticipated for and implemented.

5 Discussion

A sound and unified decision structure will give everyone a voice in the functionality and services provided by the CM SSC. Bramscher & Butler [37] identify three different roles that are critical to the success of a content management system as a technology that enables an organization to meet the needs of its users. They identify the *content role*, responsible for pushing out digital material or objects by non-technical staff, the *management role* responsible for facilitating decisions regarding the architecture and distribution of authorship and editorial roles, and the *technology role* responsible for providing the technological platform and mechanisms to carry this out enables an organization to meet the needs of its users [37]. We have used their framework to map these roles on the different stakeholders involved in the Commonwealth's decision process in order to show where the different responsibilities are located, as shown in figure 1.

The *management role* is associated with *coordination theory* as it's mainly concerned with the management of interdependencies between organizational business processes, while the *technology role* is mainly associated with *transaction cost theory* because of its responsibility for communication network and integration technology that will decrease the transaction costs and its potential to outsource certain technological activities in case a third party can provide these more cost-efficiently. The *content role* is mainly linked to *resource-based theory* and *core competency theory* because the users provide the specific knowledge that is core to the organization. The relationship between these three roles can be analyzed from the *principal-agent theory* perspective.

The case study suggests that there needs to be a good balance between the above roles during the decision process to align the business requirements with the available technology in such a way that users are able to make use of the content management system in the most efficient and effective way. This requires a holistic decision making approach.

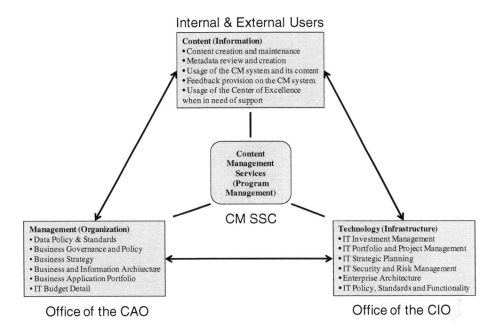

Fig. 1. Virginia's decision structure, roles and responsibilities [based on 37]

5.1 Differences between a CM SSC and SSCs in Other Areas

The case study shows that the implementation of a content management shared service center differs from shared services implementations in other areas [see for example 2, 3, 38] in several ways. These differences are related to the nature of the respective arrangements.

First, in other SSCs, activities and systems are bundled that are generally only relevant for and apply to one or more specific parts of the organization. In case of a CM SSC, activities and systems are bundled that are relevant for and apply to the whole organization. This will influence the way the applications, data and technical architecture of the underlying CM platform will have to be structured and this organization and technology dimension.

Second, SSCs in other field provide services to the internal organization and in some instances also to external customers. In general only the SSC employees do have access to the systems they are working with. In a CM SSC, this is different. Everyone within the organization is able to use the system and provide input and feedback. A content management solution therefore requires identity, access and security management, to deal with so many users. Moreover digital forms and signatures need to be introduced to ensure that external customers can securely use the documents and forms. This all involves the technology and content dimension. Finally, training, education and support will become more important, as all of the employees will potentially use the content management system (CMS).

Third, SSCs in other areas are often not as technically oriented as the content management SSC. Usually SSC start with the unbundling and concentration of business processes which are supported by technology. Whilst in CM-CSS the concentration of technology is the driver and only the supporting (helpdesk) processes are shared. Information technology pervades, affects and even shapes most organizational processes in some way [39], and this could have potential consequences for the business processes. This affects the organization, technology and content dimension. This also shows that the way governance is defined becomes more relevant as it involves coordination on all of the above mentioned dimensions.

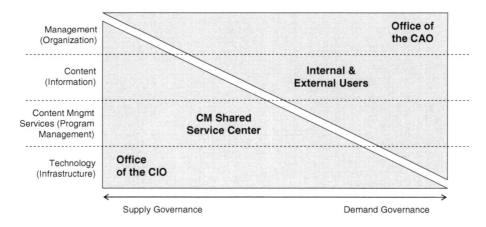

Fig. 2. Main responsibilities of the organizational entities in the CM SSC decision process

Figure 2 is an extension of figure 1, showing which organizational entities are responsible for which specific content management dimension and how the SSC relates to these entities. The CM SSC and the Office of the CIO are involved with supply governance, implying that they are providing content management and its related IT services to the internal and external users. The office of the CAO is responsible for demand governance in terms of defining the policies, standards and functionality of the CM system. Besides using the content management system and creating content that is used as input for the system, users are also supposed to provide feedback on its functionality in order to further improve the system.

6 Conclusions

For most governments the management of content is its core business. The availability of consistent and correct content is necessary for ensuring trust in governments. The choice for a SSC requires considerable organizational changes and should be based on a long term strategy. In this paper we explored an emerging new form of shared services, a Content Management SSC (CM SSC). CM SSCs have some peculiar aspects which makes them different from SSCs in other areas. Whereas in other areas activities and systems are bundled in a SSC that are generally only relevant for and apply to a specific part of the organization, in case of a CM SSC, activities and systems are bundled that are relevant for and apply to the whole organization. Most persons in the organization are involved in content management. Moreover, in other SSC arrangement generally only the SSC employees do have access to the systems they are working with, while in a CM SSC everyone within the organization is able to use the system and provide input and feedback. Another difference is that a SSC normally includes business processes and is not as technically oriented as the CM SSC. In the investigated case study no business processes are included in the SSC and the CM system itself is the central service that is shared.

To better understand the typical decision choices when implementing a CM SSC, a case study was analyzed. The peculiar characteristics of CM influence the way the CM SSC has to be implemented and highlight the decision-making issues that need to be resolved before implementation. These include decisions about the applications, data and technical architecture of the underlying CM platform, the way the governance needs to be defined, access and security management, digital forms and signatures that need to be introduced, training and support that needs to be given, and a procurement function that needs to be skilled to procure licenses, software, hardware. In this view, content management is often linked to other areas like procurement, Human Resources (HR), ePayment, Business Intelligence, and Portals. In this light, greater economies of scope and scale might be created by taking these areas also in account.

The CM SSC was introduced based on expectations about cost reduction and service improvement, but these depend on the economies of scope that can be achieved and the adoption rate, which are again dependent on factors as training, functionality, data security and governance mechanisms and infrastructure systems like digital signature. The factors relevant for the implementation affect the decision-making factors to introduce a CM SSC and vice versa. The design of a CM SSC business model seems to be a compromise balancing the management, technology, content and governance dimensions and as such it is of key importance that the decision making process of a CM SSC follows a structured, systematic and holistic approach, constantly using the potential feedback that is received on the various dimensions form the different stakeholders involved.

To our knowledge this is the first research analyzing the decision process concerning the introduction of a Content Management SSC and therefore we opted for investigating a case study. The case study has limited generalizability, however, the implementation strategy and issues presented in this paper can help decision-makers to understand the various dimensions associated with the introduction of a CM SSC. For further research we suggest to investigate the factors, dimensions, benefits, disadvantages, risks, types of organizational arrangements and decision-making processes in more detail to get better grip on these types of arrangements.

References

1. Doculabs: ECM as a Shared Service: The new frontier (2009)
2. Janssen, M., Joha, A.: Motives for Establishing Shared Service Centers in Public Administrations. International Journal of Information Management 26, 102–116 (2006)
3. Bergeron, B.: Essentials of Shared Services. John Wiley & Sons, Chichester (2003)
4. Accenture: Shared Services: Government Shared Services Model for High Performance (2006)

5. Layne, K., Lee, J.: Developing fully functional E-government: A four stage model. Government Information Quarterly 18, 122–136 (2001)
6. Yang, D.-H., Kim, S., Nam, C., Lee, I.-g.: The Future of e-Government: Collaboration Across Citizen, Business, and Government. In: Traunmüller, R. (ed.) EGOV 2004. LNCS, vol. 3183, pp. 558–559. Springer, Heidelberg (2004)
7. Hodgkinson, S.L.: The Role of the Corporate IT Function in the Federal IT Organization. In: Earl, M.J. (ed.) Information Management: The Organizational Dimension, pp. 247–269. Oxford University Press, Oxford (1996)
8. Bauer, B.T.: Is a Centralized or Decentralized IT Organization Better? Darwin Magazine (October 2003)
9. Goodwin, S., Vidgen, R.: Content, Content Everywhere... Time to stop and think? The process of web content management. Computing and Control Engineering Journal 13, 66–70 (2002)
10. Suh, P., Addey, D., Thiemecke, D., Ellis, J.: Content Management Systems. Peer Information Inc. (2002)
11. Asprey, L., Middleton, M.: Integrative Document & Content Management: Strategies for Exploiting Enterprise Knowledge. IGI Global (2003)
12. Boiko, B.: Content Management Bible. Wiley, Chichester (2004)
13. Singh, P.J., Craike, A.: Shared services: towards a more holistic conceptual definition. International Journal of Business Information Systems 3, 217–230 (2008)
14. Grant, G., McKnight, S., Uruthirapathy, A., Brown, A.: Designing Governance for shared service organizations in the public service. Government Information Quarterly 24, 522–538 (2007)
15. Borman, M.: Identifying Appropriate Governance Principles for Different Types of Sourcing Arrangement. In: Americas Conference on Information Systems, AMCIS 2009, Paper 553 (2009)
16. Lee, J.N., Huynh, M.Q., Kwok, R.C.W., Pi, S.M.: IT Outsourcing Evolution. Past, Present and Future. Communications of the ACM 46, 84–89 (2003)
17. Jayatilaka, B., Schwarz, A., Hirschheim, R.: Determinants of ASP choice: an Integrated Perspective. European Journal of Information Systems 12, 210–224 (2003)
18. Joha, A., Janssen, M.: The Strategic Determinants of Shared Services. In: Garson, D., Pour, M.K. (eds.) Handbook of Research on Public Information Technology. Information Science Reference, Hershey PA, USA, pp. 544–555 (2008)
19. Malone, T.W., Crowston, K.: The Interdisciplinary Study of Coordination. ACM Computing Surveys (CSUR) 26, 87–119 (1994)
20. Pfeffer, J., Salancik, G.R.: The external control of organisations. Stanford Business Classics, Stanford (2003)
21. Coase, R.H.: The Nature of the Firm. Economia 4, 386–405 (1937)
22. Jensen, M., Meckling, W.: Theory of the Firm: Managerial behavior, agency costs, and capital structure. Journal of Financial Economics 5, 305–360 (1976)
23. Yin, R.K.: Case study research: design and methods. Sage Publications, Newbury Park (1989)
24. Orlikowski, W.J., Baroudi, J.J.: Studying Information Technology in Organizations: Research Approaches and Assumptions. Information Systems Research 2, 1–28 (1991)
25. Benbasat, I., Goldstein, D.K., Mead, M.: The Case Research Strategy in Studies of Information Systems. MIS Quarterly 11, 369–386 (1987)
26. US_Census_Bureau: Virginia Profile (2008)
27. Somashekhar, S.: Government Takes Top Honors in Efficiency. The Washington Post (2008)

28. Virginia: Report to the Information Technology Investment Board, Chairman, House Appropriations Committee, and Chairman, Senate Finance Committee in response to 2008-2010 Budget Bill. vol. 2009 (2008)
29. Virginia: Strategic Plan for Applications, vol. 2009 (2009)
30. Virginia: ECM Benefits Statement, vol. 2009 (2008)
31. Virginia: Enterprise Content Management Initiative, vol. 2009 (2008)
32. Malone, T.W.: What is coordination theory. National Science Foundation Coordination Theory Workshop (1988)
33. Virginia: Shared Services Example: Enterprise Content Management, vol. 2009 (2009)
34. Feldmann, P.: Virginia Enterprise Applications Program. General Government Subcommittee, vol. 2009 (2008)
35. Virginia: Change Readiness Assessment, vol. 2009 (2007)
36. Bruijn, J.A.d., Heuvelhof, E.F.t., in 't Veld, R.J.: Process Management; Why Project Management Fails in Complex Decision Making Processes. Kluwer Academic Publishers, Boston (2002)
37. Bramscher, P.F., Butler, J.T.: LibData to LibCMS: One library's evolutionary pathway to a content management system. Library Hi Tech. 24, 14–28 (2006)
38. Janssen, M., Joha, A.: Emerging shared service organizations and the service-oriented enterprise: Critical management issues. Strategic Outsourcing: An International Journal 1, 35–49 (2008)
39. Kern, T., Willcocks, L.: Exploring relationships in information technology outsourcing: the interaction approach. European Journal of Information Systems 11, 3–19 (2002)

EGES Session 5:
New Applications

Process Modeling Semantics for Complex Business Environments

I.T. Hawryszkiewycz

School of Systems, Management and Leadership
University of Technology, Sydney
igorh@it.uts.edu.au

Abstract. Process management is becoming more complex especially when business units work together to create new systems constructed from many components. The complexity arises both from the growing number of components and relationships as well as continual changes in product requirements and business arrangements. The complexity impacts on process management as support systems are needed to provide the communications and coordination to support the complex relationships and their continuing change. This paper proposes a systematic way to model such processes by developing the semantics to describe complex processes in meaningful ways. The semantics include perspectives other than those found in process flows to provide a more meaningful way to describe and model complex processes. The paper then outlines ways to convert the models to lightweight platforms that directly support the modeling concepts. The paper shows the application to complex tendering processes, which many of which now require greater flexibility and collaboration.

Keywords: Complexity, Modeling, Business Processes.

1 Introduction

Increasing complexity within the current business environment is introducing new approaches to system design. Such approaches must pay more attention to system complexity now found in the increasingly dynamic business environment. This complexity arises from an increasing trend to business networking and responding to changing service demands. One common example of such environments is supply chains based on business networking and usually supported by ERP systems. They appear in many industries as for example telecom [1] and automotive [2] industries. Complex tendering processes found in many government projects also include the coordination of different suppliers in large projects followed by the integration and testing of supplied components. Each supplier is often one component of the workflow and is required to provide a service that is coordinated by a project manager. Whereas ERP systems focus on optimizing information flows, the increasing complexity and greater emphasis on collaborative supply chains, requires other perspectives to be considered, in particular social networks and knowledge to continuously develop new knowledge to optimize and rearrange supply chain processes. Rye [3] for

M. Janssen et al. (Eds.): EGES/GISP 2010, IFIP AICT 334, pp. 155–166, 2010.

example calls for knowledge hubs to be established at all supply chain transitions. Pralahad and Krishnan [4] also argue that social networking will play an increasingly important role in such coordination. In many cases coordination is through the exchange of knowledge, much of it of a tacit nature, created by process participants.

These trends have a number of implications for the design of engineering systems and the management of processes. Such systems require support for collaboration between the different units to work towards common goals. These support systems must maintain awareness across the different processes, coordination within and between teams in the environment, and facilitate the knowledge sharing.

- The emergence of process ecosystems [5], where links between the different processes are continually changing and awareness must be maintained between process participants to keep track of outcomes in distant units that may impact on their own work,
- The trend to a more service oriented environment where systems must continually respond to changing customer needs requiring the continuous sharing of knowledge across units through the business processes, and
- Greater client involvement in the design [6] where solutions are created through collaboration between supplier network and the customer network.

The paper provides systematic ways to describe processes in such complex environments emphasizing the increasing role of social relationships [4] in knowledge creation. It particularly addresses the question as to whether new modelling concepts are needed to design such systems. The paper proposes that such new concepts can be derived from complexity theory. The paper identifies some such concepts and suggests that they become criteria in system design. It then defines how the criteria can be met using a number of perspectives to allow complexity to be managed in a systematic manner. It then describes modelling methods to describe systems from the different perspectives and the kinds of design processes needed to create systems to support complex processes.

2   Design Guidelines from Complexity Theory

To some people complexity is seen as arising from the interconnection on many objects. This is often referred to as combinatorial complexity. This can be the design of a complex communication systems or circuits as those found in modern day computer systems. Many of these can be solved by tools that deal with such complexity. Complex systems are seen to be different as they need to deal with unanticipated events that cannot be addressed using existing rules. Hence there is much more emphasis on social structures to address such problems and resolve them.

McElroy [7] identifies a number of fundamental ideas arising from complexity theory. These are illustrated in Figure 1, which identifies three main dimensions for design. These see the growing importance of knowledge management as the driver of innovation. Such knowledge must be developed as part of an increasingly complex environment that calls for increased emphasis on organizational learning. It stresses

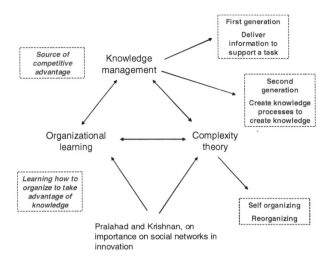

Fig. 1. Important Dimensions in Complexity Theory

that knowledge needs to be created during processes and not just information that may be consolidated to support a task. At the same time, Figure 1 also builds on the importance of social networks within complex systems by suggesting the appropriate networks e "injected" into systems to facilitate productive evolution.

In summary, the following design criteria are identified as important in system design. These are:

Learning both as organizations and individuals,
Knowledge capture and sharing,
Perception of the environment and responding to changes in the environment,
Communication and relationship building, and
Technology to provide system support.

These criteria are related as social structures must be chosen in ways that people collaborate to create new knowledge. At the same time they learn ways to do to things better and retain this knowledge for subsequent use and to support change. A number of papers such as that of Merali [9, 10] define the nature of change based on concepts of evolution found in complexity theory. These are derived from complexity theory and summarized [8] and in terms meaningful to system designers. These include:

- Ability to self-organize at local levels in response to wide variety of external changes
- Quick establishment of self-contained units that address well-defined parts of the environment
- Loose connections between system elements and a way to reorganize the structure to respond to external change
- Ability to organize connections into larger components with consequent changes to connections and interactivity
- Aggregation of smaller units into larger components

All of these become check points in a design. Not each of these is relevant to each level of design.

2.1 The Impact on Systems Modeling

Writers such as Merali [9, 10] or Kovacs [11] suggest that IS system design no longer focus on the design of deterministic systems that attempt to reduce complexity through structure but on systems that support evolution and change.

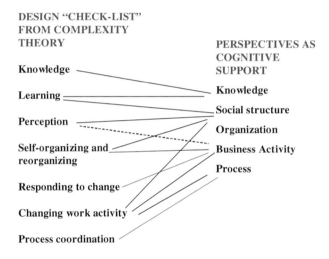

Fig. 2. Design Checklist

The complex business environment requires process management that goes beyond managing simple workflows but require systematic ways to manage complexity. These require systems to support the design criteria described in the previous section. The paper proposes that such design criteria can be met from the following perspectives:

- The **business activities** and their actions and what they create,
- The **process workflow** or sequence of activities and the interdependence between activities,
- The **social structure** that describes roles and their responsibilities and the assignment of roles to individuals to describe the increasing importance of social interactions in any design.
- The **knowledge** created and used during the activities, and
- The **technology** and how it can be used to assist process management.

Figure 2 shows the relationship between the criteria and perspectives. For example learning is related to the knowledge and social perspectives as learning requires the sharing and creation of knowledge within social environments.

3   Choosing Modeling Methods

The options for designers of systems that satisfy complex criteria are:

- Using the traditional methodologies to model other perspectives,
- Extending existing methodologies with new perspectives either by providing new modelling techniques or extending current modelling structures, or
- Creating new modelling methods.

Traditional methods include various project management tools, or modelling methods such as E-R or workflow modelling, which have been successful in developing structured systems in the past. Their purpose is to define the terms needed to describe systems in terms natural to users and then a way to convert models in these terms to computer systems. There are now a number of such models in practice mainly used to develop structured deterministic systems. These do not contain specific constructs to address the new criteria introduced through complexity. The alternative described here is to develop models for each of the perspectives and to integrate the models into a holistic system.

3.1   Choosing the Semantics

The paper describes the kinds of concepts used to model the different perspectives and ways to integrate them [12]. It focuses on using the knowledge perspective as central driver in the more emergent knowledge based processes.

Figure 3 illustrates a modeling method called the business activity model (BAM) that shows the combination at a high level. It includes concepts both from the business, social and knowledge perspectives. It is principally a high level diagram that shows the main entities in the system. It uses concepts of a conceptual model for collaborative systems [13]. These focus on collaborative business systems and have been verified in earlier research [14, 15]. As shown in Figure 3, the main modelling concepts are the activity (shown as ellipses), role (shown as black dots), and artefact

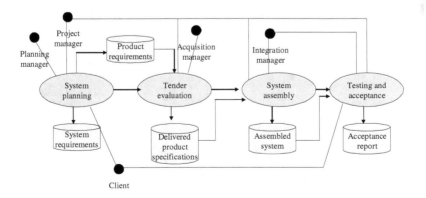

Fig. 3. Process for system development

(shown as disk shapes). It is also possible to add participants or people who tale on the roles by attaching their names to the roles. Figure 3 illustrates one instance of such model showing the main activities in a tendering process to create a new engineering system. The Figure also illustrates the links to both social structures through roles and to explicit knowledge through artifacts. Later knowledge creation through interactions is described using the enterprise social network (ESN).

Figure 3 shows the following activities:

- System planning where client requirements are developed. These specify the various components needed to construct the system,
- Tender construction for the components and evaluation of response,
- System assembly of delivered products, and
- Testing and Acceptance of the constructed system.

The activities in Figure 3 are on-going. The ability to self organize is through the governance structure within the activity. Learning and knowledge are specified as responsibilities with the social structure, which is modelled by the ESN illustrated in Figure 4.

The ESN diagram is introduced in this paper as an extension of social networks. The roles here define responsibilities of people assigned to the roles. It includes the following concepts:

- Roles that define responsibilities. These responsibilities are shown by the attached text; for example, the project manager organizes the project. One important responsibility defined at this level focuses on knowledge and learning. Thus for example the project manager needs to develop knowledge on improving project management techniques in their environment,

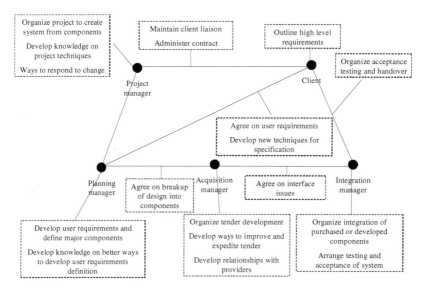

Fig. 4. ESN Diagram

- Participants who take on these roles can be shown by faces;
- Interactions shown by lines between the roles showing the kind of interactions between people assigned to these roles; for example the major interaction between client and integration manager is to organize acceptance tests.

As is normal in most design processes the high level business activities are described at lower levels. Figure 5 for example illustrates the expansion of system planning into more detailed business activities

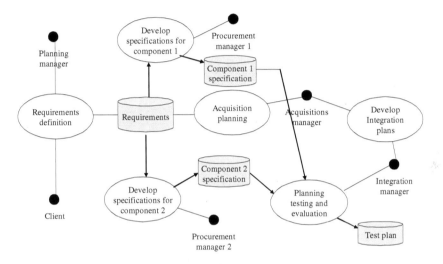

Fig. 5. System planning activities

The activities are now shown in more detail that includes:

- The definition of requirements
- The decomposition of the requirements into components and identifying the component specifications to tendering teams,
- Specifying acquisitions planning to ensure components are delivered as needed,
- Development of integration plans to put the components together, and
- Specifying the test procedures

These specifications are used in later stages.

Knowledge is gathered during the system planning stage to be used later in the tendering and system construction activities as well as in integration and testing.

3.2   Integrating the Knowledge and Social Perspectives in the Business Context

The enterprise social network (ESN) is also constructed for lower level business activities. It shows the responsibilities of the project manager in more detail and introduces any additional roles found at lower level activities. In this case these procurement managers who will be later responsible for developing tenders and accepting supplied components. Their main responsibility during planning is to develop the component specifications that are later used to construct the tender. The ESN contains an additional construct to indicate interactions between three or more roles. Thus for example the procurement managers and planning manger together interact to develop the acquisitions schedule and tender requirements.

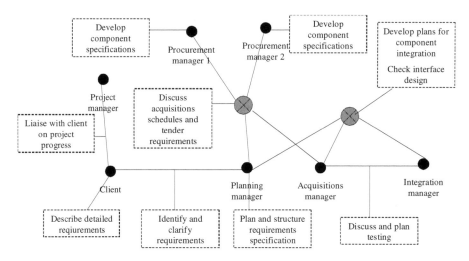

Fig. 6. Enterprise Social Network for System Planning

Figure 5 describes the social network in the system. Here each role is represented by a black circle.

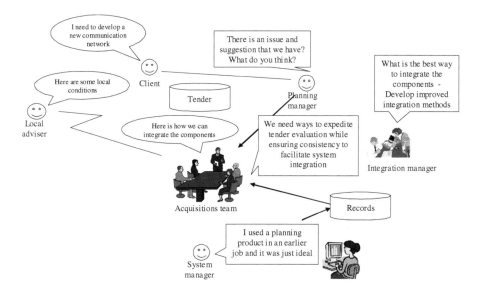

Fig. 7. A Rich Picture Model of the Knowledge Perspective

3.3 Modeling the Knowledge Perspective

Knowledge is a less structured and visible perspective and it can be shown using rich pictures that illustrate the knowledge needs of the different roles. The goal here is to capture the knowledge needed to improve activities.

The paper now shows the integration of the knowledge and social perspectives.

3.4 Specifying Change in Terms of Perspective Semantics

Change can now be specified in different perspectives and easily converted to implementation. The changes specified in Table 1 can be described in terms of the semantic concepts. For example:

Change to the organization can be implemented by creating new business activities, then adding roles and interactions as needed,

Changes to the activity can be described by changing its roles or artifacts,

Changes to the role can be expressed by changes to role responsibilities and interactions.

Assign a person to a role is expressed by linking a participant to a role.

The next requirement is for such models and their creation and change to be directly implemented using software.

4 Defining the Supporting Technology Infrastructure

The two steps to be satisfied in an implementation are to identify the services needed to support the interactions within the system and ways to integrate the services into platforms that present a holistic environment to system participants.

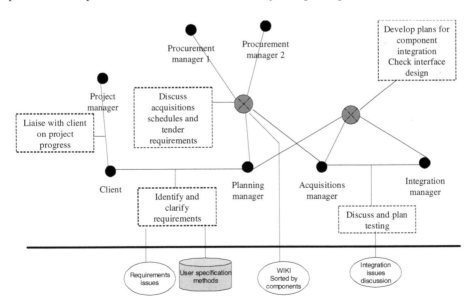

Fig. 8. Collaborative Infrastructure

4.1   Identifying the Required Services

Services must be chosen to support the interactions between the roles in the system. The main aspect of collaboration is to support the interactions between the different roles. The choice is illustrated in Figure 8. The interactions in the ESN are now mapped to social software. For example a blog is provided for client discussions, whereas alliance discussions are supported by a WIKI.

4.2   Software Infrastructure Requirements

Most current systems are supported by workflow technologies that follow a predefined set of steps. Any required social networking is carried out outside such systems using a limited set of collaborative technologies. Knowledge sharing between the two is often minimal. Complex dynamic systems that align the collaborative interactions to formal processes are better supported by:

- Middleware - this provides a solution where workspaces can be customized to roles with links to corporate databases. They can be used to develop special interfaces for roles or activities. However middleware change is more difficult than change using lightweight technologies, and the expectation is that change would not happen frequently. In most cases it would require information technology specialists to construct an interface for each individual and change it as needed.
- Lightweight technologies - these provide better abilities for change but in many cases cannot easily connect to corporate wide databases or other lightweight systems. They can be used to develop the one-fits-one option or for mass personalization, which is ideal for knowledge workers. Many allow users themselves can create and manage their workspace.

Software must be chosen to support change specified in terms of natural semantics. Thus software must include commands that actually create a workspace, add a new role, setup a new interaction and place it in the context of the activity. Lightweight platforms are an important option. However to support user driven change they must provide users with commands based on the modeling concepts as a guideline. They should include the concepts defined for the collaborative model while providing commands to easily create and change the structures of workspaces. Our experimental system, LiveNet, demonstrates the kind of support needed by workspace systems. Figure 9 shows the LiveNet interface and its typical commands.

It provides a menu that can be used to create new collaborative objects, including activities, roles, and artifacts. It also enables people to be assigned to the roles. Apart from these elementary operations the system includes ways to implement governance features as for example allowing roles limited abilities to documents. The system includes support for sharing artifacts across workspaces and a permissions structure to control such sharing. Social software such as blogs or discussion systems is supported and can be shared across workspaces.

Commercial systems in this area focus on middleware software that provides the commands that allows users to use the middleware functionality to create workspaces. Furthermore, it should allow users to change the workspaces as work practices change. Many manufacturers are now providing ways to integrate the kind of software with enterprise applications. A typical example here is Websphere provided by IBM. The challenge in many such systems is to provide ways to share knowledge across activities. They provide access to corporate databases but often do not support the sharing of knowledge collected in the course of knowledge work in identifying and solving problems, and making decisions.

Fig. 9. A Demonstration Workspace

5 Summary

The paper began by describing the increasing complexity of business processes and a systematic way to describe it. It described how complexity adds new criteria to design processes and discussed the implication for system modelling. It suggested that such criteria can be met by seeing systems from a number of perspectives and using the perspectives to specify ways to meet the criteria. It developed models to represent the perspectives and illustrated them in the context of tendering processes.

References

1. Heikkila, J.: From supply to demand chain management: efficiency and customer satisfaction. Journal of Operations Management 20, 747–767 (2002)
2. Howard, M., Vidgen, R., Powell, P.: Automotive e-hubs: Exploring Motivations and barriers to collaboration and interaction. Journal of Strategic Information Systems 15, 51–75 (2006)
3. Rye, K., Lee, S., Choi, H.: Modularization of web-based collaboration systems for manufacturing Innovation. In: Proceedings of the Tenth International Conference on Enterprise Information Systems, Barcelona, June 12-16, pp. 174–177 (2008)
4. Prahalad, C.K., Krishnan, M.S.: The New Age of Innovation. McGraw-Hill, New York (2008)
5. Vidgen, R., Wang, X.: From business process management to business process ecosystem. Journal of Information Technology 21, 262–271 (2006)
6. Cova, B., Salle, R.: Marketing solutions in accordance with S-D logic: Co-creating value with customer network actors. In: Industrial Marketing Management, vol. 37, pp. 270–277. Elsevier Press, Amsterdam (2008)
7. McElroy, M.W.: Integrating Complexity theory, knowledge management and organizational learning. Journal of Knowledge Management 4(3), 195–203 (2000)
8. Hawryszkiewycz, I.T.: Supporting Complex Adaptive Systems with Lightweight Platforms. In: Luis, M., Camerinha-Matos, P.W. (eds.) Pervasive Collaborative Networks: IFIP TC 5 Ninth Working Conference on Virtual Enterprises, Poznan, Poland, September 2008, pp. 381–388. Springer, Heidelberg (2008)
9. Merali, Y., McKelvey, B.: Using Complexity Science to effect a paradigm shift in Information systems for the 21st century. Journal of Information Technology 21, 211–215 (2006)
10. Merali, J.: Complexity and Information Systems: the emergent domain. Journal of Information Technology 21(4), 216–233 (2006)
11. Kovacs, A.I., Ueno, H.: Towards Complex Adaptive Information Systems. In: Proceedings of the 2nd International Conference on Information Technology and Application (2004)
12. Hawryszkiewycz, I.T.: Knowledge Management: Organizing the Knowledge Based Enterprise. Palgrave-Macmillan, Basingstoke (2010)
13. Hawryszkiewycz, I.T.: A Metamodel for Modeling Collaborative Systems. Journal of Computer Information Systems XLV(3), 63–72 (Spring 2005)
14. Hawryszkiewycz, I.T.: Providing Computer Services For Business Networks. In: Proceedings of the Ninth International Conference on EDI-IOS, Bled, pp. 398–411 (June 1996), ISBN-961-232-000-4
15. Hawryszkiewycz, I.T.: A Framework for Strategic Planning for Communications Support. In: Proceedings of The Inaugural Conference of Informatics in Multinational Enterprises, Washington, pp. 141–151 (October 1997)

A Role-Involved Conditional Purpose-Based Access Control Model

Md. Enamul Kabir[1], Hua Wang[1], and Elisa Bertino[2]

[1] Department of Mathematics & Computing
University of Southern Queensland
Toowoomba, QLD 4350, Australia
{kabir,wang}@usq.edu.au
[2] Department of Computer Science and CERIAS
Purdue University, West Lafayette, Indiana, USA
bertino@cs.purdue.edu

Abstract. This paper presents a role-involved conditional purpose-based access control (RCPBAC) model, where a purpose is defined as the intension of data accesses or usages. RCPBAC allows users using some data for certain purpose with conditions. The structure of RCPBAC model is defined and investigated. An algorithm is developed to achieve the compliance computation between access purposes (related to data access) and intended purposes (related to data objects) and is illustrated with role-based access control (RBAC) to support RCPBAC. According to this model, more information from data providers can be extracted while at the same time assuring privacy that maximizes the usability of consumers' data. It extends traditional access control models to a further coverage of privacy preserving in data mining environment as RBAC is one of the most popular approach towards access control to achieve database security and available in database management systems. The structure helps enterprises to circulate clear privacy promise, to collect and manage user preferences and consent.

Keywords: Access control, Conditional Purpose, Privacy.

1 Introduction

Nowadays privacy becomes a major concern for both consumers and enterprises and thus privacy preservation is a challenging problem. Enterprises collect customer's private information along with other attributes during any kind of marketing activities. It is a natural expectation that the enterprise will use this information for various purposes, this leading to concerns that the personal data may be misused. As individuals are more concerned about their privacy, they are becoming more reluctant to carry out their businesses and transactions online, and many organizations are losing a considerable amount of potential profits [9]. Therefore without a clear compromising between individuals and enterprises, data quality and data privacy cannot be achieved and so many organizations are seriously thinking about privacy issues of consumers. By demonstrating good

M. Janssen et al. (Eds.): EGES/GISP 2010, IFIP AICT 334, pp. 167–180, 2010.

privacy practices, many businesses are now trying to build up solid trust to customers, thereby attracting more customers [4]. Considering the privacy of customers, enterprise has to develop a secure privacy policy to remove the fear of customers. Thus in an internal management system, a reliable, efficient, effective and secure privacy policy should be established depending on customer's requirements.

One of the most popular approach for protecting private information is the access control model. Access control is the process of limiting access to the resources of a system only to authorized users, programs, processes, or other systems [23]. The traditional access control model focus on which user is performing which action on which data objects and completely ignores which purpose data will be used. It also overlook to take consent from customers of using their private data. Thus it can be said that personal information can be collected, stored and used without any consent of customers that make them fear of breaching privacy. So the access control model should be developed in such a way that satisfy customer requirement as well as specify which purpose data will be used for. Observing the lack of adequate privacy protecting systems, Byun *et al.* [7] proposed a privacy preserving access control model for relational databases based on the notion of purpose following an idea of Agrawal [1].They argue that the notion of purpose must play a major role in access control models and that an appropriate metadata model must be developed to support such privacy centric access control models in order to protect data privacy. An approach is developed that is based on intended purposes and access purposes corresponding to the data object and the data access respectively which makes access control clearer. Usually, during the data collection procedure customers are informed about the purposes of enterprises. Customers then decide whether their information could be used or not for a certain purpose. That means data providers are given an option of using their data with certain purposes. If an individual mentions that his/her data could not be used for a certain purpose, then his/her information is not accessible for the purpose. Generally data providers are reluctant to use any part of their information for any purposes and so there is a possibility of losing information. But more information can be extracted from data providers by providing more options of using their information. An intended purpose is divided (IP) into two parts: Allowed Intended Purposes (AIP) (explicitly allows to access the data for the particular purpose) and Prohibited Intended Purpose (PIP) (data access for particular purposes are never allowed). In our previous work [11], we included another term conditional intended purpose (CIP) (Conditionally allows to access the data for the particular purpose) to extract information from PIP, which referred to conditional purpose-based access control (CPBAC) model. The key characteristics of CPBAC model was that it allows users using some data with certain conditions and multiple purposes can be associated with each data element. Our previous work exploited query modification techniques to support data access control based on the conditional purpose information. However, RBAC is one of the most popular approach towards access control to achieve database security and available in many database management system, need to address it in CPBAC. To implement this, we need to expand CPBAC model with the conventional well-known RBAC. Such an extension of CPBAC with roles which we refer to role-involved conditional purpose-based access control (RCPBAC) model is presented in this paper. Both access purposes and intended purposes are specified with respect to a hierarchical structure that organizes a set of purposes for a given enterprise.

Role based access control (RBAC) proposed by Sandhu *et al.* [18] has been widely used in database system management and operating system products because of its significant impact on access control systems. RBAC is described in terms of individual users being associated with roles as well as roles being associated with permissions (each permission is a pair of objects and operations). As such, a role is associated with users and permissions. A user in this model is a human being and a role is a job function or job title within the organization associated with its authority and responsibility. RBAC model also includes a role hierarchy, a partial order defining a relationship between roles, to facilitate the administration tasks. In this paper we utilize RBAC which supports conditional purpose into our model. Thus RCPBAC model has the following features:

- It satisfies data providers requirements and allows users using data with conditions. The data provider express his/her own privacy preferences through setting intended purpose with three levels (AIP, CIP and PIP), while the data owner is responsible for working out the policies for authorization of access purpose.
- Its algorithm utilizes RBAC to achieve the compliance computation between access purpose and intended purpose.
- It extracts more information from data providers by providing more possible options of using their information assuring privacy of private information that maximizes the usability of data.
- It determines the compliance computation between access purpose and intended purpose. Intended purposes are associated with the requested data objects during the access decision to the well-designed hierarchy of private metadata.

The reminder of this paper is organized as follows. We present a brief overview of privacy related technologies in Section 2. Since purpose is used as the basis of access control, a brief description of the notion of purpose is described in Section 3. In Section 4 we present comprehensive descriptions of our proposed access control model with roles. Access decision of the proposed RCPBAC model is illustrated in Section 5. Concluding remarks are included in Section 6.

2   Related Work

This work is related to several topics in the area of privacy preservation in data mining atmosphere. The most notable technique to protect privacy is the W3C's Platform for Privacy Preferences (P3P) that formally specify privacy policy by service providers [13]. Byun *et al.* [7] indicate that P3P does not provide any functionality to keep promises in the internal privacy practice of enterprise. Thus it can be said that a striking privacy policy with inadequate enforcement mechanism may place the organizations at risk of reputation damage. The concept of Hippocratic database introduced by Agrawal *et al.* [1] that amalgamates privacy protection in relational database system. A Hippocratic database includes privacy policies and authorizations that associate with each attribute and each user the usage purpose(s) [3]. Agrawal *et al.* [1] presented a privacy preserving database architecture called Strawman which was based the access control on the notion of purposes, and opened up database-level researchers of privacy protection technologies. After that, purpose based access control introduced by Byun *et al.* [6,7] and Yang *et al.* [21], fine grained access control introduced by Agrawal *et al.* [2] and Rizvi *et al.* [15] are widely used access control models for privacy protection. In IT system the proposed Enterprise Privacy Authorization Language (EPAL) of IBM [10] is a language for writing enterprise privacy policies to run data handling practices.

A lot of works [5,8,16,17,19] provide many valuable insights for designing a fine-grained secure data model. In a multilevel relational database system, every piece of information is classified into a security level, and every user is assigned a security clearance [7]. LeFevre *et al.* [12] proposed an approach to enforcing privacy policy in database setting. This work focus on ensuring limited data disclosure, based on the premise that data providers have control over who is allowed to see their personal data and for what purpose. Peng *et al.* [22] proposed an approach for privacy protection based on RBAC. The key feature of their approach is dynamic and they proposed Dynamic purpose-based access control. This method however works based on subject attribute and system attribute but does not guarantee to extract more information. Byun *et al.* [7] present a comprehensive approach for privacy preserving access control model. In their access control model multiple purposes to be associated with each data elements and also support explicit prohibitions. Massacci *et al.* [14] also mention that most privacy-aware technologies use purpose as a central concept around which privacy protection is built.

All of these works proposed different approaches to protect the privacy of individuals through different models without being considering to extract more information. Our aim is to preserve privacy of individuals as well as extracting more information. With this aim, this paper investigated RBAC to extend our previous work on CPBAC [11]. It has improved in four different ways. First, we introduce conditional purpose in the intended purpose in addition to explicit prohibitions that make data providers more flexible to give information. Second, the enterprise can publish an ideal privacy policy to manage data in a sensitive, effective and trustworthy way. Third, it reduces the information loss as it shows that we can extract more information from data providers and fourth it can easily be implemented in RBAC, where a RBAC model has made a significant impact on many access control systems.

3   Purpose, Access Purpose and Intended Purpose

Data is collected for certain purpose. Each data access also serves a certain purpose. Thus a privacy policy should concern which data object is used for which purposes.

Purpose

Purpose is the most important thing to researchers as it directly shows how access to data elements has to be controlled. P3P defines purpose as "the reason(s) for data collection and use" and specifies a set of purposes [20]. In commercial surroundings purposes normally have a hierarchical associations among them; i.e., generalization and specialization relationships. We borrow the purpose definition from [7].

Fig. 1. Purpose Tree

Definition 1 (Purpose and Purpose Tree): A purpose describes the intentions for data collection and data access. A set of purposes, denoted as ω, is organized in a tree structure, referred to as Purpose Tree and denoted as Ω, where each node represents a purpose in ω and each edge represents a hierarchical relation between two purposes. Figure 1 is an example of purpose tree. Purposes, depending on their association with objects and subjects, may be called intended purposes or access purposes respectively.

Definition 2 (Access Purpose): An access purpose is intensions for accessing data objects, and it must be determined by system when data access is requested. So access purpose specifies the purpose for which a given data element is accessed.

Definition 3 (Intended Purpose): An intended purpose is the specified usages for which data objects are collected. That is, purpose associated with data and thus regulating data accesses as intended purpose. According to our approach an intended purpose consists of the following three components.

Allowable Intended Purpose (AIP): This means that data providers explicitly allow accessing the data for a particular purpose. For example data providers may consider that his/her information can be used for marketing purpose without any further restrictions.

Conditional Intended Purpose (CIP): This means that data providers allow accessing the data for a particular purpose with some conditions. For example data providers may consider that his/her income information can be used for marketing purpose through generalization.

Prohibited Intended Purpose (PIP): This means that data providers strictly disallow accessing the data for a particular purpose. For example data providers may consider that his/her income information cannot be used for marketing purpose. In that case data provider's income attribute is strictly prohibited to use for marketing purpose. Notice that each data element is stored in three different purposes each of which corresponds to a particular intended purposes.

So an intended purpose IP is a tuple $\langle AIP, CIP, PIP \rangle$, where $\text{AIP} \subseteq \omega$, $\text{CIP} \subseteq \omega$ and $\text{PIP} \subseteq \omega$ are three sets of purposes. The set of purposes implied by IP, denoted by $\text{IP}^\star$ and the set of conditional purposes, denoted by $\text{IP}^\star_c$ are defined to be $\text{AIP}^\downarrow\text{-CIP}^\updownarrow\text{-PIP}^\updownarrow$ and $\text{CIP}^\downarrow$ $\text{-PIP}^\updownarrow$ respectively, where

$\text{R}^\downarrow$, is the set of all nodes that are descendants of nodes in R, including nodes in R themselves,

$\text{R}^\uparrow$, is the set of all nodes that are ancestors of nodes in R, including nodes in R themselves, and

$\text{R}^\updownarrow$, is the set of all nodes that are either ancestors or descendants of nodes in R, that is, $\text{R}^\updownarrow = \text{R}^\uparrow \cup \text{R}^\downarrow$.

Definition 4 (Full Access Purpose Compliance): Let Ω be a purpose tree. Let IP= $\langle AIP, CIP, PIP \rangle$ and AP be an intended purpose and an access purpose defined over Ω, respectively. AP is said to be compliant with IP according to Ω, denoted as $\text{AP}_{\Leftarrow\Omega}\text{IP}$, if and only if $\text{AP} \in \text{IP}^\star$.

Definition 5 (Conditional Access Purpose Compliance): Let Ω be a purpose tree. Let IP= $\langle AIP, CIP, PIP \rangle$ and AP be an intended purpose and an access purpose defined over Ω, respectively. AP is said to be conditionally compliant with IP according to Ω, denoted as $\text{AP}_{c\Leftarrow\Omega}\text{IP}$, if and only if $\text{AP} \in \text{IP}^\star_c$.

Example 1: Suppose IP= $\langle\{\text{Admin, Direct}\}, \{\text{Third-party}\}, \{\text{D-mail}\}\rangle$, then $\text{IP}^\star$ = {Admin, Profiling, Analysis, D-Phone} and $\text{IP}^\star_c$ = {Third-party, T-Email, T-Postal}, where subscript c indicates that customers information can be used for the purpose with some conditions.

4   Conditional Purpose-Based Access Control (CPBAC)

In the CPBAC model data providers are asked three possible options for usage of each data item. Permissible usage means data providers allow to use of their data, prohibited means data providers don't allow to use their data and conditional permissible usages means data providers conditionally allow to use of their data item. Consider Table 1 that describes the intended purpose, types of data and possible data usages. For example, a data provider may select his/her name is permissible for **Admin** purpose, address is not permissible for **Shipping** purpose but income information is conditionally permissible for **Marketing** purpose. That is, data provider does not have any privacy concern over the name when it is used for the purpose of administration, great concern about privacy of

Table 1. Intended purpose, data type and data usage type

Term	Description	Example
Intended Purpose	Intended usage of data specified by data provider	AIP, CIP, PIP
Data item	Types of data being collected (i.e. attributes)	Name, Age, Income
Data usage Type	Types of potential data usage (i.e. purpose)	Marketing, Admin

Table 2. Conditional records and intended purposes

	name	age	address	income
AIP	Alice	35	21, West St., TBA, QLD 4350	35000
CIP	A	30-40	West St., TBA, QLD 4350	30000-40000
PIP	⋆	⋆	⋆	⋆

⋆ means data providers are reluctant of any usage of their
data items.

the address information (and so does not want to disclose address) when it is
used for the purpose of shipping, but his/her income information can be used for
marketing purpose with some conditions. Here the term "conditions" means that
data providers ready to release his/her certain information for certain purpose
by removing his/her name or id or through generalization. This information
is then stored in the database along with the collected data, and access to the
data is tightly governed according to the data provider's requirements. For using
the term condition data providers feel more comfortable to release their data.
Table 2 shows conditional records and intended purposes of a data provider Alice.
The design of intended purposes supports permissive, conditions and prohibitive
privacy policies. This construction allows more squash and flexible policies in
our model. Moreover, by using CIP and PIP, we can assure that data access
for particular purposes are allowed with some conditions or never allowed. Note
that an access decision is made based on the relationship between the access
purpose and the intended purpose of the data. Access is allowed only if the
access purpose is included in the implementation of the intended purpose; in
that case the access purpose is compliant with the intended purpose. The access
is accepted with conditions if the implementation of intended purpose includes
the access purpose with conditions; in this case we say that access purpose
is conditionally complaint with intended purpose. The access is denied if the
implementation of the intended purpose does not include the access purpose, in
this case access purpose is not complaint with the intended purpose.

4.1 Role-Involved CPBAC (RCPBAC)

RBAC model is a landmark in the field of access control models and become a
NIST standard [18]. The key concept of RBAC model is role which represents
certain job function or job title within the organization. The permission of performing certain operations on certain data is assigned to roles instead of to single
users. Users are thus simply authorized to play the appropriate roles, thereby

acquiring the roles authorizations. When the user makes a request, the system activates specific roles predefined for him/her. Thus he/she gains the permission of operating directly or indirectly from roles, which considerably simplifies the authorization management. Because roles represent organizational functions, an RBAC model can directly support security policies of the organization. In the recent development of privacy preserving data mining environment many researchers have been confessed the importance of purpose, but in the RBAC model purpose is not yet fully investigated. Based on RBAC, CPBAC model extends mainly in the following aspects.

- The access permission is no longer a 2-tuple ⟨*Object, Operation*⟩, but a 3-tuple ⟨*Object, Operation, AccessPurpose*⟩ which is called the access purpose permission.
- The access purpose permission is assigned to roles and after the purpose compliance process, only the objects which are purpose compliant or conditionally compliant can be returned to the users.

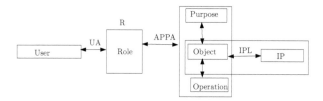

Fig. 2. RCPBAC Model

In RCPBAC model, the entity User is defined as a human being, a machine, a process, or an intelligent autonomous agent, etc. The entity Role represents the working function or working title assigned within the organization according to different authorities and obligations. Roles are created for the various job functions in an organization and users are assigned roles based on their authority and qualifications. Users can be easily reassigned from one role to another. Roles can be granted new permissions as new applications and systems are incorporated and permission can be revoked from roles as needed. The entity Object stands for the data which the user requests and can be abstracted as data set. The entity operation signifies certain action that the user wants to perform on the object. The entity Purpose represents all the possible access purposes in the system and IP signifies the intended purposes with three levels (AIP, CIP, PIP) attached with each data object. Permission is an approval of a particular operation to be performed on one or more objects. The RCPBAC model is illustrated in Figure 2. The formalized definition of RCPBAC model is shown as follows:

Definition 6 (RCPBAC model):

– *User, Role, Operation, Object, Purpose* represent the set of users, roles, operations, objects and purposes.
– $IP=\{\langle aip, cip, pip\rangle | aip \subseteq \omega, cip \subseteq \omega, pip \subseteq \omega\}$ is the set of object's intended purposes, where aip signifies the object's permitted intended purpose, cip is the conditionally permitted intended purpose and pip represents the object's forbidden intended purposes [11].
– $R=\{r|r \in Role\}$ is the set of roles.
– $APP=\{\langle o, opt, ap\rangle | o \in Object, opt \in Operation, ap \in Purpose\}$ is the set of access purpose permissions.
– $IPL=\{\langle o, ip\rangle | o \in Object, ip \in IP\}$ represents the set of data objects and their predefined intended purpose.
– $RH \subseteq Role \times Role$ is a partial order on roles, called the inheritance relationship among roles. We also define a partial order $\geq$ which is the transitive closure of RH. For example, $r_1 \leq r_2$ means r_1 inherits all permissions of r_2. Figure 3 is an example of role hierarchies of Marketing department for a hypothetical company.
– $PT \subseteq Purpose \times Purpose$ is a partial order on purposes (generalization/ specialization) shown in the purpose tree. Figure 1 is an example of purpose tree.
– *User Assignment* $UA \subseteq User \times Role$ is a many-to-many mapping relation between users and their assigned roles.
– *Access Purpose Permission Assignment* $APPA \subseteq Role \times APP$ is a many-to-many mapping relation between roles and access purpose permissions. It signifies the action that certain role performs on certain object on certain access purpose.
– *Purpose Compliance* $PC \subseteq APP \bowtie IPL$ ia a one-to-one relation between each access purpose permission and data object as well as its predefined intended purposes.

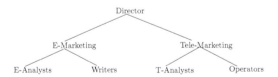

Fig. 3. Example of Role Hierarchies

Now we are at the stage to provide function definitions to facilitate the discussion of RCPBAC model.

– $assigned\_role : User \rightarrow 2^{Role}$, the mapping of a user u onto a set of roles. Formally,
$assigned\_role(u) = \{r \in Role | \langle u, r\rangle \in UA\}$

- $assigned\_access\_purpose\_permission : Role \rightarrow 2^{APP}$, the mapping of a role r onto access purpose permissions. Formally,
  $assigned\_access\_purpose\_permission(r) = \{app \in APP | \langle app, r \rangle \in APPA\}$
- $Purpose\_binding : Object \rightarrow IP$, the mapping of a data object o onto intended purposes ip with three levels, which means finding the bound intended purposes of the object.
- $Purpose\_compliance : AP \times IP \rightarrow \{True, Conditionally True, False\}$, is used to determine the compliance between the access purpose and the object's intended purposes [11]. Formally,
  $Purpose\_compliance(ap, ip)=$True iff $ap \in IP^\star$,
  $Purpose\_compliance(ap, ip)=$Conditionally True iff $ap \in IP_c^\star$.

In RCPBAC model, the users are required to explicitly state their access purpose(s) when they try to access data. That is, the users present an access purpose for each query they issue. During the access decision process, the system combines the requested data with its intended purposes according to privacy metadata and sends the data whose intended purposes are fully compliant or conditionally compliant with the access purpose to the requester. As the model respects customers requirement regarding their data usages and also support RBAC, it prevents private information from disclosure.

4.2   Authorization and Authentication

Access purpose is the reason for accessing a data item and it must be determined by the system when a data access is requested. There are different possible methods for determining the access purpose [7]. Among the various possible techniques to determine access purpose, in this paper we utilize the method where the users are required to explicitly state their access purposes when they try to access data. In the RCPBAC model, access purposes are authorized to users through roles. Users are required to state their access purposes along with their queries and the system confirms the stated access purposes by ensuring that the users are indeed allowed to access data for the particular purposes. Now we formally define access purpose authorization and its authentication.

Definition 7 (Access Purpose Authorization): Let Ω be a purpose tree and ω be the set of purposes in Ω. Also let R be the set of roles defined in a system. An access purpose is authorized to a specific set of users by a pair $\langle ap, r \rangle$, where ap is a access purpose in ω and r is a role defined over R.

   Usually in the typical situation, roles and access purpose are organized in a hierarchical structure. All users authorized for a role r_i are also authorized for any role r_j where $r_i \geq r_j$. Thus, activating a role r_i automatically activates all roles r_j, such that $r_i \geq r_j$. Similarly, authorizing an access purpose ap for a role r_i implies that the users belonging to r_i (or the users belonging to r_j, where $r_i \geq r_j$) are authorized to access data with ap as well as all the descendants of ap in the purpose tree. The access purpose authentication definition below confines the implications of access purpose authorizations.

Definition 8 (Access Purpose Authentication): Let Ω be a purpose tree, ω be the set of purposes in Ω and R be the set of roles defined in a system. Suppose that an access purpose ap and a role r_i activated by a user u. We say that ap is legitimate for u under r_i if there exists an access purpose authorization $\langle ap_l, r_i \rangle$, where ap_l in ω and r_i is a role defined over R such that $ap \in$ Descendants (ap_l) and the users belongs to role r_i (or any descendants role of r_i.)

Consider the purpose tree in Figure 1 and the role hierarchies of Marketing department for a hypothetical company in Figure 3. Suppose that access purpose "Service-Updates" are assigned to the "E-Marketing" role. Then the users who activate the role "E-Marketing" (or the two descendants role) can access data for the purpose of "Service-Updates".

Table 3. Intended purposes table

Sl_No.	Table_ID	Table_Name	Cus_ID	Attr_Name	Intended_Purpose
1	1	Customer_info	22	Customer_Name	$\langle \{$General$\}, \{$Admin$\},$ $\{$Shipping$\} \rangle$
2	1	Customer_info	25	Income	$\langle \{$Marketing$\}, \{$Admin$\},$ $\{$Shipping$\} \rangle$
3	1	Customer_info	52	Address	$\langle \{$Shipping$\}, \{$Admin$\},$ $\{$Marketing$\} \rangle$

By access purpose authorization and authentication, users get access purpose permission from access control engine. Now it is necessary to check whether users access purpose is fully or conditionally compliant with data's intended purpose for access decision. In the following Section we discuss the compliance computation for access decision.

5 Access Decision

In our model customers are given three more possible options of using their data. These make them comfortable to release their data fully or conditionally and the private information will be protected. After data are collected, intended purposes with three different levels will be associated with data. As intended purpose is assigned to every data element, an intended purposes table (IPT) is formed. Consider a typical IPT table in Table 3 which consists of six columns, where Sl_No is the serial number, Table_ID is the identification of the original table, Cus_ID is the hidden attribute which is added when tables are created, Table_Name is the name of the table in the database and Attr_Name is the attribute name in the table. Thus the storage of intended purposes and data are separated. Data providers (customers) are able to control the release of their data by adding privacy levels into the IPT which will not affect data in the database. After authorizing access purpose, users get access purpose permission from access control engine. The access control engine needs a match process to finish the compliance computation

Table 4. Compliance computation and access decision algorithm

Comp_Check$_1$ (ap, $\langle AIP, PIP \rangle$)
/$\star$ This function is required for access decision $\star$/
1. if $ap \in PIP^{\downarrow}$ then
2.   return False;
3. else if $ap \in AIP^{\downarrow}$ then
4.   return True;
5. end if

Comp_Check$_2$ (ap, $\langle CIP, PIP \rangle$)
1. if $ap \in PIP^{\downarrow}$ then
2.   return False;
3. else if $ap \in CIP^{\downarrow}$ then
4.   return True;
5. end if

Access Decision (ap, Object O)
/$\star$ IPT means intended purpose table $\star$/
1. For each tuple of IPT where Sl_No.$= i (i = 1$ to n)
2.   c_id$=\prod_{Cus\_ID} (\sigma_{Sl\_No.=i}(IPT))$
3.   attr$=\prod_{Attr\_Name} (\sigma_{Sl\_No.=i}(IPT))$
4.   if O$=\prod_{Table\_Name}(\sigma_{Sl\_No.=i} (IPT))$,
        attr $\in \{A | A$ is one of O's attributes$\}$
        and c_id$\in \prod_{O.Cus\_ID} (O)$
5.   ip$=\prod_{Intended\_Purpose}(\sigma_{Sl\_No.=i}(IPT))$
6.   if (Comp_Check$_1$ (ap, $\langle AIP, PIP \rangle$)= False)
7.   O$\leftarrow \prod_{attr_1,attr_2,...,attr_n=null}$
              $(\sigma_{O.Cus\_ID=c\_id}(O))$
8.   else if Comp_Check$_2$ (ap, $\langle CIP, PIP \rangle$)= False
9.   O$\leftarrow \prod_{attr_1,attr_2,...,attr_n=null}$
              $(\sigma_{O.Cus\_ID=c\_id}(O))$
10. return O

fully or conditionally between access purposes and intended purposes. If the requester's access purpose is fully compliant with the intended purposes of requested data, the engine will release full data to the requester. On the other hand, if the access purpose is conditionally compliant, the engine will release conditional data to the requester, otherwise returned data will be null. Thus in this model the search engine needs to evaluate two compliance checks, the first one is for fully compliance and the second one is for conditionally compliance. The compliance computation and the access decision algorithm of the model is illustrated in Table 4. Method Comp_Check returns the result of the purpose compliance check (fully or conditionally) for the given intended purpose with three levels as described in Section 4. Method Access Decision is based on the Comp_Check and the Intended_Purpose of a particular attribute in the IPT table.

6   Conclusion

Purposes play a significant role in the field of database management system privacy preserving techniques. In this paper we presented a CPBAC and injected it with RBAC which we referred to RCPBAC model that enables enterprise to operate as a reliable keeper of their customers data. The basic concepts of the proposed model is discussed and it has shown the possibility to extract more information from customers by providing a secure privacy policy. We also analyzed an algorithm to achieve the compliance check between access purpose and intended purposes. The effect of the proposed access control can be useful for internal access control within an organization as well as information sharing between organizations as many systems are already using RBAC mechanisms for the management of access permission. This technique can be used by enterprises to enforce the privacy promises they make and to enable their customers to maintain control over their data.

References

1. Agrawal, R., Kiernan, J., Srikant, R., Xu, Y.: Hippocratic databases. In: 28th International Conference on Very Large Databases, Hong Kong, pp. 143–154 (2002)
2. Agrawal, R., Bird, P., Grandison, T., Kiernan, J., Logan, S., Xu, Y.: Extending relational database systems to automatically enforce privacy policies. In: 21st International Conference on Data Engineering, Tokyo, pp. 1013–1022 (2005)
3. Al-Fedaghi, S.S.: Beyond Purpose-based privacy access control. In: 18th Australian Database Conference, Ballarat, pp. 23–32 (2007)
4. Barker, S., Stuckey, P.N.: Flexible access control policy specification with constraint logic programming. ACM Transaction on Information and System Security 6(4), 501–546 (2003)
5. Bertino, E., Jajodia, S., Samarati, P.: Data-base security: Research and practice. Information Systems 20(7), 537–556 (1995)
6. Byun, J.W., Bertino, E., Li, N.: Purpose based access control of complex data for privacy protection. In: 10th ACM Symposium on Access Control Model And Technologies, Stockholm, pp. 102–110 (2005)
7. Byun, J.W., Bertino, E., Li, N.: Purpose based access control for privacy protection in relational database systems. VLDB J. 17(4), 603–619 (2008)
8. Denning, D., Lunt, T., Schell, R., Shockley, W., Heckman, M.: The seaview security model. In: 1988 IEEE Symposium on Research in Security and Privacy, Oakland, pp. 218–233 (1988)
9. Forrester Research: Privacy concerns cost e-commerce $15 billion. Technical report (2001)
10. IBM. The Enterprise Privacy Authorization Language (EPAL), http://www.zurich.ibm.com/security/enterprise-privacy/epal
11. Kabir, M.E., Wang, H.: Conditional Purpose Based Access Control Model for Privacy Protection. In: 20th Australisian Database Conference, Wellington, pp. 137–144 (2009)
12. LeFevre, K., Agrawal, R., Ercegovac, V., Ramakrishnan, R., Xu, Y., DeWitt, D.: Disclosure in Hippocratic databases. In: 30th International Conference on Very Large Databases, Toronto, pp. 108–119 (2004)

13. Marchiori, M.: The platform for privacy preferences 1.0 (P3P1.0) specification. Technical report, W3C (2002)
14. Massacci, F., Mylopoulos, J., Zannone, N.: Minimal Disclosure in Hierarchical Hippocratic Databases with Delegation. In: 10th Europran Symposium on Research in Computer Security, Milan, pp. 438–454 (2005)
15. Rizvi, S., Mendelzon, A.O., Sudarshan, S., Roy, P.: Extending query rewriting techniques for fine-grained access control. In: ACM SIGMOD Conference 2004, Paries, pp. 551–562 (2004)
16. Powers, C.S., Ashley, P., Schunter, M.: Privacy promises, access control, and privacy management. In: 3rd International Symposium on Electronic Commerce, North Carolina, pp. 13–21 (2002)
17. Sandhu, R., Jajodia, S.: Toward a multilevel secure relational data model. In: 1991 ACM Transactional Conference on Management of Data, Colorado, pp. 50–59 (1991)
18. Sandhu, R.S., Coyne, E.J., Feinstein, H.L., Youman, C.E.: Role-based access control models. IEEE Computer 29(2), 38–47 (1996)
19. Sandhu, R., Chen, F.: The multilevel relational data model. ACM Transaction on Information and System Security 1(1), 93–132 (1998)
20. World Wide Web Consortium (W3C).: Platform for Privacy Preferences (P3P), http://www.w3.org/P3P
21. Yang, N., Barringer, H., Zhang, N.: A Purpose-Based Access Control Model. In: 3rd International Symposium on Information Assurance and Security, Manchester, pp. 143–148 (2007)
22. Peng, H., Gu, J., Ye, X.: Dynamic Purpose-Based Access Control. In: IEEE International Symposium on Parallel and Distributed Processing with Applications, Sydney, pp. 695–700 (2008)
23. Hung, P.C.K.: Towards a Privacy Access Control Model for e-Healthcare Services. In: Third Annual Conference on Privacy, Security and Trust, New Brunswick (2005)

Part 2

Global Information Systems Processes (GISP)

GISP Preface

The process-based view is now an established paradigm for the design of organizations and their supportive systems. Business process management (BPM) is the discipline that comprises the set of methodologies, tools and techniques which facilitate the enterprise-wide establishment of process capabilities and project-specific process lifecycle management support. Over the last decade, the field of BPM has matured substantially in terms of its practical uptake and impact as well as in terms of the corresponding academic body of knowledge. The Information Systems discipline has become a main intellectual home for BPM-related research and BPM as a topic has inspired fruitful new research directions.

However, an increasingly globalized world leads to new demands, and the domain of BPM is no exception. The design of processes needs to be tailored to the regional circumstances, while headquarters of multi-national organizations are aiming towards global process standards.

The First Conference on Global Information Systems Processes was dedicated to the development of a better understanding of the differences in which organizations adopt the process-centered approach. This covers both the detailed analysis of the adoption in a specific region with an individual cultural and legislative setting as well as the rollout of business processes in multinational corporations.

Jointly organized with the E-Government and E-Services Conference, GISP 2010 attracted 13 submissions that were all reviewed by 2-3 carefully selected expert reviewers. As part of a competitive process, we selected six papers (46% acceptance rate) for inclusion in the inaugural GISP program. These papers cover both of the facets of global process design. First, we have four papers covering global case studies on process design issues. These cases cover the contextual settings of Singapore, Kuwait, Finland and South Africa. Second, two papers deal with the challenge of globalized process design, i.e., the demands of large-scale process models as they emerge in global projects and an investigation of a process design project covering two continents. A panel discussion on "Process Design in an Increasingly Globalized Society" completed the program.

We are grateful to all authors of submitted papers. The quality of the submissions in such a young field was high, making the paper selection a difficult task. We are grateful to the careful revisions that were conducted by the authors of successful papers. In particular, we would like to thank all of our reviewers. Their critical feedback and constructive inspirations were a key success factor for this conference.

The challenges of process design in a globalized world will remain of high significance in the coming years. We hope that the contents presented and discussed at this conference will provide guidance for practitioners and academics involved in this field.

September 2010

Jan Pries-Heje
Michael Rosemann

GISP Session 1:
Global Case Studies on Process Design Issues

Process Model of Customer-Centric E-Government Enabled Service Transformation: Insights from MINDEF's Portal Implementation Experience

Satish Krishnan, Barney C.C. Tan, and Shan L. Pan

Department of Information Systems, National University of Singapore, 3 Science Drive 2,
Singapore 117543, Singapore
{satishk,tancheec,pansl}@comp.nus.edu.sg

Abstract. Information Technology (IT) enabled transformation in an organization enhances the business value by improving its performance. Though a lot has been documented on this topic, a review of information systems literature reveal that the research on how e-government enabled transformation affects firm performance remains under-examined. With this motivation, this piece of research aims to focus on the mechanisms through which e-government enabled service transformation improves the performance of an organization. Analyzing the case study of e-government implementation experience of Ministry of Defense (MINDEF), Singapore in the light of Resource Based View (RBV) and Dynamic Capabilities perspective, we build a process model of customer-centric e-government enabled service transformation showing how MINDEF enhanced its performance. With its findings, this study contributes to the theoretical discourse on firm performance and provides implications to the practice for enhancing firm performance.

Keywords: E-government, Resources, Capabilities, Core competencies, Firm Performance, Case study.

1 Introduction

Rapid advances in IT and advent of Internet have not only changed the way the private sectors work but also the public sectors. This is due to increased exposure to the offerings of Internet which has redefined the expectations of citizens on their government and its services by demanding faster and more efficient services [33]. Thinking customer-centric and attracted by potential benefits such as cost savings and better governance, bureaucratic government organizations are now transforming to anticipative and responsive government organizations [36]. This is brought about by adopting IT and making the best use of new and emerging technologies which in turn is termed as 'Electronic Government' or 'E-Government'.

Although governments have been actively engaging in efforts to digitalize the public sector [17], they face great challenges in reinventing such vast enterprises and resources [33]. Difficulties involved in digitalizing the public sector are reflected by

M. Janssen et al. (Eds.): EGES/GISP 2010, IFIP AICT 334, pp. 187–200, 2010.

the contrast between the number of e-government projects being initiated and the number of e-government projects that have progressed beyond creating a web presence [33]. Despite these initiatives and emerging programs on e-government throughout the world in all levels of government, there has been a lack of academic literature on understanding the process of e-government enabled service transformation and the mechanisms through which it affects firm performance.

With this knowledge gap, our work is aimed at studying the process of customer-centric e-government enabled service transformation. In specific, the research question we strive to address is, *'How does customer-centric e-government development enhance the firm performance?'* We answer this question by analyzing a case study of e-government implementation experience of MINDEF in the light of RBV and Dynamic Capabilities perspective.

In the remainder of the paper, we first review the existing perspectives of e-government, then present the arguments on RBV and Dynamic Capabilities, report the methodology adopted for studying the above research question, describe and analyze the MINDEF case, and discuss our findings. We conclude by highlighting the shortcomings of our research and the implications of our study for theory and practice.

2   Theoretical Background

The term *'E-Government'* has wide ranging interpretations. Organisation for Economic Co-operation and Development (OECD) defines E-Government as, "the use of information and communication technologies and particularly Internet as a tool to achieve better government". E-government discipline has received attention among researchers for more than a decade and is significantly increasing [36]. Though researchers have focussed on various dimensions of e-government like maturity [34], transformation management [36], evolution and success [17], stakeholders' interest [37] and customer relationship management [26], there are several dimensions that remains uncovered [30]. One such dimension is the relationship between 'IT-enabled transformation' and 'firm performance'. Though this term is overused in e-commerce and private sector research [30], it has received less attention in public-sector research. One key reason is because of the general misconception that the public sectors are rigid and risk-averse establishments [37].

Like e-government, the term *'Firm Performance'* also has different interpretations. Literature on organizational effectiveness indicates that the definition of firm performance varies depending on how firms are viewed [4]. It has been argued that there are at least three main perspectives on firm performance [35]. First, if firms are viewed as rational and goal-seeking entities, successful goal accomplishment would be an appropriate measure of performance. Second, if firms are viewed as coalitions of power constituencies, degree of satisfaction of employees and/or customers would be an appropriate measure of performance. And third, if firms are viewed as entities involved in a bargaining relationship with their surroundings, firm's ability to garner scarce resources and productivity would be the appropriate measures of effective performance. Though MINDEF as an organization could be viewed from all three perspectives, our interest, however is to look at the service transformation from the view point of customer. Accordingly, we choose two measures of firm performance: 'Customer Satisfaction' and 'Service Delivery'.

To study the relationship between IT-enabled transformation and firm performance, we use two complementary perspectives as our theoretical lens: (1) RBV and (2) Dynamic Capabilities. *'RBV of a firm'* is an influential framework within the field of strategic management describing how sustainable competitive advantage can be developed [2, 40]. RBV positions a firm as a bundle of heterogeneous and imperfectly mobile resources which are valuable, rare, inimitable, durable, transparent, transferable and replicable and delivers value to the company [2, 14, 27]. Penrose [27] indicates that it is not the resources themselves that deliver value, but it is the core competencies (i.e., services rendered by resources) which organizes the resources to generate or deliver value. Core competencies are collective learning in an organization that coordinate diverse production skills and integrate multiple streams of technologies [29]. Though RBV is comprehensive [2], it has been criticized to be vague and tautological [12], observed to be lacking of empirical grounding and being more suited for only relatively stable environments [20]. This implies that it cannot be used to explain sustained competitive advantage in situations of rapid and unpredictable changes [12, 38].

To overcome the shortcoming of RBV in addressing why firms have competitive advantage in situations of rapid and unpredictable market change or dynamic markets, *'Dynamic Capabilities'* perspective was developed and characterized as an organization's processes that integrate, reconfigure, gain and release resources to match and even create market change [12]. That is, dynamic capability is a company's ability to integrate, build and reconfigure internal and external competencies to address rapidly changing environments [38]. These capabilities act as an innovative basis for competitive advantage in terms of path dependencies and market positions and act as mediators determining a firm's market position and overall performance [20].

In summary, we use both these complementary perspectives as our theoretical lens to study the mechanisms underlying e-government enabled system transformation and firm performance enhancement.

3 Research Methodology

Case research methodology was adopted for this study as our research question is a *"how"* question [39] that delves into the process of customer-centric e-government service transformation and the underlying mechanisms through which it enhances firm performance. Based on our research question, we selected MINDEF to study the phenomenon, as it has effectively implemented e-government system for performance gains. Research access was negotiated and granted in July 2008 and a total of 17 interviews were conducted. All the interviews were transcribed for data analysis and lasted an hour on the average. Secondary data from newspaper articles, company brochures, internal publications, the corporate website and notes from direct observation were also used to corroborate the data obtained. We followed a three-step procedure for analyzing our case data [22]. First, we did *'data reduction'* which helped us to sharpen, sort, focus, discard and organize the data in a way that allowed for 'final' conclusions to be drawn and verified. We used several means such as selection, summary and paraphrasing. After the data reduction step, we *'displayed the data'* by organizing the reduced data in a compressed way so that the conclusions could be easily drawn. Finally, we *'drew conclusions and verified them'* by noting regularities, patterns (differences/ similarities), explanations, possible configurations, causal flows and propositions.

4   Case Description

MINDEF, established in 1966 is responsible for the recruitment, training and administrative needs of the National Servicemen (NSmen) of Singapore. The ministry is tasked with overseeing the defense, manpower and technological capabilities of the Singapore. More than 40 years on, there are currently more than 300,000 NSmen in active service, forming the backbone of the national defense. As a serviceman transitions through his NS lifecycle, taking on several roles, he will require the administrative services provided by various agencies of MINDEF. Yet, with hundreds of different transactions provided by over 60 different agencies available, coordinating the administrative processes that underlie the needs of the servicemen was complex, paperwork-intensive and tedious. MINDEF slowly realized the needs for implementing e-government and started taking initiatives to move from an ordinary government to a 'Customer-centric E-Government'. Following paragraphs summarizes phase wise case details.

Phase 1: Service Delivery via Traditional Counter and Queue System (Before 1999). MINDEF's transactions were characterized by repetitive, manual work processes and each agency is responsible for their own administrative procedures. The operations were tedious, error-prone, labour-intensive and manual because of minimal integration and data sharing between the different entities. These resulted in a deep-seated inefficiency within the organization which was overcome by ample resources of MINDEF.

Phase 2: Defense Town I and II (April 1999-April 2001). First corporate website was launched in June 1996 and consisted only of static informational pages organized along departmental lines. Within a year, electronic transactions (inadequate, uncoordinated and decentralized) were made available. 18 different online transactions housed in different websites and more than 13 telephone hotlines were available which was difficult for servicemen to obtain the services they require. By the end of the Defence Town phase I, detailed information about the services and all 18 electronic transactions were made available on Defense Town. Backend processing of the submitted electronic forms remained a laborious, manual process and integration and data sharing problems remained unresolved. To look into the problem, a study team (comprising several members from different departments of MINDEF) was established to review the existing business processes. An extensive Business Process Improvement (BPI) Study was sought to streamline the operations and business process of MINDEF.

Phase II of the Defense Town project was launched in September 1999 with an aim to fully integrate online service center. Electronic transactions were integrated with relevant backend databases of MINDEF. Through this integration, manual, backend processing is no longer required after an electronic form has been submitted. In addition, benefits include: (1) Marked improvements in service cycle time, (2) reduction in the generation and mailing of paperwork, (3) diversion of labour resources to more meaningful job functions, (4) error reduction through the incorporation of computation and business rule checks into the system, and (5) marked increase in convenience for users.

Phase 3: MIW Portal Implementation (April 2001-April 2006). Defense Town project lacked strategic coherence and was curtailed by a low rate of adoption. A committee was established for the purpose of examining the organizational implications of the technology-induced upheaval in the external environment. Top management realized that Internet was a promising solution to the chronic inefficiency and bureaucratic mindset and MINDEF.com initiative was eventually launched. A closed tender was called and management of MINDEF eventually decided to award the contract to Green Dot Internet Services (GDIS).

Phase 3a: Ensuring Information and Basic Services Availability (Apr 2001-Oct 2001). MIW portal was eventually built from scratch within eight months and focus was to make all related information and existing e-services available. Initial phase was characterized by a tentative, trial-and-error approach to systems development due to the relative inexperience. Communication and coordination problems also existed. In addition to the technical challenges, there was also a sense of apprehension among internal MINDEF departments and agencies. A steering committe was formed to overcome the resistance of internal stakeholders. The initial MIW portal was not well received due to poor navigability, lack of aesthetic appeal and poor content organization of the website. A decision was made to revamp the portal just 6 months after its initial launch.

Phase 3b: Improving the Quality of Services (Nov 2001-Apr 2004). A series of usability studies were conducted and user interface was revamped to improve the usability, utility and attractiveness. Contents of the portal were reorganized and accessibility of the services was enhanced. Usage of new platforms like WAP, SMS, etc resulted in a greater flexibility and continuous stream of new applications and e-services were introduced. Internal stakeholders at MINDEF were often apprehensive about experimenting new technologies. To overcome this, the management of MINDEF was highly supportive, encouraging and tolerant of failure. As a result, the portal was well received by the customers with approximately 300,000 transactions per month.

Phase 3c: Providing a Positive National Service Experience (May 2004-Apr 2006). The "stickiness" of MIW portal was increased through a comprehensive rebranding initiative. A comprehensive change management exercise was conducted to overcome the data sharing, coordination and collaboration challenges. Toward the attainment of this strategic objective, a number of new features (e.g., My MIW, MIW Shopzone and MIW Game Center) were implemented on the MIW portal. In addition, MINDEF sought to foster the creation and maintenance of social relationships between servicemen through the cultivation of virtual communities hosted on the MIW portal. As a result, volume of transactions handled by the MIW portal doubled to an average of more than 600,000 a month.

Phase 4: NS Portal Implementation (May 2006-Present). MINDEF needed to collaborate with Ministry of Home Affairs (MHA) to ensure the security and the defense of the country. A joint decision was made to collaborate on the development of an integrated portal. Decision was made to not pursue the contractual option of continuing with GDIS for the next five years and call for an open tender. MINDEF used 'Analytic Hierarchy Process' to form an objective judgment. The contract was eventually awarded to the vendor (NCS) with the highest cost benefit ratio.

Phase 4a: The Challenges of Migration (May 2006-Apr2007). The first stage of migration involved the migration of static and non-transactional websites and the second stage involved the migration of the main Internet portal. Issue of brand confusion and inexperience of NCS in running a full-fledged e-government portal were two main challenges. A third related challenge concerned the inevitable, "starting over" of the cultivation of virtual communities. MINDEF invested extensive resources and efforts in trying to overcome these challenges. The URL for the new portal (http://www.ns.sg) was carefully formulated to be easier to remember and more relevant to NS as compared to the old URL. Customer satisfaction with the new NS portal tumbled to 88.12%. Yet, within a year, NCS was able to restore operational excellence by reinstating and improving on most of the features of the previous portal.

Phase 4b: Promoting NS Commitment (Apr 2007-Present). With the teething issues of portal migration resolved, NCS was ready to bring the quality of the public services of both MINDEF and MHA to the next level. Accordingly, the focus of e-government development had shifted beyond providing a positive NS experience to the overarching strategic vision of promoting NS commitment among Singapore's NS community. To this end, NCS designed and deployed a number of new features on the NS portal in accordance with a two-pronged strategy. First, NCS is seeking to enhance the relationship and community building capabilities of the NS portal further by developing website features that facilitate the creation of social bonds and a sense of belonging. Second, NCS is looking to enhance the variety and richness of the applications on the mobile channel through the launch of the Mobile eServices Hub (MeSH); a sophisticated bundle of mobile applications consisting of a comprehensive suite of mobile e-services, a messaging system, lifestyle content and location-based services.

5   Case Analysis and Discussion

As e-government success is necessarily defined by the end-user satisfaction [36], our knowledge on how e-government implementation success can be achieved is contingent on understanding the inherent process through which e-government development enhances the services of a public organization. Toward this end, a model of this underlying process; which we term '*Customer-centric E-government Enabled Service Transformation*', is constructed based on empirical evidences from the MINDEF case study (see Figure 1). Through this process model we gain insights into: (1) the resources necessary for successful e-government implementation, (2) the organizational capabilities and the organizational core competencies that are developed or enhanced through the e-government implementation, and (3) how these resources, capabilities, and core competencies enhance the organizational performance.

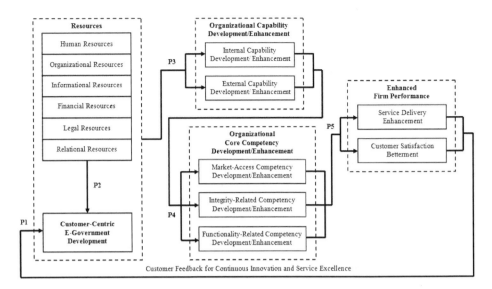

Fig. 1. Process Model of Customer-centric E-government Enabled Service Transformation

5.1   Customer Satisfaction for Continuous Innovation and Service Excellence

Before we proceed to know the importance of resources-capabilities-core competencies in the process of customer-centric e-government enabled service transformation, it is necessary to know what a customer-centric e-government is and how it is different from an organization-centric e-government. An organization-centric e-government is developed giving less or no importance to the customer's needs and feedbacks. This is called as treating the *'customers as outsiders'* and *'customers as clients'* during the service transformation [36]. As a result, his satisfaction level with the services provided by the e-government is either negligible or low and no value or only an internally-focused operational value is created [36]. On the other hand, a customer-centric e-government is developed by involving the customers in each and every phase of e-government development. This is called as treating the *'customers as valued customers'*, *'customers as strategic partners'*, and *'customers as strategic value networks'* during the service transformation [36]. As a result, the satisfaction level with the services provided by the e-government is high or sustained or complete (total) respectively and the value created is either operational or strategic or multi-directional strategic [36].

MINDEF initially treated its 'customer as outsiders'. Proceeding through the process of service transformation, MINDEF realized the importance of engaging the end-user in the e-government development and gradually started treating its customers as clients, valued customers, strategic partners, and finally as strategic value networks. During the phase 1 and phase 2 of service transformation, MINDEF treated its customer as 'outsiders'. As a result, the customer satisfaction was low. During the first, second and third phase of MIW portal implementation (phase 3a, 3b and 3c), MINDEF treated its customers as 'clients', 'valued customers', and 'strategic partners' respectively. Accordingly, the customer satisfaction was increased, high and sustained. During the final phase of service transformation (phase 4a and phase 4b),

MINDEF treated its customers as 'strategic partners' and 'strategic value networks' respectively. Accordingly, the customer satisfaction was sustained and complete (total). This facilitated continuous innovation and service excellence which in turn led to total customer satisfaction and multi-directional strategic value creation. Accordingly, we propose:

Proposition P1: *Involving customers during the process of service transformation and satisfying their needs and expectations are the necessary conditions for developing a successful customer-centric e-government.*

5.2 Resources Required for Customer-Centric E-Government Development

A customer-centric e-government cannot happen accidently. Large number of resources is required for developing it successfully. To achieve competitive advantage [2], the resources of the firm must be *valuable* (the resource can enable a firm to conceive or implement strategies that improve its efficiency or effectiveness), *rare* (the resources should not be possessed by a large number of competing firms), *imperfectly imitable* (the resources should not be easily imitated due to unique historical conditions, causally ambiguous, or social complex) and n*on-substitutable* (the resource should not be easily replaced by other substitutes).

In MINDEF's case, six categories of resources were identified as valuable, rare, imperfectly imitable and non-substitutable for the developing a customer-centric e-government successfully and improving the performance of the organization: (1) Human Resources, (2) Organizational Resources, (3) Informational Resources, (4) Financial Resources, (5) Legal Resources, and (6) Relational Resources. We categorize personal networks, individuals' experience and education/skill level of the individuals in MINDEF and other personal attributes as *'Human Resources'*. Culture, structure, routines, processes, and brand/reputation of MINDEF are classified as *'Organizational Resources'*. Information related to the customer, vendor (partner), and services are categorized as *'Informational Resources'*. The funds and financial instruments in developing the e-government are classified as *'Financial Resources'*. The assets like agreements, licenses and government regulations are categorized as *'Legal Resources'*. Relationships inside the firm, relationships with the partner organization and agencies and relationships with the customer are categorized as the *'Relational Resources'*.

These six categories of resources facilitated the development of customer-centric e-government thereby improving the firm performance [31]. These resources acted as triggers or drivers for developing a customer-centric e-government. With this, we posit that the above resources are necessary (1) to successfully build a customer-centric or customer-focused e-government and (2) to enhance the performance of the organization. Accordingly, we propose:

Proposition P2: *Existence of human, organizational, informational, financial, legal and relational resources in an organization determines the development of successful customer-centric e-government and the enhancement of firm performance.*

5.3 Capability Development/Enhancement

Though resources can have direct effect on firm performance, several researchers argue that the effect of valuable resource may need other factors. While researchers on one hand argue that integration of different complementary resources can generate synergy that can lead to better performance [21, 41] others propose that the factors such as strategic fitness can enhance firm performance [6, 7, 25]. Among those possible factors, organizational capabilities are the most liked mediators in existing literature [1, 5, 6, 16, 30, 32]. The rationale is that valuable resources can provide or enhance capabilities to deal with customers' needs and expectations.

In MINDEF, the above six categories of resources facilitated the development and enhancement of capabilities which paved the way for firm's performance enhancement. Top management and project team developed these capabilities based on several initiatives. We use Montealegre's process model of capability development [23] to explain the key initiatives taken by MINDEF to develop and enhance the capabilities.

Global Benchmarking and Training. Benchmarking was used to evaluate the effectiveness and relevance of MINDEF's operations. Extensive BPI study was conducted and change management exercises were initialized to overcome several challenges like streamlining the operations and the business process of MINDEF. The executives' awareness and heightened sensitivity to the service environment enabled the organization to identify and adapt best practices in its management and operations [18], which also helped MINDEF in identifying the customer needs and expectations.

Learning from Past Experiences and History. Learning from unique organizational history implies path dependency, which contributes to the inimitable nature of an organization's resources or capabilities [2]. In our case, MINDEF had in-depth knowledge on the mechanisms of e-government service delivery as it was delivering services for several years. It also enjoyed close coordination with many of its operational departments and agencies.

Absorbing Knowledge as a Unified Group at the Top of the Organization. Exchanging ideas through shared narratives of individual experiences contributes to the development of corporate vision [24]. MINDEF's top management was committed to supporting an open learning environment, in which the experiences of its employees were highly valued. Top management of MINDEF was highly supportive, encouraging and tolerant of failures. MINDEF made the resources in terms of funding and manpower readily available. Constant encouragement was provided to develop new ideas.

Integrating Resources into Core Activities. In order to build the capabilities, resources must be sufficiently integrated with key activities and organizational routines [38]. At MINDEF, valuable resources were allocated appropriately to ensure that the organization would not lose focus on essential operations while executing its new strategies. To minimize disruptions in the daily operations, several committees were established by the top management of MINDEF which met frequently. These committees (1) examined the organizational implications of the technology-induced upheaval in the external environment and (2) periodically conducted comprehensive studies of servicemen population to understand their needs and expectations and on the quality of the services delivered.

Experimenting. Experimentation is a mechanism for capability building through performing incremental improvements to operational routines [11]. Continuous experimentation is a key characteristic of successful firms [9]. At MINDEF, experimentation with new technologies and testing them were mechanisms used iteratively to improve service delivery continually. Experience gained from experimentation resulted in an optimal service model. Employees' feedback coupled with the customer needs and expectations and regulatory requirements paved the way for developing optimal and user-friendly applications and services.

Investing in, Leveraging, and Co-opting Resources. MINDEF aimed to surpass customer expectation by developing and improving its capability to provide more value-added services. This aim was achieved by improving its business processes and leveraging the existing manpower. Leveraging technology as a resource to improve processes within and across business functions developed capabilities [15].

Gaining Internal Commitment. MINDEF adopted the selective use of high-involvement work practices, which helped to increase job satisfaction and positive attitudes, thereby leading to increased profitability [3]. For example, during the meetings that spanned various functional divisions, steering committee were involved in fostering greater commitment with the team members to implement the changes. Furthermore, by empowering service representatives with greater autonomy to make decisions increased their ability to solve customer problems and helped to foster an open and innovative culture in MINDEF [10, 18].

Investments in complementary Infrastructure. Infrastructure frameworks are necessary to facilitate successful transfer of processes and activities. MINDEF invested in technology infrastructure to optimize its daily operations, which then formed the strong foundation of resources that were leveraged to develop capabilities. For instance, MINDEF developed iMIS for computerization and process automation.

Strengthening External Relationships. Effective management of collaborative relationships through close communication between vendors and customers can allow a high level of internal coordination and process integration [9]. Establishing and maintaining strategic partnerships with various stakeholders were essential to MINDEF in maintaining its ability to deliver customized services [26]. MINDEF built a long-term strategic partnership with its vendors and other government agencies (e.g., MFA) through close communications and interactions.

Based on the above explanations and chain of evidences we posit that resources available with the organization facilitate development and enhancement of capabilities of an organization. These newly developed capabilities and enhanced existing capabilities mediate the resources that can enhance the performance of a firm. Accordingly, we propose:

Proposition P3: *Existence of human, organizational, informational, financial, legal and relational resources determines the development of new capabilities and the enhancement of existing capabilities. These newly developed capabilities and enhanced existing capabilities are necessary for improving firm performance.*

5.4 Core Competencies Development/Enhancement

Core competences are those that make a disproportionate contribution to ultimate customer value, or to the efficiency with which that value is delivered and provide a basis for entering new markets [29]. Core competencies which can be developed or enhanced by developing or enhancing the organizational capabilities can be categorized into three types [30]: market-access competencies, integrity-related competencies and functionality-related competencies.

'*Market-access Competencies*' include all those that allow an organization to be in close proximity to its customers, identify their needs effectively and respond in a timely manner to shifts in customer needs and tastes [30]. MINDEF developed/enhanced the market-access competencies through comprehensive branding/rebranding initiatives and by tailoring the offerings to match the demands of the customer. '*Integrity-related Competencies*' include those that allow a firm to offer reliable products and services at competitive prices and deliver them with minimal inconvenience [30]. MINDEF developed/enhanced the integrity-related competencies by investing in new technologies. '*Functionality-related Competencies*' are those that enable a firm to offer unique products and services with distinctive customer benefits [30]. MINDEF developed/enhanced the functionality-related competencies by doing innovations in the new services.

All these three core competencies enhanced the performance of MINDEF by enhancing the service delivery and increasing the customer satisfaction thereby making a significant contribution to customer perceived value and customer perceived benefits. Accordingly, we propose:

Propositions P4 and P5: *Developing new capabilities and enhancing existing capabilities are necessary for successful development and enhancement of core competencies. These newly developed core competencies and enhanced existing core competencies are necessary for improving firm performance.*

---

6 Conclusion

By addressing the research question set forth at the beginning of the paper, this study makes two important contributions to the theory. First, while significant research has focused on IT-enabled system transformation and firm performance relationship in e-commerce and private sector research [30], the mechanisms through which how e-government enabled system transformation affects firm performance remain underexamined. This study, based on RBV and dynamic capabilities perspective, has attempted to bridge this gap. Previous studies on the related topics have focused on (1) how IT system could be used to exploit the unique structural characteristics of a firm [8], and (2) how the value of IS resources could be enhanced in the presence of other business resources such as an innovative culture [28]. Our study extends this line of research by examining the mechanisms through which e-government service transformation affects firm performance. Second, the process model of e-government enabled service transformation developed here can serve as a basis for firm performance evaluation using two measures: customer satisfaction and service delivery. Our study adds to the performance research and provides a basis for the development of performance assessment tools for managerial use from the view point of customer [13, 31].

From a practical standpoint, this study makes two main contributions. By providing evidences that core competencies can affect firm performance, this study highlights that managers have to do more than investing in the latest technologies or developing a strong IS department. To do so, the managers have to clearly understand the strategic thrust of the organization and institute mechanisms to ensure that the capabilities are channeled toward areas of importance to the organization [30]. Second, our study provides evidences for the types of resources that are necessary to build a customer-centric e-government through which organizational capabilities and core competencies can be enhanced/developed thereby enhancing the firm's performance.

Findings of this study should be viewed within the context of its limitations. In particular, although the single case research methodology adopted in this study is a "typical and legitimate endeavor" in qualitative research [19], a common criticism of the methodology is the problem of generalizability or external validity [39]. However, while it must be readily acknowledged that the single case research methodology makes statistical generalization impossible, we nevertheless assert that our study is valid and generalizable beyond its singular context as the developed process model is not only grounded in the empirical reality of a real world organization, but also corroborated by the propositions of some of the most established works in management and IS literature. As such, this study invokes the principles of "analytic generalization" [42] or what some researchers refer to as *"generalizing from description to theory"* [19]. Nevertheless, future research can be directed at statistically validating the propositions of our process model, so that the boundary conditions of our study can be better defined.

In summary, based on the evidences from MINDEF's portal implementation experience, we would like to reiterate that the existence of resources and involving the customers during the transformation process would trigger successful development of customer-centric e-government. The newly developed customer-centric e-government system along with the resources would facilitate development of new organizational capabilities and enhancement of existing organizational capabilities which in turn would lead to development and enhancement of core competencies. In short, resources, capabilities and core competencies would facilitate the enhancement of firm performance by improving the customers' satisfaction and enhancing the service delivery mechanisms.

References

1. Bharadwaj, A.S.: A Resource-Based Perspective on Information Technology Capability and Firm Performance: An Empirical Investigation. MIS Quarterly 24, 169–196 (2000)
2. Barney, J.: Firm resources and sustained competitive advantage. Journal of Management 17, 99–120 (1991)
3. Batt, R., Moynihan, L.: The viability of alternative call centre production models. Human Resource Management Journal 12, 14–34 (2002)

4. Bedeiart, A.G., Zammuto, R.F.: Organizations: Theory and Design. The Dryden Press, New York (1991)
5. Bhatt, G.D., Grover, V.: Types of Information Technology Capabilities and Their Role in Competitive Advantage: An Empirical Study. Journal of Management Information Systems 22, 253–277 (2005)
6. Chan, Y.E., Huff, S.L., Barclay, D.W., Copeland, D.G.: Business Strategic Orientation, Information Systems Strategic Orientation, and Strategic Alignment. Information Systems Research 8, 125–147 (1997)
7. Choe, J.M.: The effect of environmental uncertainty and strategic applications of IS on a firm's performance. Information and Management 40(4) (2003)
8. Clemons, E.K., Row, M.: Sustaining IT advantage: The role of structural differences. MIS Quarterly 15, 275–292 (1991)
9. Day, G.S.: The capabilities of market-driven organizations. Journal of Marketing 58, 37–53 (1994)
10. Deery, S., Kinnie, N.: Call centres and beyond: A thematic evaluation. Human Resource Management Journal London 12, 3–13 (2002)
11. Dosi, G., Nelson, R.R., Winter, S.G.: Introduction: The nature and dynamics of organizational capabilities. In: Nature and Dynamics of Organizational Capabilities, pp. 1–22 (2000)
12. Eisenhardt, K.M., Martin, J.A.: Dynamic Capabilities: What are they? Strategic Management Journal 21, 1105–1121 (2000)
13. Galetta, D.F., Lederer, A.L.: Some cautions on the measurement of user information satisfaction. Decision Science 20, 419–438 (1989)
14. Grant, R.M.: The Resource-Based View of Competitive Advantage: Implications for Strategy Formulation. California Management Review 33, 114–135 (1991)
15. Jarvenpaa, S.L., Leidner, D.E.: An information company in Mexico: Extending the RBV of the firm to a developing country context. Information Systems Research 9, 342–361 (1998)
16. Karimi, J., Somers, T.M., Bhattacherjee, A.: The role of information system resources in ERP capability building and business process outcomes. Journal of Management Information System 24, 221–260 (2007)
17. Ke, W., Kee Wei, K.: Successful E-Government in Singapore. Communications of the ACM 47, 95–99 (2004)
18. Lawson, B., Samson, D.: Developing innovation capability in organizations: A dynamic capabilities approach. International Journal of Innovation Management 5, 377–400 (2001)
19. Lee, A.S., Baskerville, R.L.: Generalizing generalizability in information systems research. Information Systems Research 14, 221–243 (2003)
20. Leonard-Barton, D.: Core Capabilities and Core Rigidities: A Paradox in Managing New Product Development. Strategic Management Journal 13, 111–125 (1992)
21. Melville, N., Kraemer, K., Gurbaxani, V.: Review: Information technology and organizational performance: an integrative model of IT business value. MIS Quarterly 28, 283–322 (2004)
22. Miles, M.B., Huberman, M.A.: Qualitative Data Analysis, 2nd edn (1994)
23. Montealegre, R.: A process model of capability development: Lessons from the electronic commerce strategy at Bolsa de Valores de Guayaquil. Organization Science 13, 514–531 (2002)
24. Nonaka, I.: A dynamic theory of organizational knowledge creation. Organization Science 5, 14–37 (1994)

25. Palmer, J.W., Markus, M.L.: The Performance Impacts of Quick Response and Strategic Alignment in Specialty Retailing. Information Systems Research 11, 241 (2000)
26. Pan, S.-L., Tan, C.-W., Lim, E.: Customer Relationship Management (CRM) in E-Government: A Relational Perspective. Decision Support Systems 42, 237–250 (2006)
27. Penrose, E.T.: Theory of the Growth of the Firm. Oxford Publishing (1959)
28. Powell, T.C., Dent-Micallef, A.: Information technology as competitive advantage: The role of human, business, and technology resources. Strategic Management Journal 18, 375–405 (1959)
29. Prahalad, C.K., Hamel, G.: The core competence of the corporation. Harvard Business Review 90, 79–91 (1990)
30. Ravinchandran, T., Lertwongsatien, C.: Effect of Information Systems Resources and Capabilities on Firm Performance: A Resource-Based Perspective. Journal of Management Information Systems 21, 237–276 (2005)
31. Saunders, C.S., Jones, J.W.: Measuring performance of the information systems function. Journal of Management Information Systems 8, 63–82 (1992)
32. Santhanam, R., Hartono, E.: Issues in Linking Information Technology Capability to Firm Performance. MIS Quarterly, vol 27, 125–153 (2003)
33. Seneviratne, S.J.: Information Technology and Organizational Change in the Public Sector. In: David Garson, G. (ed.) Information Technology and Computer Applications in Public Administration: Issues and Trends, pp. 41–61. Idea Group Publishing, PA (1999)
34. Shackleton, P., Fisher, J., Dawson, L.: From Dog Licences to Democracy: Local Government Approaches to E-Service Delivery in Australia. Paper Presented at the Thirteenth European Conference on Information Systems, Regensberg, Germany (2005)
35. Soh, C., Markus, M.L.: How IT creates business value: A process theory synthesis. In: Proceedings of the 16th International Conference of Information Systems, Amsterdam, The Netherlands (1995)
36. Tan, C.W., Pan, S.L.: Managing e-transformation in the public sector: an e-government study of the Inland Revenue Authority of Singapore. European Journal of Information Systems 12, 269–281 (2003)
37. Tan, C.W., Pan, S.P., Lim, E.T.K.: Managing stakeholder interests in e-government implementation: lessons learned from a Singapore e-Government project. Journal of Global Information Management 13, 31–54 (2005)
38. Teece, D.J., Pisano, G., Shuen, A.: Dynamic Capabilities and Strategic Management. Strategic Management Journal 18, 509–533 (1997)
39. Walsham, G.: Doing interpretive research. European Journal of Information Systems 15, 320–330 (2006)
40. Wernerfelt, B.: A Resource-based view of the firm. Strategic Management Journal 5, 171–180 (1984)
41. Wade, M., Hulland, J.: Review: The Resource-Based View and Information Systems Research: Review, Extension, and Suggestions for Future Research. MIS Quarterly 28(1), 107–142 (2004)
42. Yin, R.K.: Case Study Research: Design and Methods. Sage, Thousand Oaks (2003)

User's Satisfaction of Kuwait E-Government Portal: Organization of Information in Particular

Huda R. Farhan and Mark Sanderson

Department of Information Studies University of Sheffield, UK
Sheffield, UK
H.farhan@shef.ac.uk, m.sanderson@shef.ac.uk

Abstract. Assessing the success of an information system might help in locating weak and strong points of the system leading to the improvement of system under assessment. A popular system evaluation construct is user's satisfaction. Different measuring instruments were developed to assess this construct at the organization environment. In addition to the traditional instruments that were develop to assess information system success, new instruments need to be adapted that can cope with the internet context. This paper presents a measuring instrument that was developed to evaluate Kuwait e-government user's satisfaction while seeking information via Kuwait e-government portal. The instrument was based on several satisfaction factors. The application of this instrument indicated that the suggested factors predict the overall user satisfaction.

Keywords: User's satisfaction, e-government portals, evaluation of information systems, satisfaction factors.

1 Introduction

Consulting e-government portals to fulfill information needs was considered as an information seeking process [21]. In order to fulfil information needs related to government facilities and services, citizens might consult e-government portals instead of visiting the government institutions. The e-government portal's ability to satisfy citizens' information needs will affect how users perceive, revisit and use the portal and determine their degree of satisfaction. Thereby, measuring citizens' satisfaction will help in determining the success or failure of the portal from a user perspective and lead to the improvement of the portal, increase usage and loyalty [10].

Citizens' satisfaction as information seekers in an e-government context was not the focus of the literature in the field. Most of the studies were focusing on either the technical design of e-government portals [14]; [3], service quality [16];[18] or proposed evaluation methods [21]. Thereby, a need was identified to explore the success of an e-government portal from a user's perspective. The Kuwait e-government portal was chosen for this purpose. Knowing that it is a newly lunched portal and never been evaluated for success based on user's satisfaction. To measure users' satisfaction while using Kuwait e-government portal, a measuring instrument was developed based on Bailey and Pearson's users' information satisfaction instrument. The developed

M. Janssen et al. (Eds.): EGES/GISP 2010, IFIP AICT 334, pp. 201–209, 2010.

instrument was designed based on several satisfaction factors that were introduced in previous literature. In addition to the subjects' overall satisfaction the measuring instrument is expected to assess a particular dimension of users' satisfaction which is the organization of information. Another aim of this study was to measure the ability of the suggested satisfaction factors to predict the overall satisfaction.

The measuring instrument was applied surveying 229 Kuwaitis. In this paper user's satisfaction as an evaluation measure was discussed, followed by related studies. After that, the design of the measuring instrument was introduced along with the data collection and methodology. Finally, a discussion of the findings was provided, followed by the conclusion.

2   Can User's Satisfaction Work as an Evaluation Measure?

[2] Defined user satisfaction in a certain situation as "*the sum of one's feelings or attitudes toward a variety of factors affecting that situation*". Measuring user's satisfaction of information systems would facilitate detecting weaknesses and strength of a system from a users' point of view [12]. In addition, users' satisfaction "*measures how users view their information system rather than the technical quality of the system*"[15]. [17] Assumed the lack of theoretical assessment of user satisfaction as a measure of information system effectiveness, concentrating only on user's satisfaction rather than exploring attitude in its broad meaning. [17]Questioned the relation between user satisfaction and information system effectiveness in the organization environment where the system use is mandatory. In organization context -where most of the user's satisfaction studies were conducted- users' satisfaction was perceived as "*a reflection of the context to which the information needs of manager have been met*" [13]. Different measuring instruments were developed to measure UIS. The most common used measures are: "Bailey and Pearson, 1983; Baroudi and Orlikowski, 1988; Doll and Torkzadeh, 1988; Goodhue, 1988; Ives, et al., 1983; Jenkins and Ricketts, 1979, Doll et al., 1994).

[2] Developed a measuring instrument consisting of 39 factors to measure satisfaction. [8] Developed an instrument to measure the end user satisfaction with a specific application. The instrument consisted of five factors; content, accuracy, format, ease of use, time line. The factors measured via 12 items. The instrument was tested for validity and reliability. Asking 618 end users distributed at 44 different firms to fill out the questionnaire supported the generalizeability of the instrument. The instrument was found to be able to measure end user satisfaction of specific application, compare between applications and general satisfaction. [19] Believed that Jenkins and Ricketts 1979 instrument was "*one of the few (if not the only) approaches that develops an instrument to measure user satisfaction that is well grounded in a widely accepted theoretical model*"

[17] emphasized the need for an argument to relate user satisfaction and system use and system effectiveness. In addition, [17] called for studying the reverse direction of influence relation between attitude and behavior (the effect of behavior on attitude). [17] Believed that "*user satisfaction instruments are currently employed to assess (relative) user dissatisfaction, to diagnose possible causes for dissatisfaction, and to suggest corrective action*"

[15] Investigated a number of users' satisfaction instruments to test their reliability as information system measures. [15] Investigation was based on four criterion; empirically derived measure, with adequate empirical support, which covers both the information system product and general system services, and provides multiple indicators. In this study it was found that Pearson's measure (1983) as having more potential as a UIS measure, which leads [15] to further investigate Pearson's measure (1983) to test its reliability and validity. Testing the measure on 800 managers with 25% response rate, [15] concluded that the measure is valid and can be considered as a step towards the establishment of standard measures of UIS, and suggesting further testing to validate the measure. [15] Modified the measure to make it shorter to meet general evaluation process.

[12] investigated the test and retest reliability of the *detailed* UIS measure – Bailey and Pearson's instrument (1983) that was refined and abbreviated by [1]. The summary part of the instrument was modified to represent each factor individually instead of having one global summary question owing to the heterogeneity of the instrument factors. Three groups of MBA students were recruited to answer the questionnaire. One group was exposed to system failure materials; the second group was exposed to system success materials, where the third group answered the questionnaire without prior preparation. The findings indicated that the instrument "*lack test and retest reliability*". Also, it was noticed that the summary questions were more reliable than the detailed questions. The researcher recommended further testing and retesting of the user's satisfaction *detailed* measure.

Using the confirmatory factor analysis, [9] tested the validity and reliability of Doll and Torkzadeh's end user computer satisfaction measuring instrument [8]. Applying the instrument on 409 computer end users affiliated with 18 organizations two of them government agencies – which support the generalizability of the results –, the researchers confirmed the validity and reliability of the instrument. Also, the findings of the study indicated that the instrument "*explains and measures the users satisfaction construct*", hence, can work as a standardized instrument to measure user's satisfaction with specific computer applications.

User satisfaction has been tested for reliability as a measure to evaluate information systems' success or failure. [13] Conducted a study to validate the use of user satisfaction and system usage as two measures of information systems success. A modified questionnaire (based on Doll and Torkzaddah) was deployed to investigate the relation between both measures and performance. The questionnaire addresses 5 dimensions of user's satisfaction: satisfaction with the content, accuracy, format, time line, ease of use. The findings of this study indicated that user's satisfaction is a reliable measure of information system success. Also, the study showed that satisfied users are more likely to use the system frequently. Regardless of researchers' different attitudes towards deploying user's satisfaction as a measure of information system success, [7] stated that "*user information satisfaction continues to be the most commonly used and developed success measure*".

3 Related Studies

In system management literature, several models had been developed to measure information system success in an organizational context (e.g. [7]; [11]). It was noticed that a common aspect to information system success models was the inclusions of user's satisfaction as a success construct whether to measure overall success or particular aspect of success.

User's satisfaction interacting with an electronic medical record system was evaluated by [20]. The evaluation instrument was especially designed for this study covering four satisfaction dimensions; overall user reactions, screen design and layout, terms and system information, learning and system capabilities. Seventy five physicians participated in the survey. The findings indicated that satisfaction was higher with screen design and layout more than system capabilities. The researcher recommended the use of terms preferred by physicians rather than terms chosen by the system developers.

Just like other research fields, research focussing on information system success was influenced by the existence of the internet. The impact of the internet on user satisfaction research can be understood from the call to redesign user satisfaction measuring instruments to meet the internet environment. Hence, new users' information satisfaction instruments were developed especially to measure users' information satisfaction in the internet context based on the assumption that internet environment differ from the organization environment in terms of usage and type of users [6]. In the internet environment, [4] evaluated Australian academics' satisfaction of the information seeking experience on the internet, and the relation between information seeking satisfaction and previous training, success expectation, and frequency of internet usage. Using the magnitude estimate method as well as questionnaire and structured interviews, 37 randomly selected Australian academics were recruited as subjects to report their satisfaction regarding information seeking experiences. [4] Didn't find any significant effect between information search previous training, frequency of internet usage and users' level of satisfaction. A moderate positive relation between information seeking satisfaction and success expectations was noticed, although this finding needed further investigation owing to the fact that subjects were asked to report success expectation after the completion of the information seeking process. Hence, the success expectation could be affected by the information seeking experience results. Finally, [4] research indicated that Australian academics have high expectation of information seeking in the internet and they were highly satisfied.

[6] Modified Goodhue's model to meet the requirements of the web environment to evaluate user's information satisfaction outside an organizational context. The model consisted of six concepts in addition to the Goodhue concepts that were seen as appropriate for the web environment. [6] Emphasized the importance of considering web users in developing web information system at the success of the system. The focus of the model wasn't only users' satisfaction instead two other dimensions were addressed; web usage and individual performance. The reliability of the instrument was low indicating the need for further improvement of the instrument.

4 Methodology

A user centric study was conducted to assess how citizens' are satisfied with their information seeking experience at the Kuwait e-government portal. The study was expected to explore the difficulties related to information classification and descriptive terms citizens encounter while retrieving government information. Our study was not concerned with information seeking behaviour. Instead our study focused on Kuwait e-government portal's ability to organize information in a way that adhered to citizens' information needs and information seeking preferences. In addition, the study did not focus on the well known measure of information retrieval systems (recall and precision), instead it focused on the users' perception of the success of the information retrieval system based on predefined satisfaction factors. A quantitative method was deployed to collect data for the purpose of this study. This study evolved based on investigating the following aims;

1. To assess how satisfied users are with their information seeking experience at the Kuwait e-government portal.
2. To investigate the effect of the methods used to organize information on the users' decision to revisit Kuwait e-government portal.
3. To develop a theoretically justifiable and empirically tested user satisfaction measuring instrument.
4. To explore the ability of the suggested satisfaction factors to predict user's overall satisfaction.

In order to meet the previous mentioned aims the following questions will be answered:

- What is the degree of citizen's information satisfaction regarding finding needed information in Kuwait e-government portal?
- To what extent can the suggested satisfaction factor reflect user's overall satisfaction?

Using [2] abbreviated user's satisfaction instrument as a starting point, a questionnaire was designed to collect data. Believing that user satisfaction is "*a bi-dimensional attitude affected by a variety of factors*" [2], the developed instrument consisted of seven factors with more than 3 indicators each. A summery section was included summarizing users' overall satisfaction. The questionnaire was detailed to assess particular dimension of satisfaction which was the organization of information. According to [12] "*User satisfaction is a state at a given point in time (rather than a lasting trait) and more easily influenced by experience*". Hence, the questionnaire was intended to address user's satisfaction of information seeking for information related to multiple real life events. This decision was made to eliminate the expected bias that may occur from a single failure incident. Seven factors of [2] were the base for our questionnaire; currency, understanding of the system, expectation as well as repeated visit [7] and recommendation (we believe that a user will recommend a system to his network if he is satisfied with this system), organization of information and ease of use [8]. Whenever applicable, relevant questions were adapted from previously tested and validated user's satisfaction measuring instruments and added to our instrument. In addition to addressing the satisfaction factors the questionnaire included several questions addressing users' computer skills, access to internet and hearing of the portal. The inclusion of these questions was to eliminate the effect of these factors on users' satisfaction. Hence, assure the assessment of the intended factors only. The questionnaire was piloted prior to the actual application to test reliability, design and language suitability to the participants. Changes and modifications were applied whenever needed based on the pilot test.

Six hundred questionnaires were distributed at the main public libraries in Kuwait. The response rate was 55.1% representing 331 responses. Around 104 questionnaires were labeled as invalid and were not used. The excluded questionnaires suffer from missing information, contradicted answers that shows the participants answers were haphazard and not based on reading the questionnaire. The valid responses were 229 entered and manipulated using SPSS.

5   Findings and Discussion

The purpose of this evaluation was to investigate how satisfied users are of the information seeking experience at Kuwait e-government portal. The majority of subjects indicated that they can access computer with internet connection easily. Also, the majority of subjects believed that they have computer and internet skills that allowed them to search the internet and bookmark and describe documents they find. Therefore, Computer skills and computer and internet access were excluded as factors that affect usage and satisfaction. Also, Knowledge of the portal was excluded as a factor that might affect the portal usage and satisfaction. This decision was made based on the subjects responses indicating that they have heard about the portal.

Although technical issues such as pages slow downloads and dead links were not the focus of this study, it was noticed that technical issues do affect the usage of the portal. Around 68.2% of the respondents believed that technical issues they faced when using the portal prevented them from wanting to revisit the portal. Thereby, all conclusions derived from this study took into considerations the effect of the technical issues on user's satisfaction.

1- Understanding of the System
To explore subjects' understanding of Kuwait e-government portal, subjects were asked if they knew the goal of the portal as well as the type of information and services available at the portal. In addition, subjects were asked if they knew how to use the portal in their everyday life. The majority of subjects expressed a good understanding of the system. Around 97.6 % understood the goal of the portal, and 87.1 % knew the type of information and services available at the portal. Also, 92.9% knew how to make use of the portal in their everyday life. Furthermore, it was noticed that 79.6% of the subjects that expressed a good understanding of the portal indicated a high level of overall satisfaction with the information seeking experience using the system. The indication of this observation supported the assumption that understanding the system might be used to predict the overall satisfaction.

2- Ease of Use
Knowing that "*the basic premise behind ease of use is designing a website that builds on the user's perspective*" [5]. Subjects were asked if they found the portal easy to use when performing an information seeking process. More than 80% of subjects believed that the portal was easy to use. Around 90.6% consulted the portal when they didn't know where to search. Also, 83.5 % found information in the portal more than other information resources. Finally, subjects who believed that using the portal helped them avoid going to the government institution building were around 80%. As for the possibility of ease of use to act as a satisfaction factor, 80.5% of subjects who believed in the ease of use of the portal expressed a high level of overall satisfaction.

Hence, supporting the assumption that ease of use can be used to predict the overall satisfaction.

3- Currency of Information

Subjects were asked to show their opinion about the currency of information available at the portal. Around 87% believed information available at the portal were current meeting their information needs. Also, 85% of subjects who believed information available at the portal was current also showed a high level of satisfaction. Hence, subjects' opinion about the currency of information can be used to anticipate the overall satisfaction.

4- Repeated Visit

To investigate the interval of visiting, the portal subjects were asked to state their frequency of visits on a five point scale. Subjects visiting the portal daily or once a week were considered as frequent users. Subjects that visited the portal less than that were considered less frequent users. A small number of subjects 20.0% considered themselves as more frequent users visiting the portal from daily to once a week. Although, 88% of subjects who considered themselves as frequent users expressed a high level of satisfaction, it was noticed that the majority of satisfied subjects 72.05% considered themselves as less frequent users. Therefore, repeated visit don't necessarily reflect the level of overall satisfaction. This finding goes in line with previous literature in both obligatory system usage and optional system usage. [4] No significant relationship between subject level of satisfaction and frequency of internet usage was found.

5- Recommendation

Believing that users recommend information channels that satisfy their information needs conveniently, and attempting to measure recommendation as a satisfaction factor, subjects were asked to recommend an information channel to other people based on two incidents; traffic violations and fines related to car insurance. The Kuwait e-gov portal came as the second preferable information channel for the incidents discussed. However, the number of subjects recommending the portal was low. Most subjects (50%) recommended a relevant ministry web site. Also, from the findings it was noticed that recommendation might reflect the overall satisfaction, around 84.9% of subjects that recommended the portal for both incidents investigated also, expressed a high level of satisfaction. The recommendation section of the questionnaire revealed a different preference pattern. The highest recommended information channel was the government institution web site followed by the e-government portal. This finding questions the appropriateness of considering recommendation as a user's satisfaction factor.

6- Expectation

The number of subjects that recommended the portal was low. However, Most of subjects (96.9%) that recommended the portal had good expectation about the information seeking experience using the portal. The number of subjects with high expectations of the portal being of use to others for traffic violation and car insurance incidents were highly satisfied at the same time, respectively 82.8% and 60%. This indicates that user expectation predicts overall satisfaction. [4] Findings indicated a moderate significant positive relationship between subject's expectation and the level of satisfaction.

8- Organization of Information

Amongst the difficulties that [5] identified with users searching the internet for health information are; information overload and disorganization of information in addition to the need to know jargon and technical terms. Assessing how subjects perceived the way information was organized at the portal was another factor of satisfaction explored in this study. Subjects were asked about the effect of the way information was organized at the portal on their decision to revisit the portal. Also, subjects were asked whether they found the descriptive terms available at the portal easy to understand or ambiguous. 76.5 % of subjects believed information organization on the portal didn't affect their decision to revisit the portal. Most of subjects (78.4%) believed that terms were clear. As for the relation between user's opinion about the way information was organized and the overall satisfaction, it was noticed that subjects with positive opinions expressed a high level of overall satisfaction. This finding suggested the possibility to consider organization of information as factor that might predict the overall satisfaction.

6 Conclusion

Although the number of subjects that actually used the portal in comparison to the subjects who heard of the portal was low (37.1%), the majority of those subjects expressed a high level of overall satisfaction with the portal. The findings raised a need to locate effective methods to motivate users to consult the Kuwait e-government portal. In addition to assessing user's satisfaction with the information seeking experience using the Kuwait e-government portal, the data were analyzed to investigate the possibility of the suggested satisfaction factors to predict the overall satisfaction. The findings revealed the possibility of six factors to predict the overall satisfaction. These factors were; understanding of the system, ease of use, currency of information, recommendation and expectation and organization of information. The only factor that failed to reflect the overall satisfaction was repeated visit. This finding indicates the ability of the developed measuring instrument to measure user's satisfaction. Some modifications need to be applied to the instrument though. These modifications related to the factors that failed to predict the overall satisfaction.

Being part of an ongoing research, this study will be followed by a user's centric study. An exploratory lab controlled study will be conducted. Cross users comparative system success assessment will be performed. In this study, the focus will be on the method used to organize information at the portal in particular. Users will be introduced to two system interfaces. One interface with a previously generated folksonomy by end users and the other interface will be the original portal interface without folksonomy. The success of the portal will be based on comparing user's satisfaction utilizing the developed and modified measuring instrument

References

1. Baroudi, J.J., Olson, M.H., et al.: An Empirical Study of the Impact of User Involvement on System Usage and Information Satisfaction. Communication of the ACM 29(3), 232–238 (1986)
2. Baily, J.E., Pearson, S.W.: Development of a Tool for Measuring and Analyzing Computer User Satisfaction. Management Science 29(5), 530–545 (1983)

3. Becker, S.A.: E-Government Visual Accessibility for Older Adult Users. Social Science Computer Review 22(1), 11–23 (2004)
4. Bruce, H.: User Satisfaction with Information Seeking on the Internet. Journal of the American Society for Information Science 49(6), 541–556 (1998)
5. Cline, R.J.W., Haynes, K.M.: Consumer Health Information Seeking on the Internet: the State of the Art. Health Education Research 16(6), 671–692 (2001)
6. D'Ambra, J., Rice, R.E.: Emerging Factors in User Evaluation of the World Wide Web. Information and Management 38, 373–384 (2001)
7. Delone, W.H., Mclean, E.R.: The Delone and Mclean Model of Information System Success: A Ten- Year Update. Journal of Management Information Systems 19(4), 9–30 (2003)
8. Doll, W.J., Torkzadeh, G.: The Measurement of End -User Computing Satisfaction. MIS Quarterly 12(2), 259–274 (1988)
9. Doll, W.J., Torkzadeh, G.: A Confirmatory Factor Analysis of the End-User Computing Satisfaction Instrument. MIS Quarterly 18(4), 453–461 (1994)
10. Freed, L.: American Customer Satisfaction Index: E-Government satisfaction Index (2005), http://www.fcg.gov/documents/12-2007.pdf (retrieved June 16, 2008)
11. Gable, G.G., Sedera, D., et al.: Enterprise Systems Success: A measurement Model. In: Twenty-Fourth International Conference on Information Systerms, Seattle, USA (2003)
12. Galletta, D.F., Lederer, A.L.: Some cautions on the measurement of user information satisfaction. Decision Science 20, 419–438 (1989)
13. Gelderman, M.: The relation between user satisfaction, usage of information systems and performance. Information and Management 34, 11–18 (1998)
14. Ho, A.T.-K.: Reinventing Local Governments and the E-Government Initiative. Public Administration Review 62(4), 434–444 (2002)
15. Ives, B., Olson, M.H., et al.: The measurement of user information satisfaction. Communication of the ACM 26(10), 785–793 (1983)
16. Marcella, R., Baxter, G., et al.: The effectiveness of parliamentry information services in the United Kingdom. Government Information Quarterly 20(1), 29–46 (2003)
17. Melone, N.P.: Atheoretical assessment of the user satisfaction construct in information systems research. Management Science 36(1), 76–91 (1990)
18. Parent, M., Vandebeek, C.A., et al.: Building Citizen Trust Through E-government. Government Information Quarterly 4(22), 4720–4736 (2005)
19. Srinivasan, A.: Alternative measures of system effectiveness: associations and implications. MIS Quarterly 9(3), 243–253 (1985)
20. Sittig, D.F., Kuperman, G.J., et al.: Evaluating physician satisfaction regarding user interactions with an electronic medical record system. In: Proc. AMIA Symp., pp. 400–404 (1999)
21. Wang, L., Bretschneider, S., et al.: Evaluating Web-Based E-Government Services with a Citizen-Centric Approach. In: 38th Annual Hawaii International Conference on System Sciences (HICSS 2005)-Track 5, Hawaii, vol. 5. IEEE Computer Society, Los Alamitos (2005)

ICT-Based Improvement
of Construction Procurement Process

Olli Martikainen[1,2], Raija Halonen[1,3], and Valeriy Naumov[1]

[1] University of Oulu, Department of Information Processing Science, Oulu, Finland
[2] The Research Institute of the Finnish Economy, Helsinki, Finland
[3] National University of Ireland, Centre for Innovation & Structural Change, Galway, Ireland
{olli.martikainen,raija.halonen,valeriy.naumov}@oulu.fi

Abstract. The research by Maliranta and Rouvinen based on the Finnish industrial statistics confirms that the productivity improvements in ICT services in
firms correlate to organizational and process changes. These results implied a
further question: Which types of process changes create the most beneficial
productivity improvements in different environments? In this paper we apply
the Three Viewpoint Method (3VPM) approach, originally developed for the
productivity analysis of process changes, to analyze the improvement of the
construction procurement process of a large Scandinavian construction company when an IT system for procurement was taken into use in the Finnish
offices. The analysis revealed that implementing the procurement IT system decreased worker utilization rates and improved the procurement process
throughput.

Keywords: Business process analysis, procurement process, IT-system, process
improvement, Three Viewpoint Method.

1 Introduction

The productivity increase results from ICT (Information and Communication Technologies) in the industry and in the society are of rather recent origin [1, 2]. Furthermore, the benefits derived from ICT have been experienced arduous to calculate [3].
The history of ICT implementations is still lacking a positive signal as a mark of successful accomplishment in business improvements [4, 5].

According to the prior research it seems that the excess productivity effect of ICT-
equipped labor typically ranges from eight to eighteen per cent. The effect tends to be
larger in services than in manufacturing. The effect is often manifold in younger and
can even be negative in older firms. Since organizational changes are easier to implement in younger firms and recently established firms have by definition a new
structure, this can be interpreted as evidence for the need for complementary organizational changes. Manufacturing firms seem to benefit from ICT-induced efficiency
in internal whereas service firms benefit from efficiency in external communication.
These results, however, fail to explain, what really happens in the organization, when
large productivity improvements are observed.

M. Janssen et al. (Eds.): EGES/GISP 2010, IFIP AICT 334, pp. 210–219, 2010.

The literature has contributed to IT benefit measurement and management in four major areas: Performance improvements, the issue of information systems reach tangible and intangible benefits and benefit evolution [6]. The benefits from process changes when workflow systems have been introduced are measured in [7]. In their extensive literature review Melville et al. [8] introduced a model of a resource-based view of a firm (RBV) that builds on intellectual foundations (theory of imperfect competition, theory of monopolistic competition, theory of firm growth) and theory development (resource-based view of the firm, resource heterogeneity and above normal firm performance, identification of resources that confer a sustained competitive advantage, bundling of resources). Melville et al. [8] confirm that IT is valuable and offers potential benefits ranging from flexibility and quality improvements to cost reduction and productivity enhancement. They also propose that the high degree of complexity leads to a context-contingent set of synergistic combinations of IT and other organizational resources such as workplace practices, change initiatives, organizational structure and financial condition. Therefore they suggest further case and field studies of specific organizational contexts. Our work continues this research by presenting a formal process modeling and analysis framework, the Three Viewpoint Method (3VPM), for the calculation of the benefits created by the process changes enabled by the new ICT services. The approach is appropriate in any business process analysis that fulfills the required steps [9].

Prior literature has only little knowledge so far of what the best practices in organizing ICT-assisted work will be. Nevertheless, it is obvious that in the future when the ICT benefits are optimally applied in new process forms, the job descriptions will ultimately differ considerably from the current ones. Likewise, prior research sets forth experiences from computational approaches to business process design and positive sign concerning the possibility of analytical support for business process design is visible [10, 11]. The productivity improvements created by ICT services are a result of customer process changes enabled by the IT service. Depending on customer process types different improvements are possible. The benefits from customer process changes should be larger than the cost of the IT service in order the IT service to be feasible.

2 Business Process Modeling

Business process was defined by Davenport [12] as a specific ordering of work activities across time and place, with a beginning and end, and with clearly defined inputs and outputs. First approaches of business process development were published in the early 1990's [13, 14, 15]. The term business process re-engineering (BPR) was also introduced at that time [15]. The management and improvement of business processes has after that generated a large amount of literature, including topics Re-engineering the Corporation [16], Process Innovation [12], Improving Performance [17], Business Process Management [18] and Business Process Change [19]. All approaches have the same notion of improving the performance of the organization by developing the business processes.

The first task in business process development is the process modeling, where the necessary features of the process are documented. There are several modeling approaches for this purpose based on Business Process Diagrams such as Business Process Modelling Notation (BPMN) by Object Management Group (OMG) [20],

Ericsson Penker extension of Unified Modelling Language (UML) [21] and Work-flow Nets [22, 23]. Here we apply the UML Activity Diagram notation [21].

When a service is provided for customer's business process or personal process the interaction with the service process changes the customer process in a way that creates the productivity improvements. Usually the utility of the productivity improvements should be larger than the cost of the service. However, in public services the utility is not only the performance improvement in the customer's process but also the utilities created through externalities in the society (Fig. 1).

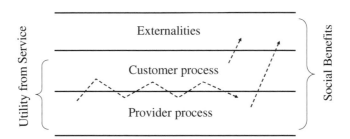

Fig. 1. The benefits created by a service process

In addition to the process diagrams, both performance and cost modeling of the process are needed when productivity improvements are analyzed. We call the modeling approach that uses these three viewpoints: 1) diagrams, 2) performance and 3) cost, as Three Viewpoint Modelling (3VPM). For performance we use queuing network models to calculate the throughput and waiting times of events or tasks in the process and the utilizations of the resources related to the activities of the process [24]. In cost analysis the fixed costs in the process are related to the costs per time unit of the fixed resources involved as well as to the fixed quality costs and fixed risk costs. The variable costs of the process are related to the product of the utilization and the cost per time unit of the variable resources involved as well as to the waiting costs, quality costs and risk costs that depend on the load of the system.

3 Business Process Analysis

The micro level analysis of a system of processes is based on the following four steps: Drawing the logical process diagrams of the original and transformed processes, calculating the process performance analysis of the obtained models, calculating the activity based costs of the models and comparing the results of original and transformed models.

3.1 Create the Logical Process Diagrams

The first task, with the employees, is to create a cognitive description (a swim line model) of the work process. There are several descriptive models and corresponding graphical editors that can be used. In our analysis we apply the activity diagram notation based on the OMG Unified Modelling Language (UML) with Eriksson Penker business process extensions (see [20, 25]). Both the service processes and the corresponding customer processes and their proposed changes should be modeled. The process diagrams specify the logical process model denoted by M.

3.2 Analyze the Process Performance

For performance analysis we use the queuing network solution G for the model M to calculate the throughput and waiting times of events or tasks in the process and the utilizations of the resources related to the activities of the processes [24]. When the processes are analyzed using the queuing network model, the modeling results can be calibrated with the real system. The calibration often reveals problems or unknown features in the system, and discussion with the process personnel is needed to solve possible inconsistencies. Only after successful calibration the possible process changes can be modeled and their effects analyzed.

3.3 Calculate the Activity Based Costs

In the cost analysis the fixed costs in the processes are related to the costs of the fixed resources as well as to the fixed quality costs and fixed risk costs. The variable costs of the processes are related to the product of the utilization and the cost per time unit of the variable resources involved as well as to the waiting costs, quality costs and risk costs that depend on the load of the system. The cost function F divided by the number of service transactions and calculated as a function of load represents the average variable cost curve generated by the production function of the system.

3.4 Combine the Three Models

In the Three Viewpoint Model (3VPM) approach the three viewpoints: 1) diagrams, 2) performance and 3) cost are related to each other with common variables (Fig. 2).

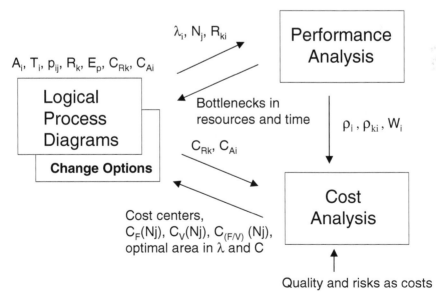

Fig. 2. The 3VPM approach

In the process diagram the activities (A_i), related resources (R_k), tasks or customers (E) served and the corresponding task arrival intensities (λ_i), routing probabilities (ρ_{ij}), service times in activities (T_i), population sizes (N_i) and costs of resources (C_{Rk}) are given for the model M. The results are calculated in the 3VPM analysis using the queuing network solution denoted by G and the cost analysis solution denoted by F. The variables used as input and results obtained as output are displayed in Table 1 and they are related as shown in formulas 1, 2 and 3.

Table 1. Input and output parameters in the 3VPM analysis

Inputs		Outputs	
Activities	A_i	Customer time in activity ...	W_i
Task classes	E_p	Customers p in activity i	N_{pi}
Routing probability	ρ_{ij}	Utilization of activity	ρ_i
Service time in activity	T_i	Utilization of resource k in activity i	ρ_{ki},
Arrival intensity	λ_i	Fixed costs	C_F
Customers p in system	N_p	Variable costs	C_V
Resource	R_k		
Resource time in activity	R_{ki},		
Resource k cost in time	C_{Rk}		
Activity I other costs	C_{Aj}		

$$M = (A_i, T_i, r_{ij}, E_p, C_{Rk}, C_{aj}) \tag{1}$$

$$(\rho_i, \rho_{ki}, W_i) = G(\lambda_{ij}, N_i, R_{ki}, M) \tag{2}$$

$$(C_F, C_V) = F(\rho_i, \rho_{ki}, W_i, M) \tag{3}$$

The model M includes the process components and the graphical description. The function G is the solution of the open or closed queuing network representing the process. Usually G is an algorithm that cannot be given in a closed form. The function F simply calculates the costs based on the resource utilizations and customer delays that are obtained from G.

4   Construction Procurement Process

In what follows we analyze the construction procurement process of a large Scandinavian construction company before and after an IT system for procurement was taken into use. The study focuses in the Finnish offices of the company. In order to analyze the original procurement process, the process was described with the help of a graph (Fig. 3). Several key persons from the company were interviewed to find out information about the procurement process at the time. The actual procurement process started with searching the suppliers after the project needs had been specified. As can be seen in Figure 3, the process was partly iterative. The procurement process under inspection is located at the lower half of the chart.

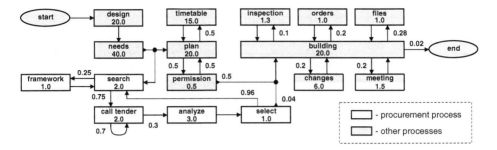

Fig. 3. Procurement Process

As shown in Figure 3, the sample process was loaded with changes that required a lot of resources (6 hrs) parallel to the actual building phase despite the design phase (20 hrs) and requirement analysis ("needs" 40 hrs) that lead to the plan phase (20 hrs).

In the case company, cross-trained employees were qualified and authorized to perform more than one task type. The company had identified six employee categories: 1) architects, 2) engineers, 3) project managers, 4) site managers, 5) area managers, and 6) procurement managers.

The employees were classified according to their skill patterns, which were described by a skill matrix (Table 2). Besides employee categories, the skill matrix included the tasks that were described to be included in the construction procurement process (see Fig. 3). The skill matrix revealed that in the company there were both tasks managed by several professionals and professionals who managed several skills. The skill matrix also revealed the total quantity of each group of professionals per profession and per task type. Furthermore, the skill matrix enabled the estimation of potential changes in the process when the employee-related parameters were changed in the analysis framework 3VPM.

Table 2. Skill matrix

	Total quantity	Design	Needs	Plan	Timetable	Building	Orders	Meeting	Search	Framework	Call	Analyze	Select	Database	Permission	Inspection
Architect	10	X	X													
Engineer	15		X	X												
Project manager	15		X	X	X											
Site manager	100					X	X	X						X	X	X
Area manager	6					X	X	X								
Procurement manager	25							X	X	X	X	X	X			

5 Process Transformations

Next, we present the new process, based on the elaborated skill matrix, cost analysis and original process description influenced by the new procurement IT system Pursys that was recently implemented to manage the procurement process. As the implementation still was in process, Pursys was not in use in every task in the process. The process graph of the sample project (Fig. 4) reveals that the modified procurement process (located at the lower half of the graph) produces significant improvements in two distinct tasks, namely "search" and "changes".

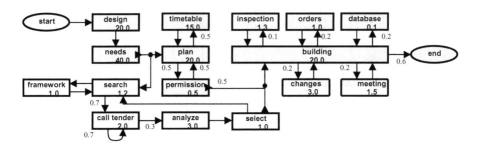

Fig. 4. Improved Procurement Process

The influence of Pursys was theoretically analyzed in relation to the procurement process. While the 3VPM made it possible to estimate and evaluate the process outcomes, the response time was evaluated in three hypothesized cases (Fig. 5).

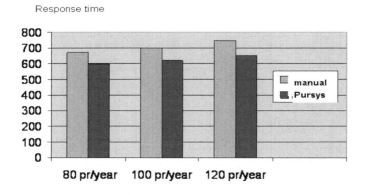

Fig. 5. Improvements in response time (no construction time, arrival rate = 1.6)

As described in Figure 5, the improvement of the procurement response time, when one replaces the manual procurement process with the Pursys managed one seems to be almost independent on the number of annual construction projects.

The use of Pursys was further compared with manual process management as the employee utilization (Fig. 6) was evaluated with the 3VPM.

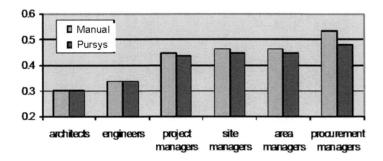

Fig. 6. Improvements in employee utilization (no construction time, arrival rate = 1.6)

The use of Pursys did not improve the workload of architects or engineers compared to the legacy system as described in Figure 6. However, even project managers benefited from Pursys even if the change is only modest. The workload of procurement managers was decreased more visibly. The same tendency was seen in the process chart as tasks managed by architects and engineers were not affected by implementing Pursys. On the other hand, procurement managers were in charge when searching suppliers that definitely was improved when Pursys was implemented (see Fig. 4).

All in all, the calculated savings based on the changes in employee utilizations made it possible to assess the Pursys system payback time and to justify the Pursys system investment.

6 Conclusions

Prior research has revealed that it is complicated and challenging to investigate the role of ICT when seeking for improvements in productivity in the industry sector [1, 8]. The problem is not rare in several other sectors [4]. Also, research on productivity increase resulting from ICT in the industry and in the society is of rather recent origin even if it shows that the productivity improvements in ICT services in firms correlate to organizational and process changes [1, 2]. While Melville et al. [8] propose that ICT infrastructure is a complementary asset that shapes the extent to which firms can apply ICT to improve organizational performance; our study highlights the need to evaluate the business processes from three different angles simultaneously.

In our approach we were able to evaluate the existing processes that covered three distinct viewpoints that were related to each other with specified parameters (see Fig. 2). Not only did the model notice the business process that was defined by key professionals in the company but it also paid attention to the costs and performance that were varied according to the presupposed circumstances in the company.

Since there were several improvements but also some drawbacks in the Pursys supported procurement process, compared to the manual one, it was not possible at the beginning to make an expert opinion on the productivity improvement enabled by the Pursys system. After the system was modeled and analyzed with the 3VPM method, the overall productivity improvement and the resource utilizations could be calculated. Also different improvement options could be compared. The drawbacks of the 3VPM method were the need of interviews and modeling work. Methods and tools which could at least partially automate the data collection are under study.

In practice, the study showed that in a large enterprise it is important to recognize the several viewpoints that influence the business process. Even small changes in the separate input parameters may lead to great changes in the output. Therefore our study suggests additional research to find out the dependent factors that one by one influence business processes. After that, to further combine those to be used when suggesting future improvements in business processes.

A near future improvement of the 3VPM method will be the automated process data measurement by the aid of a wireless data logging system. A long time goal for the research could be the classification of the best process improvement practices depending on the process type and the ICT application.

Acknowledgments. The authors kindly acknowledge the support from the Protura project from ETLA. The project has been financed by the Finnish Funding Agency for Technology and Innovation (Tekes) and several firms. In addition, SESC and VESC projects financed by Academy of Finland have supported the 3VPM methodology development, which is greatly appreciated.

References

1. Maliranta, M., Rouvinen, P.: Informational mobility and productivity – Finnish evidence. Econ. Innov. New Techn. 15(6), 605–616 (2006)
2. Martikainen, O.: Productivity Improvements Enabled by ICT based Process Transformations. In: 3rd Balkan Conference in Informatics BCI 2007, Sofia, September 27-29, pp. 1–8 (2007)
3. Remenyi, D.: The Elusive Nature of Delivering Benefits from IT Investment. EJISE 3(1) (2000), http://www.ejise.com
4. Gunasekaran, A., Ngai, E.W.T., Gaughey, R.E.: Information technology and systems justification: A review for research and applications. Eur. J. Oper. Res. 173, 957–983 (2006)
5. Barclay, C.: Towards an integrated measurement of IS project performance: The project performance scorecard. Inf. Syst. Front. 10, 331–345 (2008)
6. Rummler, G., Brache, A.: Improving Performance. Jossey-Bass, San Francisco (1995)
7. Smith, H., Fingar, P.: Business Process Management. Meghan-Kiffer Press, tampa (2002)
8. Melville, N., Kraemer, C., Gurbaxani, V.: Review: Information technology and organizational performance: An integrative model of IT business value. MIS Quart 28(2), 283–322 (2004)
9. Martikainen, O., Alasalmi, A.: Multichannel Contact Strategy helps Outpatient Healthcare Access. J. The Institute of Telecommunications Professionals 2, part 2, 43–47 (2008)
10. Hofacker, I., Vetschera, R.: Algorithmical approaches to business process design. Computers & Operations Res. 28, 1253–1275 (2001)
11. Kallrath, J.: Solving planning and design problems in the process industry using mixed integer and global optimization. Ann. Oper. Res. 140, 339–373 (2005)
12. Davenport, T.H.: Putting the Enterprise into the Enterprise System. Harvard Business Review (July 1998)
13. Davenport, T.H., Short, J.E.: The new industrial engineering: Information technology and Business Process Redesign. Sloan Management Review 31(4), 11–27 (1990)

14. Davenport, T.H.: Process Innovation. Harvard Business School Press (1993)
15. Hammer, M., Champy, J.: Reengineering the Corporation. Harper Business (1993)
16. Harmon, P.: Business Process Change. Morgan Kaufman Publishers, San Francisco (2003)
17. Choenni, S., Bakker, R., Baets, W.: On the Evaluation of Workflow Systems in Business Processes. EJISE 6(2) (2003), `http://www.ejise.com`
18. van der Aalst, W.M.P.: The Application of Petri Nets to Workflow Management. J. Circuits, Systems and Computers 8(1), 21–66 (1998)
19. Maliranta, M., Rouvinen, P.: Productivity effects of ICT in Finnish business. ETLA DP 852 (2003)
20. Object Management Group: Business Process Modeling Notation Specification, Final Adopted Specification dtc/06-02-01, OMG (February 2006)
21. Gelenbe, E., Pujolle, G.: Introduction to Queueing Networks. Wiley, Chichester (2001)
22. Reijers, H.A.: Design and Control of Workflow Processes: Business Process Management for the Service Industry. Springer, Heidelberg (2003)
23. Denning, P.J., Buzen, J.P.: The Operational Analysis of Queueing Network Models. ACM Computing Surveys 10(3), 225–261 (1978)
24. Hammer, M.: Re-engineering Work: Don't automate, obliterate. Harvard Business Review 68(4), 104–113 (1990)
25. Eriksson, H.-E., Penker, M.: Business Modeling with UML: Business patterns at Work. Wiley, Chichester (2001)

The Case for Improvisation in Information Security Risk Management

Kennedy Njenga[1] and Irwin Brown[2]

[1] Department of Business IT, University of Johannesburg,
Tel.: +27 11 559 1253
knjenga@uj.ac.za
[2] Department of Information Systems, University of Cape Town,
Tel.: +27 21 650 2677
irwin.brown@uct.ac.za

Abstract. Information Security (IS) practitioners face increasingly unanticipated challenges in IS risk management, often pushing them to act extemporaneously. Few studies have been dedicated to examining the role these extemporaneous actions play in mitigating IS risk. Studies have focused on clear guidelines and policies as sound approaches to ISRM (functionalist approaches). When IS risk incidents occur in context and differ one from another, incrementalist approaches to ISRM apply. This paper qualitatively draws viewpoints from IS management on the functionalist and incrementalist viewpoint of managing IS risk. We examine improvisation as an expression of extemporaneous action using a selected case study and argue that improvisation is a fusion of functionalist and incrementalist approaches. Discussions with information security practitioners selected from the case study suggest the presence of improvisation as a positive value-add phenomenon in ISRM. This paper presents a case for improvisation in ISRM.

Keywords: Improvisation, Information Security, Risk Management Functionalism, Incrementalism.

1 Introduction

Business reliance on integrated computing globally has brought about many information security concerns. There has been a need to ensure confidentiality, integrity and availability of information in global integrated computing systems. This need has driven business and particularly information security practitioners to rely on various normative theories as frameworks that can help create stable environments (Siponen and Iivari 2006). Information Security Risk Management (ISRM), applies these normative theories within business contexts to ensure that technical and soft solutions exist for securing organizations' systems (Dhillon and Backhouse 2001; Siponen and Iivari 2006). Normative theories within ISRM usually have two main practical functions, namely a) to evaluate human/practitioners' action and b) to guide people's/practitioners' behaviour (Siponen and Iivari 2006). These two are based on normative logic that suggests action as either good or bad. In the present world of

M. Janssen et al. (Eds.): EGES/GISP 2010, IFIP AICT 334, pp. 220–230, 2010.
© Springer-Verlag Berlin Heidelberg 2010

unpredictability in information systems security, judging action as good or bad based on kernel normative theories has proved difficult.

Anecdotes from information security practitioners suggest that during times of heightened uncertainty and exceptional situations, normative logic, (stemming from normative theories focused on imposing control and order) is usually followed. There has not yet been conclusive research which suggests that these control and order measures are sufficient. Emphasis of discussion on this paper is the 'exceptional situations' (Siponen and Iivari 2006) that give rise to the inconsistent application of normative theories in information security by practitioners in the course of their work. Exceptional situations have been recognized in Information Systems (IS) security literature (Baskerville1995; Dhillon and Backhouse 2001). While current research does not explicitly address or illustrate how these exceptional situations are handled in ISRM (Siponen and Iivari 2006), this paper recognises and promotes *improvisation* as a distinct way of handling exceptional situations.

The following sections discuss approaches in ISRM by practitioners: Section 2 discusses general issues in ISRM in brief. Section 3 discusses improvisation and the philosophy underlying these approaches. Section 4 contextualises research undertaken to examine these alternative approaches. This section also explains the research methodology. Section 5 discusses the research findings while section 6 gives a conclusion.

2 Information Security Risk Management

Historically, ISRM activities have been conducted in order to establish controls and security over information systems (Choobineh, *et al.* 2007). ISRM has therefore been a consistent way of strengthening security controls and practices at the organization level through risk analysis and continual improvement. The ISRM process has mechanisms in place designed to facilitate information security risk mitigation (Wiander and Holappa 2006) and is driven by organizational objectives. Baskerville (2005) has described two problems faced by information security practitioners, which limit the effectiveness of risk analysis practices. These include the lack of reliable empirical data concerning the frequency and amount of losses attributable to information security compromises, and the relative rarity of many kinds of information security compromises. Researchers have tried to examine information security risk in terms of the common challenges faced by information security practitioners in approaching and executing the ISRM process (Baskerville and Portugal 2003). Conventional methods of examining information security risk proposed by these studies include checklists, risk analysis and evaluation (Baskerville 1993; Birch and McEvoy 1992; Dhillon and Backhouse, 2001). The limitations of these techniques have been exacerbated by not including the socio-organisational aspects of information security, which researchers have found to be an important element in the development of an information security strategy (Backhouse and Dhillon 1996; Dhillon and Backhouse 2001).

3 The Improvisation Effect in Information Security

Researchers such as Bjo¨rck (2004) realized the need to look at ISRM in organizations afresh by postulating a neo-institutional theory in studying IT security issues in organizations. Bjo¨rck (2004) argues that the revolutionized modern organization requires new ways of explaining why formal security structures (*functionalism*) and actual security behavior (*incrementalism*) differ and why organizations often create formal security structures *without implementing them fully*. Such observations have lead us to have a closer look at organizational *improvisation* as a potentially relevant phenomenon for ISRM in current competitive environments (Crossan & Sorrenti 1997; Moorman & Miner 1998). Improvisation occurs in various forms as either individual improvisation or collective improvisation. *Individual Improvisation* is where planned or deliberate individual behaviour creates *improvisation* (Moorman and Miner 1998). As an illustration, an individual's deliberate behaviour may play an important role in speeding the development of highly iterative and experiential new products (Moorman and Miner 1998; Eisenhardt and Tabrizi 1995). *Collective Improvisation* is the combined effort of several individuals/organizations (Cunha 2004). Research suggests that interactions among people who are improvising frequently produce collective *improvisation* (Cunha 2004; Crossan and Sorrenti 1997). There are suggestions that collective *improvisation* often builds on and incorporates individual *improvisation* (Moorman and Miner 1998).

   Ciborra *et al.* (2000) considered *improvised* activities as **simultaneously structured** (functionalist) and **unpredictable**; planned but emergent; discernible after the fact but spontaneous (incrementalism) in manifestation. *Improvisation* in organisations has been a phenomenon researched by social scientists due to its perceived importance in contextually relating content and sequence of previous processes and routines in novel ways that affect outcomes (Cunha 2004). The perspective illustrated in Figure 1 below shows *improvisation* **as a fusion** between functionalism and incremental approaches to ISRM (Njenga 2007).

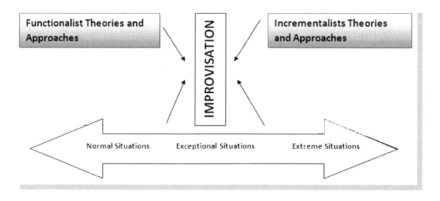

Fig. 1. The holistic view of Improvisation in ISRM (Adopted from Njenga 2007)

   Figure 1 provides a framework for conceptual thinking regarding IS security related improvisation that is guided by suggested kernel theories (i.e. both functionalist and incrementalist). IS security related improvisation manifests in two ways; First improvisation can result from short-comings or "functional gaps" in existing information systems. This primarily occurs in unanticipated (exceptional) situations and is often referred to as "*workarounds*" (McGann and Lyytinen 2008). Secondly, improvisations can result from an actor seizing new opportunities to configure existing IS capabilities into new functionality - referred to as *"configurable IT improvisations"* (McGann and Lyytinen 2008). Improvisation occurs in a continuum from normal to extreme situations and can arise from events for which no applicable rule (functionalist) exists (Saastamoinen 1995). Weick (1998) views the attributes of improvisation as a continuum ranging from taking minor liberties and adding "accents" to systems known as *"interpretation"*; through anticipating, rephrasing, regrouping, and adding clusters not originally included - known as *"embellishment"*. This latter aspect results in full-scale "improvisation" meaning that there is transformation that results in the revised system having little resemblance to the original system (Weick 1998).

The framework discussed in **Figure 1** offers a baseline for a comprehensive analysis of improvisation in ISRM. It integrates functionalist kernel normative theories and incrementalist perspectives (planned, reflexive). Such phenomena are also referred to as being rational adaptive (Segars & Grover, 1999).. Having this framework in mind, the next section illustrates its application in an organisational setting through an in-depth case study. In this case study, we explored how information security practitioners handled exceptional situations within contexts of information security. The analysis illustrates improvisation in ISRM. Empirical data is deployed to illustrate interplay and fusion between kernel normative functionalist and incrementalist approaches to ISRM.

4 Research Methodology

4.1 Research Approach

The research combined theory building (Glaser and Strauss 1967) and a single case study (Yin 1994). The single case study research was exploratory, interpretivist and contextual. The case study approach was used because the study involved the examination of a complex social phenomenon. The selected case was also uniquely *positioned* to generate a full variety of evidence including documents, artefacts, interviews and observations. The benefit of interpretivism was that the researcher could retain "holistic and meaningful characteristics of real-life events" occurring within the context of information security in this organisation. The research method models Eisenhardt's (1989) approach and involved both theory generating and validating of conceptual elements.

Units of Analysis; the following units of analysis from the case were examined. 1. Information Assets Access and Data Control; 2. Information Security Architecture; 3. Information Security Policies; 4. Information Security Event Monitoring; 5. IT Governance and Regulatory Compliance; 6. Disaster Recovery and Business Continuity. The case organisation followed set procedures as directed by the CobiT, ITIL, ISO IEC 17799 frameworks and methodologies. It was therefore easy to map out the abovementioned units of analysis as activities defined by kernel theories.

4.2 Data Collection

The primary data consisted of a series of 11 in-depth interviews. All interviews were tape recorded. After each interview, the information was transcribed verbatim in writing. In addition, notes were taken as the interviews progressed. It is from the transcribed responses from the interviewees that the research formed the contextual case for the phenomenon of *improvisation* being investigated. The interviews were conducted for 60 to 90 minutes per session. This generated close to 700 transcript minutes for data analysis.

4.3   The Use of Grounded Theory Techniques

The researcher used the grounded theory technique of open coding to inductively derive concepts of improvisation from empirical data (Glaser & Strauss 1967; Strauss & Corbin 1990; Glaser 1992) . Grounded theory techniques have been used successfully in both organizational and information systems research in the past (Orlikowski 1993; Trauth & Jessup 2000). An explanation of each step of the research procedure is shown in Table 1.

Table 1. Open Coding of Improvisational Date Incidents

STEP 1 Data Incidents (Transcribed Interviews)	STEP 2 Context of Data Incident	STEP 3 Researcher's memos	STEP 4 Level (Strategic, Tactical, or Operational)	STEP 5 Concepts generated
Extracting Data Incident; The researcher started by looking for elements of *improvisation*. The process of breaking down and analysing the data and assigning labels is described as content analysis by researchers (Glaser and Strauss 1967).	**Determining Context of Data Incident;** Through conversation analysis (Denzin et al. 2003) the researcher provided the context for selected data in the data-sets for incidents that reasonably suggested *improvisations*.	**Deriving Open Codes from Researcher's Memos;** The process of writing memos that would guide open coding (grounded theory technique) in STEP 3 involved several sub-steps. The first step was to examine in-vivo codes.	**Determining Level;** The inductive aspect of analysing data was made possible by extracting and understanding data that reflected aptitude for a fusion of structure and creative thinking simultaneously at three organisational levels.	**Creation of Codes and High Level Concepts Inductively;** Deriving codes was by way of examining data-sets in-depth and careful analyzing these.

5 Discussions and Analysis

The table above shows the methods used to extract instances of *improvisation* through discussions held with the information security practitioners. The next section is a more detailed discussion of *improvisation* as analysed by the researcher.

5.1 Functionalism and Incrementalism - Improvisation

New ways of thinking in ISRM was evident particularly in how practitioners managed information access and data control. Although there are specified procedures (functionalist) contained both in **ISO IEC 17799, Section 5.1** (prescribing how information security practitioners should treat information assets) and **Section 5.2** (prescribing acceptable ways for information control and classification), extemporaneous thinking regarding these procedures was revealed through discussions with practitioners. Discussions with Information Security practitioners firstly acknowledged the need to adhere to procedure, evidenced as follows:

> "...and without preparation, [we needed] getting to know whether there is compliance, considering, information security you know whether there are best solutions to match the technology platform... stuff like that..."

> "Roles [end users roles] are specifically split into two areas, technical response and the process, procedures and people element"

There were times when the practitioners would be forced to address information security control and access issues in an out-of-the-box, spur-of-the-moment fashion. In one particular instance, it was noted that access to sensitive information to a user who requested such access was granted spontaneously:

> "...so we quickly had to make [create] a few more categories...so it doesn't just get as simple as you just having internet access and you didn't get this..."

This act of spontaneity in determining access levels was a demonstration of the need to quickly address information access needs. The researcher proceeded to code this instance as **quick reaction.** At the heart of this kind of *improvisation* was the ability for the practitioner to react quickly and ingeniously, to overcome emergent and presented constraints. While there are specified compliance requirements for information architecture specifications, the **ISO IEC 17799 Section 12.1.1** explains the management obligation to design, operate and use information systems in ways that meet and address requirements stipulated by statutes, regulatory and contractual frameworks. The **CobiT** objectives **Section AI5.13** similarly suggests a manner for evaluation and meeting user requirements through post-implementation review to assess whether user needs are being met. **ITIL**

Section 3.5.4 (*ICT Infrastructure Management*) gives direction on system deployment and acceptance testing. Information security practitioners were aware of these requirements and had put in place procedures necessary for compliance. The organisation's architecture form was primarily responsible for this as shown by an extract of this data incident.

> "...*We have got the Architecture forum, which sits under [name withheld]... and uum, we also have [another forum], which I'm more involved in, in making sure that there is compliance architecture...*

Most of these procedures are incorporated in the overall information architecture specifications. In as much as these procedures were known to the practitioners, when faced with the challenge of identifying compliance requirements at the time, the information security practitioners showed unique ability to match compliance needs with pragmatic solutions. One information security practitioner was of the opinion that some of these compliance requirements in as much as they were important, had inherent gaps. These gaps left practitioners with little choice but to draw on their past experiences and any other cognitive or physical resource available in order to address the gaps and face IT challenges as they arose. In their words, "they did what they had to do" This was explained by one practitioner as follows:

> "...*I think our main thing here is to keep [going]... I mean we have a lot of good uses in policies when it comes to keeping the system going, certain time we do what we have to do to keep the [systems] going...and sometimes we don't...know if it is the right thing to do...*"

The context of the data incident was that when faced with challenges, there were no clear guidelines to follow hence "*sometimes we don't...know if it is the right thing to do*". While following procedure would mean following what was set, improvisation would have meant looking at procedure but re-creating new routines. This is what was done. In this case the practitioner showed that they acted outside of formal procedures. This was coded as being **rational adaptive.**

In all, 25 similar types of high level concepts (e.g., **quick reaction**, **rational adaptive**) specific to improvisation (either as individual or collective) were developed by the researcher through discussions with the information security practitioners. An important point about improvisation derived from these codes was that the phenomenon was demonstrated to be actively present at both individual and group (collective) level. If the improvisation was coded as being at the individual level, this simply meant that key information security practitioners were at an individual level altering their roles to meet the heightened demands of the emergency. Collective improvisation manifested itself as a combined effort of several information security practitioners whose aim was to create and enact novel scenes or situations simultaneously to solve problems that presented them. This can be explained as follows. During discussions the researcher could not help but notice the continued use of the word "*we*" for instance,

> "*...maybe we should actually do this in a different way... "*

> "*...I mean...a lot of it is in based on experience, and just knowing what is important and what's not, we sit...and we put together our plan...*"

The context of the data incident was that during emergencies, there were no clear guidelines to follow and practitioners relied on experience. While following procedure would mean following what was set, *improvisation* would mean looking at procedure but re-creating new routines based on experience. Although collectively the group did not anticipate challenges or problem areas, they seemed to collectively work together to simultaneously coordinate solutions. There was a lot more of this collective coordination between practitioners as opposed to practitioners acting alone. Table 2 shows that the conceptual density of collective improvisation (19 instances) was much greater than individual improvisation (6 instances) for this specific case. These specific instances, (with example quotes), are also shown in Table 2.

Table 2. Conceptual Density of Individual and Collective Improvisation

Units of Analysis	Concepts and Conceptual Density			
Activities related to:	Collective Improvisation	Individual Improvisation	Example (transcripts)	Count
1 **Information Assets Access and Data Control**	Manipulating[IMPROV-1] Quick reaction[IMPROV-2] Being deliberative[IMPROV-3]		"*...and we did and worked on exactly what they said.. and of course within the first few days.. of putting access controls in [the system]...we got hundreds and hundreds of calls...saying they couldn't get through.. they said that they wanted to go to selling sites.. whatever...and they couldn't go to see what was on hundreds of other sites...*"	3
2 **Information Security Architecture**	Novel[IMPROV-4], Rational adaptive[IMPROV-5] Deliberative[IMPROV-6]		"*and whether there is compliance, you know considering security you know whether there are best solutions to match the technology platform... stuff like that*"	3
3 **Information Security Policies**	Rational adaptive[IMPROV-7]	Lateral thinking[IMPROV-8]	"*what they did was... they took the notebooks...they gave those new notebooks to people...and they gave the old notebooks[against policy due to expired warranties] that people had that were still on working conditions to other people* "	2

Table 2. (*continued*)

Units of Analysis Activities related to:	Concepts and Conceptual Density			
	Collective Improvisation	Individual Improvisation	Example (transcripts)	Count
4 **Information Security Event Monitoring**	*Being practical*[IMPROV-9] *Being ingenuous*[IMPROV-10]	*Being creative*[IMPROV-11] *Rational adaptive*[IMPROV-12]	*"well… what you see… well what happens is that it is all about saving money " "so there are those little things…that we do just to help us and to help the business.. because it's those quick little things that…we need to do better "*	4
5 **IT Governance and Regulatory Compliance**	*Being inspired*[IMPROV-13] *Rational adaptive*[IMPROV-14] *Creativeness*[IMPROV-15] *Resourceful*[IMPROV-16] *Getting by*[IMPROV-17] *Managing*[IMPROV-18]	*Being novel*[IMPROV-19]	*"yes but …like I said…had we not adopted CobiT at the board level, we would have made it far more difficult [to implement], but … and the challenge being the audit report"*	7
6. Disaster Recovery and Business Continuity	*Being-quick-witted*[IMPROV-20] *Lateral thinking*[IMPROV-21] *Rational adaptive*[IMPROV-22] *Managing*[IMPROV-23]	*Being-quick-witted*[IMPROV-24] *Getting-by*[IMPROV-25]	*" in order to give to the people [resources] that they gave…they got the ones that [were] broken…[and modified these] they had to think quick…and make that kind of a judgment…"*	6
Total Conceptual Instances of improvisation	19	6		25

5.2 Implications for Practice

The need to encourage improvisation would be justified since improvisation offers information security practitioners and practices various ways to remain flexible and adaptive in turbulent situations while allowing for co-presence efficiency and effectiveness in detecting change and immediately taking advantage of this change. It can be seen that the sets of improvisation (collective or individual) presented in this paper were essential and proved effective in ISRM processes. In general terms, however, improvisation proves only effective provided the information security practitioners are skilled enough and are capable of utilising the best available resources within a firm to achieve the intended purpose.

6 Conclusion

A concluding suggestion is that so long as practice is endowed with practitioners who are capable of skillfully manifesting improvised acts, whether individually or collectively, these acts should not be stifled, but made to flourish since they have been shown to be of value to ISRM. Practice should establish mechanisms to cope with the fear that various improvisations will override long nurtured functionalist structures. Improvisation will actually give contextual meaning to these very functionalist structures. For improvisation to be beneficial to ISRM, information security practitioners should perceive its intrinsic and extrinsic value. It is hoped that this discussion has highlighted this. Information security practitioners should see themselves as socio-constructive agents who are creative and who create reality around themselves. They should see improvisation as leading to a rich and good ISRM practice.

References

1. Backhouse, J., Dhillon, G.: Structures of responsibility and security of information systems. European Journal of Information Systems 5(1), 2–9 (1996)
2. Baskerville, R.: Semantic Database Prototypes. Journal of Information Systems 3(2), 119–144 (1993)
3. Baskerville, R.: The Second-Order Security Dilemma. In: Orlikowski, W., Walsham, G., Jones, M., DeGross, J. (eds.) Information Technology and Changes in Organizational Work, pp. 239–249. Chapman & Hall, London (1995)
4. Baskerville, R.: Information Warfare: a comparative framework for Business Information Security. Journal of Information System Security 1(1), 23–50 (2005)
5. Baskerville, R., Portougal, V.: A Possibility Theory Framework for Security Evaluation in National Infrastructure Protection. Journal of Database Management 14(2), 1–13 (2003)
6. Birch, G.D.W., McEvoy, N.A.: Risk analysis for information systems. Journal of Information Technology 7, 44–53 (1992)
7. Björck, F.: Institutional Theory: A New Perspective for Research into IS/IT Security. In: Proceedings of the 37th Hawaii International Conference on System Sciences (HICSS-37 2004), January 5-8. IEEE Computer Society, Big Island (2004)
8. Choobineh, J., Dhillon, G., Grimaila, M.: Management Of Information Security: Challenges And Research Directions. Communications of the Association for Information Systems 14(3), 958–971 (2007)
9. Ciborra, C., Braa, K., Cordella, A., Dahlbom, b., Hanseth, O., Hepso, V., Ljungberg, J., Monterio, E., Simon, K.A.: From Control to Drift'. Oxford University Press, Oxford (2000)
10. Crossan, M.M., Sorrenti, M.: Making Sense of Improvisation. Advances in Strategic Management 14, 155–180 (1997)
11. Cunha, M.P.: Management Improvisation, FEUNL Working Paper No. 460 (2004), SSRN: http://ssrn.com/abstract=882455
12. Dhillon, G., Backhouse, J.: Current Directions in IS Security Research: Toward Socio-organizational Perspectives. Information Systems Journal 11(2) (2001)
13. Eisenhardt, K.M.: Building Theories from Case Study Research. Academy of Management Review 14(4), 532–550 (1989)

14. Eisenhardt, K.M., Tabrizi, B.N.: Accelerating Adaptive Processes: Product Innovation in the Global Computer Industry. Administrative Science Quarterly 40(1), 84–110 (1995)
15. Glaser, B.G.: Basics of Grounded Theory Analysis: Emergence Vs. Forcing. Sociology Press, California (1992)
16. Glaser, B.G., Strauss, A.L.: The Discovery of Grounded Theory: Strategies for Qualitative Research. Aldine Transaction, New Jersey (1967)
17. McGann, S.T., Lyytinen, K.: The Improvisation Effect: A Case Study of User Improvisation and Its Effects on Information System Evolution. In: Proceedings of the 29th International Conference on Information Systems (ICIS), Paris, France (2008)
18. Moorman, C., Miner, A.: Organisational Improvisation and Organisational Memory. Academy of Management Review 23(4), 698–723 (1998)
19. Njenga, K.: Conceptualising Improvisation in Information Security Risk Management Activities. In (Doctoral Consortium) Proceedings of the 11th Pacific Asia Conference on Information, Auckland, New Zealand (2007)
20. Orlikowski, W.J.: CASE tools as organizational change: investigating incremental and radical changes in systems development. MIS Quarterly 17(3), 309–340 (1993)
21. Saastamoinen, H.: On the handling of exceptions in information systems. In: Computer Science, Economics and Statistics, p. 195. University of Jvaskyla, Jvaskyla (1995)
22. Segars, A., Grover, V.: Profiles of strategic information systems planning. Information Systems Research 10(3), 199–232 (1999)
23. Siponen, M., Iivari, J.: Six Design Theories for IS Security Policies and Guidelines. Journal of the Association for Information Systems 7(7), 445–472 (2006)
24. Strauss, A., Corbin, J.: Basics of qualitative research: Grounded theory procedures and techniques. Sage Publications, Newbury Park (1990)
25. Trauth, E.M., Jessup, L.M.: Understanding computer-mediated discussions: positivist and interpretive analyses of group support system use. MIS Quarterly 24(1), 43–79 (2000)
26. Weick, K.: Improvisation as a mindset for organizational analysis. Organization Science 9(5), 543–555 (1998)
27. Wiander, T., Holappa, J.M.: Theoretical framework of ISO 17799 compliant information security management system using novel ASD method. In: Proceedings of the IAEA Technical Meeting on Cyber Security of Nuclear Power Plant Instrumentation, Control and Information Systems, Idaho Falls, USA, pp. 17–20 (2006)
28. Yin, R.K.: Case Study Research, Design and Methods, 2nd edn. Sage Publications, Newbury Park (1994)

GISP Session 2:
Globalized Process Design

BPM-in-the-Large – Towards a Higher Level of Abstraction in Business Process Management

Constantin Houy[1], Peter Fettke[1], Peter Loos[1],
Wil M.P. van der Aalst[2], and John Krogstie[3]

[1] Institute for Information Systems
at the German Research Center for Artificial Intelligence (DFKI)
Stuhlsatzenhausweg 3, Geb. D3 2
66123 Saarbrücken, Germany
{Constantin.Houy,Peter.Fettke,Peter.Loos}@iwi.dfki.de
[2] Department of Mathematics and Computer Science
Technische Universiteit Eindhoven (TUE)
Den Dolech 2
5612 AZ Eindhoven, Netherlands
w.m.p.v.d.aalst@tue.nl
[3] Department of Computer and Information Science
Norges Teknisk-Naturvitenskapelige Universitet (NTNU)
Hogskoleringen 1
7491 Trondheim, Norway
krogstie@idi.ntnu.no

Abstract. Business Process Management (BPM) has gained tremendous importance in recent years and BPM technologies and techniques are widely applied in practice. Furthermore there is a growing and very active research community looking at process modeling and analysis, reference models, workflow flexibility, process mining and process-centric Service-Oriented Architectures (SOA). However, it is clear that existing approaches have problems dealing with the enormous challenges real-life BPM projects are facing. Large organizations have hundreds of processes in place. These processes are often poorly documented and the relationships between them are not made explicit. Conventional BPM research seems to focus on situations with just a few isolated processes while in reality the real challenge is to cope with large collections of interconnected processes. Moreover, new technologies such as ubiquitous computing (sensor technologies, mobile devices, RFID tagging etc.) and pervasive networks (cf. "internet of things") generate enormous volumes of event data. Organizations have problems handling and using such data. Event data is scattered over various subsystems and not used well. This paper coins the term "BPM-in-the-Large" to describe the above situation and describes challenges and opportunities for BPM research.

Keywords: Business Process Management, BPM-in-the-Large, abstraction, complexity, Programming-in-the-Large.

M. Janssen et al. (Eds.): EGES/GISP 2010, IFIP AICT 334, pp. 233–244, 2010.
© Springer-Verlag Berlin Heidelberg 2010

1   Introduction

Business Process Management (BPM) has gained tremendous importance in the last decade and is increasingly used by organizations around the world [1]. The usage of information and communication technology (ICT) in order to manage business processes in companies and administrations has gained more and more importance in recent years [2]. BPM is characterized by a cross-fertilization of results from management science and computer science. Adequate techniques and software tools supporting the design, enactment, control as well as the analysis of operational business processes are already applied in businesses in order to facilitate an optimized value creation [3].

However, it is clear that existing approaches have problems dealing with the enormous challenges real-life BPM projects are facing. Large organizations have hundreds of processes in place. These processes are often poorly documented and the relationships between them are not made explicit. The amount of different process types which are characteristic for large enterprises are documented by well-established reference process models like Scheer's Reference Model for Industrial Enterprises [4] as well as the SAP reference model. As comprehensive and inter-corporate value chain networks keep gaining importance and as new possibilities of managing business processes have emerged on the basis of newer technologies – like mobile communication or ubiquitous computing technologies – the complexity of business processes has increased in recent years. Conventional BPM research seems to focus on situations with just a few isolated processes while in reality the real challenge is to cope with large collections of interconnected processes. In the future existing techniques and tools for BPM will not suffice to handle this ever increasing complexity.

In the following we argue for the need of new methods and technologies in BPM for the handling of the complexity mentioned ("BPM-in-the-Large"). A first overview of challenges and opportunities will be given based on conceptual consideration. Our contribution is structured as follows: In Section 2 the underlying understanding of BPM is introduced. Section 3 expatiates upon the reasons for the increasing complexity in BPM. Section 4 introduces BPM-in-the-Large as a new level of abstraction before Section 5 presents resulting challenges as well as the opportunities of BPM research. Section 6 focuses on the role of process mining in BPM-in-the-Large. Section 7 concludes the paper.

2   Business Process Management Framework

In general BPM comprises a management principle which companies apply in order to sustain their competitive advantage [5]. It focuses on business processes as a sequence of executions in a business context based on the purpose of creating goods and services [6]. There are two basic approaches to BPM and process improvement: (1) Business Process Reengineering as a radical redesign of business processes by a singular transformation [7] and (2) evolutionary improvement of business processes by continuous transformation. Today the latter is certainly of more importance for practical BPM efforts [8]. This continuous improvement approach is typically

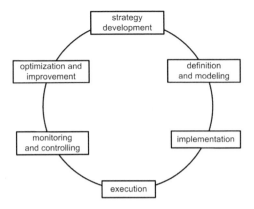

Fig. 1. BPM Life Cycle for continuous process improvement

conceptualized by a BPM Life Cycle [9] which will be used as a reference framework for the description of opportunities of BPM-in-the-Large.

3 Reasons for Increased Complexity

As emerging technologies permit new ICT system architectures, new and promising opportunities in the context of BPM arise. Based on globalization trends, new challenges pop up, particularly when multi-national companies need to coordinate their local business units in order to serve other multi-national companies in an integrated fashion. In an earlier reported case of a certification company [10, 11], there was a need to standardise the processes of the company's national branches in order to build a common image of the organization, and to support the certification of the cross-national processes of their multi-national customers, but at the same time adhere to national and cultural rules and expectations.

In such a context the integration of common technologies like mobile devices, techniques from the ubiquitous computing context, so called smart environments as well as the increasing use of sensor network technologies for the collection of process-relevant data and the application of service-oriented architectures (SOA) as well as Web 2.0 technologies can improve the flexibility of inter-corporate BPM [12] and thus increase the effectiveness and efficiency of business processes in inter-corporate value chain networks. Furthermore the options of action for human actors involved increase. Figure 2 illustrates a collaborative scenario in a value chain network applying the technologies mentioned. Scenarios like these are not only of importance in business, but also in the public administration area as described in the last EU Ministerial Declaration on eGovernment [13] which emphasizes the special need to develop and improve cross-border eGovernment services, making it easier for businesses and citizens to operate in and across any EU-member state.

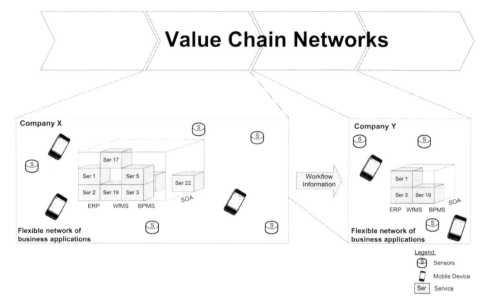

Fig. 2. Collaborative scenario in Value Chain Networks

The above scenario shows four important *trends*:

1. processes are *increasingly interconnected* and it makes no sense to look at a single process in isolation,
2. the *number of processes* an organization has to cope with *is rapidly increasing* (large organizations have hundreds of processes which need to be managed),
3. modern technology is generating unprecedented streams of event data representing the states of different processes (sensor data, RFID data, remote logging, remote services etc.) and
4. different devices are used to access the BPM System (BPMS) in different situations necessitating a flexible multi-channel support influencing which parts of the workflow are available in which manner depending on the context of use.

Based on these trends and the application of the mentioned technologies on the one hand the enterprises' agility and the handling of more and more dynamic business conditions can be improved. On the other hand Business Process Management becomes more and more complex. The *reasons for this complexity* are manifold:

1. the range of inter-corporate collaborative business processes,
2. the number of organizational units involved in a business process,
3. the need to manage and control mobile actors in business processes,
4. the need to control person-machine and machine-machine interactions,
5. the interdependencies in sensor networks, and
6. the need to manage services in a business process applying SOA etc.

The handling of this complexity which is generated by many thousands of process types, process instances and process events is a new challenge in BPM.

4 BPM-in-the-Large as a New Level of Abstraction

The study and development of accurate abstractions of relevant objects is a fundamental issue in computer science. So far business processes have been considered the highest level of abstraction in the context of information systems. This has been considered in the following figure illustrating a taxonomy of levels of abstraction within an information system based on Denning [14]. In Denning's original model business processes represent the highest level of abstraction which has to be managed by information system infrastructures. Still today business processes are being managed by distributed information system infrastructures applying different data processing units ("multimachine level"). Based on the presented facts a new level of abstraction needs to be introduced. The illustration has been expanded by a new level of management and which we entitle "BPM-in-the-Large" according to DeRemer/Kron's "Programming-In-The-Large" [15]. We think that the situation in BPM is quite similar to the situation in programming in 1975. BPM-in-the-Large (as opposed to "BPM-in-the-Small") can be understood by looking at the characteristics mentioned earlier: highly interconnected scenarios, hundreds of processes, large data streams and the usage of diverse devices within the BPMS.

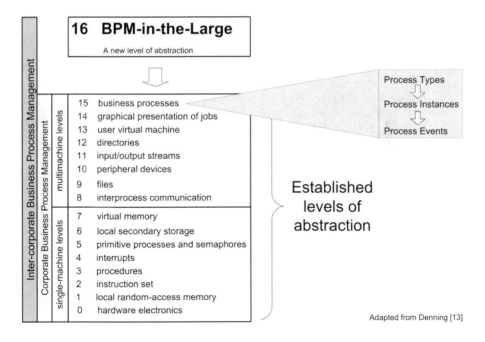

Fig. 3. Levels of abstraction within a business process-oriented information system

5   Challenges and Opportunities of BPM-in-the-Large

Based on the introduced phases of the BPM Life Cycle the various challenges and opportunities of BPM-in-the-Large are presented in the following.

Strategy development
On the level of strategy development BPM-in-the-Large can offer an improved overview and steering of comprehensive value creation networks by providing large scale process models and process-relevant data collected from Enterprise Resource Planning (ERP) Systems, Workflow Management Systems (WfMS) and lower scale BPMS. Important structures of collaborative processes can thus be controlled effectively, an improved development of the further process strategy is rendered possible and the full strategic potentials can be tapped.

The application of analytical concepts based on the data provided by different applications such as business process mining can make an important contribution to the strategy development as well. In connection with sensor networks and mobile devices the integration of analytical concepts like business process mining supports the identification of strategically important process structures from existing data by identifying patterns within this data [16].

Definition and Modeling
Managing business process models is one of the crucial points in BPM and in BPM-in-the-Large as well. Available experience in the application of business process models shows the considerable complexity of the definition and design of original business process models and the maintenance of existing ones [17]. Reasons for this complexity are:

1. the size and extensiveness of applied process models in practice,
2. the collaborative design and maintenance of process models and
3. the different usage areas of models by different stakeholders at different times [11], combined with the manifold of modifications of these models during their life cycle in the context of continuous improvement.

In order to manage the complexity mentioned, BPM-in-the-Large should integrate tools for improved collaborative business process modeling. Furthermore the support of automatic or semi-automatic discovery of complex process models and their modifications during the life cycle from event log files by advanced methods of business process mining [18] can make a substantial contribution to a successful management of business process models.

Another interesting aspect in this context is the retrieval of structural analogies in process models. Structural analogies express similarity of several model constructs and can thus be useful for the reduction of complexity by providing "common parts" of business process models [19]. Thus a once implemented module of a business process model can be used multiple times. Data provided by sensors and mobile devices offers important context information which supports not only the discovery of structural patterns, but also semantic subtleties in this context. Thus the quality of business process models and their management can effectively be enhanced. Capable methods of assessing and improving the quality of important processes support the entire following BPM Life Cycle and using these methods in BPM-in-the-Large supports a comprehensive and effective handling of business process models.

Implementation

BPM-in-the-Large should enable an optimal implementation of comprehensive inter-corporate business processes. Thus an improved inter-corporate communication is of importance. In this context, Web 2.0 technologies like Wikis, Blogs and Social Bookmarking etc. as an extension of approaches of interactive process modeling [20] can support the improvement of business process-related communication of cooperative partners [12].

Furthermore, according to defined and modelled processes the quality of models and their implementation have to be assured. As a high quality of process models is generally considered to influence the success of a company the improvement of process model quality and the quality of their implementation is of high importance.

Although the quality of models in general can be analysed as the interplay of quality at different levels (physical, empirical, syntactic, semantic, pragmatic, social, organizational [21]), existing approaches for the measurement of process model quality have not been defined consistently [22]. For BPM-in-the-Large the measurement of process model quality is therefore of high importance. Adequate instruments for the measurement of model quality support a distinctive effectiveness of business process models and their implementations on business success. The following questions are of specific importance for process model quality: (1) Does the model describe what was intended (organizational quality)?, (2) Is the model understandable (pragmatic quality)?, (3) Is the model internally consistent (e.g. absence of deadlocks) (an aspect of semantic quality)? and (4) Does the model conform to reality (semantic quality)? The latter point can be addressed using conformance checking techniques that compare the behaviour observed and recorded in event logs with the model [23]. Furthermore, the implementation of process models can be facilitated by the adequate configuration of promising "common parts" extracted in the preceding phase. It has to be noted that the need for federated process models in order to address variants of models across different cultures often makes this a difficult problem. A good sales process in India for instance will be different than the sales process in Europe or US even if the goal of the process is the same [10].

Execution

In the execution context BPM-in-the-Large envisions a wide-ranging workflow functionality which has to be adapted for comprehensive cooperative business processes in order to support an optimal execution of process instances according to the collaboratively defined process models in value creation networks. In this context the interoperability of the workflow management components has to be assured. A realization can be assured by using SOA for the implementation of the workflow components.

Monitoring and Controlling

Also in the context of monitoring and controlling of business processes BPM-in-the-Large provides an enormous potential in comparison to established BPMS. In connection with further information provided by different distributed data sources which collect process-relevant information, business process instances and anomalies during their execution can be controlled and identified more effectively. Relevant data is provided by the plethora of sensors and mobile devices. These data allow for a more comprehensive monitoring and analysis of business process instances. By utilizing this opportunity, the optimization and improvement phase which addresses process types can be better supported. Using process mining methods in this phase can furthermore support the deduction and construction of reference process models based on successfully executed process instances. Reference models play an important role in the context of successful business engineering [24].

Optimization and Improvement
The actually measured performance of business processes forms the basis for improvement initiatives and for the development of new process structures which can improve the performance of future process instances. In this context the developed quality and performance measures provide the basis for comprehensive and effective comparisons. Moreover, the identification of structural analogies provided by the application of business process mining techniques supports the improvement and the further development of process models applied in the organisation. Figure 4 summarizes these findings.

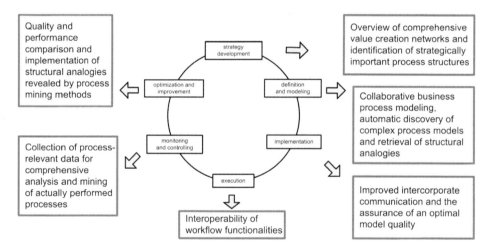

Fig. 4. BPM Life Cycle supported with BPM-in-the-Large

6   Process Mining as a Driver for BPM-in-the-Large

The importance of having short feedback-loops from actual process performance to future process support has been acknowledged for some time in areas such as emergent and interactive process support [21] and active knowledge modeling [25]. However, these techniques are appropriate mostly for knowledge intensive tasks with relatively few processes and few stakeholders involved, with primarily manual support for process knowledge management [26]. Therefore, we consider automated analysis based on event data. In the previous section there were several references to the use of process mining technology to support the various phases. Therefore, we now describe the state-of-the-art in process mining and position this work in BPM-in-the-Large.

More and more information about (business) processes is recorded by information systems in the form of so-called "event logs". IT systems are becoming more and more intertwined with these processes, resulting in an "explosion" of available data that can be used for analysis purposes. Process mining techniques attempt to extract non-trivial and useful information from event logs. One aspect of process mining is *control-flow discovery*, i.e., automatically constructing a process model (e.g., a Petri net or BPMN model) describing the causal dependencies between activities. The basic idea of control-flow discovery is very simple: given an event log containing a set of traces, these traces are used to automatically construct a suitable process model describing the behavior seen in the log. Such discovered processes have proven to be very useful for the understanding, redesign, and continuous improvement of business processes [27].

Process mining is not limited to control-flow discovery. First of all, besides the *control-flow perspective* ("How?"), other perspectives such as the *organizational perspective* ("Who?") and the *case/data perspective* ("What?") may be considered.

Second, process mining is not restricted to *discovery*. There may be existing models that can be related to the event logs. For example, process mining can be used to analyze deviations from some normative model (e.g. *conformance checking* as discussed in [23]), thus enabling auditing functionality.

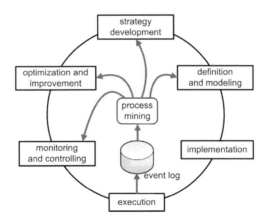

Fig. 5. Process mining positioned in the BPM Life Cycle

Figure 5 shows the central role of process mining in the BPM Life Cycle. It is used as input for four of the six phases. To conclude this section of process mining we focus on *two challenges* related to BPM-in-the-large and process mining.

The first challenge is related to difficulties in making process models which are understandable and correct in the presence of massive amounts of activities and (sub-) processes. Here we make the analogy to cartography. The first geographical maps date back to the 7th Millennium BC. Since then cartographers have improved their skills and techniques to create maps thereby addressing problems such as clearly representing desired traits, eliminating irrelevant details, reducing complexity, and improving understandability. Today, geographic maps are digital and of high quality. This has fueled innovative applications of cartography as is illustrated by modern car navigation systems (e.g. TomTom, Garmin, etc.), Google maps, Google Street View, Mash ups using geo-tagging, etc. People can seamlessly zoom in and out using the interactive maps in such systems. Moreover, all kinds of information can be projected on these interactive maps (e.g., traffic jams, four-bedroom apartments for sale, etc.). Process models can be seen as the "maps" describing the operational processes of organizations. Unfortunately, *accurate and interactive process maps are typically missing when it comes to BPM*. The challenge is to reach the same level of maturity for "business process maps". This is one of the grand challenges in process mining; how to automatically generate models which are well-understood, correct, and showing dynamic information. Furthermore new ways of visualizing the process knowledge have to be found [28].

The second challenge is related to the input data itself. BPM-in-the-large is characterized by a large number of processes and massive streams of event data. This requires a more systematic approach towards the collection and storage of event data. We use the term *business process provenance* to refer to the systematic collection of the information needed to reconstruct what has actually happened. The term signifies that for process mining it is vital that "history cannot be rewritten or obscured". For example, from an auditing point of view the systematic, reliable, and trustworthy recording of events is essential. Therefore, we propose to collect (whenever possible) provenance data outside of the operational information. This means that events need to be collected and stored persistently. Note that semantics play an important role here, i.e. *events need to refer to a commonly agreed-upon ontology*. Here we propose to use the *Semantically Annotated Mining XML* (SA-MXML) format developed in the context of the SUPER project [29]. This reflects that we would like to treat event data as a "first class citizen" in BPM-in-the-Large.

7   Conclusion

BPM-in-the-Large is of high relevance for both research and practice. The opportunities which can be offered by the implementation of BPM-in-the-Large are of the utmost importance for enterprises which aim at utilizing innovative information technology components and at rationally organizing these components in order to tap their full potential. By the usage of SOA and interchangeable components future BPM-in-the-Large implementations can be highly scalable and can thus be applied optimally in small and medium enterprises (SME) as well as in large multinationals and across governments.

Furthermore BPM-related topics gain more and more importance in IS research. The study of integration possibilities of mentioned technologies in BPM is of a very high interest as the field of research grows steadily and BPM has become a considerable trend in management as well as in computer science. The successful introduction of a higher level of abstraction can be seen as a useful and valuable challenge in BPM research.

BPM technology has been successfully implemented in many different organizations and has shown to directly influence the operational processes. Therefore, BPM-in-the-Large can have an enormous technological and economic impact. The effectiveness and efficiency, and thus the success of business processes will be enhanced by the application of BPM-in-the-Large across various industries. Furthermore, the scientific impact of the presented methods, e.g. systematically measuring process model quality and innovative process mining techniques, can be considerable, as these methods can support further innovation in practical BPM as well as BPM-related research.

Acknowledgements. The research described in this paper was supported in part by a grant from the German Federal Ministry of Education and Research (BMBF), project name: "Process-oriented Web-2.0-based Integrated Telecommunication Service (PROWIT)", support code FKZ 01BS0833.

References

1. Fettke, P.: How Conceptual Modeling Is Used. Communications of the AIS 25, 571–592 (2009)
2. ter Hofstede, A.H.M., van der Aalst, W.M.P., Adams, M., Russell, N. (eds.): Modern Business Process Automation: YAWL and its Support Environment. Springer, Berlin (2010)
3. van der Aalst, W.M.P., ter Hofstede, A.H.M., Weske, M.: Business Process Management: A Survey. In: van der Aalst, W.M.P., ter Hofstede, A.H.M., Weske, M. (eds.) BPM 2003. LNCS, vol. 2678, pp. 1–12. Springer, Heidelberg (2003)
4. Scheer, A.-W.: Business Process Engineering - Reference Models for Industrial Companies. Springer, Berlin (1994)
5. Hung, R.Y.: Business Process Management as Competitive Advantage: a Review and Empirical Study. Total Quality Management 17, 21–40 (2006)
6. Scheer, A.-W.: ARIS - Business Process Frameworks. Springer, Berlin (1999)
7. Hammer, M., Champy, J.: Reengineering the Corporation: A Manifesto for Business Revolution. Harper Business, New York (1993)
8. Weske, M.: Business Process Management: Concepts, Languages, Architectures. Springer, Berlin (2007)
9. Houy, C., Fettke, P., Loos, P.: Empirical Research in Business Process Management - Analysis of an emerging field of research. Business Process Management Journal 16 (2010) (accepted)
10. Krogstie, J., Dalberg, V., Jensen, S.M.: Harmonising Business Processes of Collaborative Networked Organisations Using Process Modelling. In: Virtual Enterprises and Collaborative Networks. IFIP, vol. 149, pp. 81–88. Springer, Boston (2004)
11. Krogstie, J., Dalberg, V., Jensen, S.M.: Process modeling value framework. In: Manolopoulos, Y., Filipe, J., Constantopoulos, P., Cordeiro, J. (eds.) ICEIS 2006. LNBIP, vol. 3, pp. 309–321. Springer, Heidelberg (2008)
12. Vanderhaeghen, D., Fettke, P., Loos, P.: Organizational and Technological Options for Business Process Management from the Perspective of Web 2.0 - Results of a Design Oriented Research Approach with Particular Consideration of Self-Organization and Collective Intelligence. Business & Information Systems Engineering 2, 15–28 (2010)

13. Ministerial Declaration on eGovernment, Malmø, Sweden, 5th Ministerial eGovernment Conference (2009)
14. Denning, P.J.: Work is a closed-loop process. American Scientist 80, 314–317 (1992)
15. DeRemer, F., Kron, H.: Programming-in-the large versus programming-in-the-small. In: Proceedings of the International Conference on Reliable Software, pp. 114–121. ACM, Los Angeles (1975)
16. Tiwari, A., Turner, C.J., Majeed, B.: A review of business process mining: state-of-the-art and future trends. Business Process Management Journal 14, 5–22 (2008)
17. Cardoso, J., Mendling, J., Neumann, G., Reijers, H.A.: A discourse on complexity of process models. In: Dustdar, S., Fiadeiro, J.L., Sheth, A.P. (eds.) BPM 2006. LNCS, vol. 4102, pp. 117–128. Springer, Heidelberg (2006)
18. van der Aalst, W.M.P., Weijters, A.J.M.M., Maruster, L.: Workflow mining: Discovering process models from event logs. IEEE Transactions on Knowledge and Data Engineering 16, 1128–1142 (2004)
19. Fettke, P., Loos, P.: Identifying Structural Analogies in Data Models - A Procedure and its Application Exemplified by Scheer's Y-CIM Reference Model. Wirtschaftsinformatik 47, 89–100 (2005)
20. Krogstie, J., Jørgensen, H.: Interactive Models for Supporting Networked Organisations. In: Persson, A., Stirna, J. (eds.) CAiSE 2004. LNCS, vol. 3084, pp. 550–563. Springer, Heidelberg (2004)
21. Krogstie, J., Sindre, G., Jørgensen, H.: Process Models as Knowledge for Action: A Revised Quality Framework. European Journal of Information Systems 15, 91–102 (2006)
22. Moody, D.L.: Theoretical and Practical Issues in Evaluating the Quality of Conceptual Models: Current State and Future Directions. Data & Knowledge Engineering 55, 243–276 (2005)
23. Rozinat, A., van der Aalst, W.M.P.: Conformance Checking of Processes Based on Monitoring Real Behavior. Information Systems 33, 64–95 (2008)
24. Fettke, P., Loos, P. (eds.): Reference Modeling for Business Systems Analysis. Idea Group, Hershey (2007)
25. Lillehagen, F., Krogstie, J.: Active Knowledge Modeling of Enterprises. Springer, Berlin (2008)
26. Jørgensen, H.D.: Interactive Process Models. PhD-thesis NTNU, Trondheim, Norway (2004)
27. van der Aalst, W.M.P., Reijers, H.A., Weijters, A.J.M.M., van Dongen, B.F., Alves de Medeiros, A.K., Song, M., Verbeek, H.M.W.: Business Process Mining: An Industrial Application. Information Systems 32, 713–732 (2007)
28. Nossum, A., Krogstie, J.: Integrated Quality of Models and Quality of Maps. In: Halpin, T., Krogstie, J., Nurcan, S., Proper, E., Schmidt, R., Soffer, P., Ukor, R. (eds.) EMMSAD 2009. LNBIP, vol. 29, pp. 264–276. Springer, Berlin (2009)
29. Alves de Medeiros, A.K., van der Aalst, W.M.P.: Process Mining towards Semantics. In: Dillon, T.S., Chang, E., Meersman, R., Sycara, K. (eds.) Advances in Web Semantics I. LNCS, vol. 4891, pp. 35–80. Springer, Heidelberg (2008)

When Global Process Fails: A Grounded Theory Study of a Case from Agile Engagement to Compulsive Outsourcing

Jan Pries-Heje, Magnus Hansen, and Sofia Bergbäck Knudsen

Roskilde University, Denmark
janph@ruc.dk, magnuha@ruc.dk, samb@ruc.dk

Abstract. In a Scandinavian company developing a healthcare information system (IS) at three Scandinavian sites they succeeded in taking agile processes into use across the three sites. After a fourth development site in India was added the use of agile development processes gradually came to an end and plan-driven processes took over. In this paper we report from a month-long study where our analysis of the case shows that the cause for giving up agile was three-fold: (1) The cultural distance between India and Scandinavia was too great. (2) There were telling differences in competence and (3) the presence of knowledge asymmetry. From this analysis we develop a grounded theory explaining the necessary preconditions for succeeding with a global process for agile IS development.

Keywords: Global Process, Agile Processes, Outsourcing, IS development.

1 Introduction

Information systems (IS) development typically unfolds as a process with stages such as analysis, design, coding and testing. Stages do not have to be carried out sequentially but can be done in parallel or iteratively. An IS development method is a prescribed process for carrying out development. The method description typically includes activities to be performed, artifacts resulting from the activities, plus some principles for organizing the activities including roles and responsibilities.

In the mid 1990s current IS development processes were typically effective in large-scale, long-term development efforts that employed stable and disciplined processes [1]. In contrast, many IS projects involved rapid changes in requirements and unpredictable product complexity. IS development approaches that achieves a balance between flexibility and disciplined method were needed [2-4] – so *agile processes* were born.

A comparative study [5] of the older traditional 'plan-driven' processes and agile processes found that IS developers in the 21st century environment in many cases adopted a considerably different set of agile practices from those associated with traditional IS development. The distinctive agile principles (those with no traditional counterpart) regard teamwork and on-the-fly software process adaptation, and they emphasize informal knowledge exchange, collaboration, and experience as important

M. Janssen et al. (Eds.): EGES/GISP 2010, IFIP AICT 334, pp. 245–258, 2010.

elements in IS development, and acknowledge more sensitivity to tailoring project practices to environmental conditions. These principles are essential for managing software projects in volatile settings where fast changing technologies and markets drive fast changing skills and knowledge.

Prominent examples of agile processes (methods) are XP (eXtreme Programming), Crystal and SCRUM. The major similarity between XP and SCRUM is the focus on close collaboration and shared experiences in order to achieve a successful developing cycle. However, this close collaboration with shared experiences is at risk when the SD team is expected to outsource part of the development process to cut costs. Interestingly enough, a recent quantitative study found that the use of agile practices like stand-up meetings in an outsourced development context where management located in the US and development in the Czech Republic was successful due to informal communication presented daily [6]. The question remains as to how agile processes fare against a team that has to share its knowledge with new developers working globally? Recent studies indicate a 'yes', when characteristics of agile and global are blended properly [7].

Outsourcing traditionally is the practice where an organization purchases goods or services ·that were previously provided internally [8]. Outsourcing involves the movement of specific tasks or entire processes to one or more outsourcing vendors, typically to a place where wages are lower [9]. Organizations have claimed that IS outsourcing reduces cost and time, increases quality and reliability of products and services, improves business performance, and releases organizations to concentrate on core competencies [9].

The traditional way of thinking outsourcing is a vendor/client-relationship, where the client organization to the greater part decides what and when the vendor organization should deliver and how the process should be carried out [10]. However, an increasing number of client organizations aim for a closer collaboration with the vendor organization. It causes IS development to take place in a *distributed environment* where a team of developers working on the same project are distributed at several locations, sometimes across larger geographical distances.

The distributed project team is heavily dependent on a developing method which can support communicating and coordinating their daily work tasks [11]. The challenge in this is to be able to share knowledge and experiences through computer mediated communication-channels, a collaboration method that has proven less successful than working in collocated projects [12]. A suggestion is to use practices such as synchronizing head milestones, frequent deliveries, use of peer-to-peer communication links, problem solving practices, information- and monitoring practices and client/vendor-relationship building practices [13, 14].

These distributed team best practices are much alike those practices argued for in agile processes. Moore and Barnett (2004) found that labor gains from outsourcing combined with agile development practices can lead to lower overall costs along with a project team that can address a high rate of change [15]. A McKinsey study even shows a saving of 58 cents is achieved for every dollar mainly on wages, and further concludes "that offshore services are identical to those they replace ..." [9, 16].

Can agile processes be the answer in achieving a successful distributed IS developing team? If we turn to scholars like Cramton [17], Olsen [12] and Cockburn [18], agile processes in a distributed environment is dismissed because of the lack of face-to-face-communication due to the large proximity between team members. However, drawing on conclusions from Kiesler & Cummings [19], we seek out to investigate the antecedents of distributed IS developing in an agile setting so the work is not constrained to the effects of lack of face-to-face communication only.

This leads to the following related research question: *Why is it difficult to get agile processes to work in a distributed environment?*

The remainder of the paper is structured as follows. First we present our research method and then our case and our case analysis. Third we discuss our findings with an emphasis on the changes that outsourcing and distributed IS development caused. Finally, we use our findings to develop a theory on what makes the use of agile processes difficult.

2   Research Method

To answer our research question we decided to use a single-case study. The main reason being that case studies is a useful way of exploring unknown phenomena based on "why" and "how" research questions [20].

The case study was conducted using semi-structured interviews and participatory observations of the team's stand-up meetings over a course of three months around New Year 2008-09. In the beginning we observed the ending of one project iteration – observing the last stand-up meetings in that iteration. In the end of our case study we observed the beginning of a new project iteration aiming for a new project goal.

The reason for choosing to observe stand-up meetings was because this was an important daily communicative event where most team members took part in the ongoing communication and coordination of the daily work. It was also a unique opportunity for us to observe how agile principles were implemented in a particular context based on globally distributed worksites. We characterized the use of agile principles by using a theoretical framework by Conboy & Fitzgerald [21] of how successful agile teams respond to a variety of types and sources of change [21]: Over time the cost of defining and fulfilling changes decreases as the learning process of the team as a whole increases. From this definition we were able to compare the team's reluctance and enthusiasm towards delegating different type of tasks with different change requests to the developers over time.

We mixed the data collection processes to obtain different insights as to how the participants contemplated themselves and others (during interviews) and how they positioned themselves and others in a social context (during observations) [22]. We interviewed team members who themselves volunteered to participate in the study. This resulted in 11 interviews and six observed stand-up meetings. Observations were transcribed and recorded. Afterwards we made very thoroughly written summaries of the interviews.

In analyzing and reducing the data we listed important passages and quotes from the interviews as well as the observations and transcribed these in further detail. Our method of coding the data were based on categories identified through a literature study of distributed teams and agile development in outsourcing. As we perceive IS development as a social act with for example formal and informal power plays we used discourse analysis in order to understand how the participants in the software team individually made sense and applied meaning to concepts, words and work structures. In the concrete we used the concepts of inter-textual and inter-discursive references in both interviews and observations to interpret how the participants made and remade values, norms and meaning to their respective work practices [23].

After having analyzed the data we decided to apply some coding procedures from Grounded Theory (GT) to develop a theory. Barney Glaser and Anselm Strauss originally developed GT [24, 25] as an inherently flexible methodology in which the researcher "should simply code and analyze categories and properties with theoretical codes which will emerge and generate their complex theory of a complex world" [26]. Glaser also makes theory generation versus theory verification the core theme of GT. As an alternative to this Strauss' version of GT emphasizes things like replicability, validation, and verification as important parts of conducting GT research. Use of GT in IS research is exemplified by a landmark paper by Orlikowski [27] on CASE tools and organizational change, over explorations on software requirements [28, 29], to a more recent study from Denmark of how the Internet is redefining information systems development methodology [30].

In the research reported in this paper we use the GT school of thought developed by Strauss [31]. According to Straus and Corbin [31], analysis in a grounded theory approach is composed of three groups of coding procedures called open, axial and selective coding. However, we only used the last third of these coding procedures called selective coding.

Selective coding involves the integration of the categories that have been developed to form the initial theoretical framework. Firstly, in selective coding, a story line is either generated or made explicit. A story is simply a descriptive narrative about the central phenomenon of study and the story line is the conceptualization of this story (abstracting). When analyzed, the story line becomes the core category, which is related to all the categories found earlier (as explained above), validating these relationships, and elaborating the categories that need further refinement and development.

3   Scandinavian IT Company Case

To answer our research question we selected a larger Scandinavian IT company which offers IT consultancy as well as development of their own IT solutions within a broad range of areas. The company has 16,000 employees primarily in Europe, and has a long tradition of virtual collaboration across geographical distances. In the concrete we were able to obtain access to the company via a healthcare IT project.

The particular project team which we examine in this case is developing a module to an Electronic Patient Journal-system with the scope of documenting patient treatment and care in a Swedish hospital. The team consists of seven developers, two software testers, a systems architect and a project manager. They are one of two teams developing the system and are nearing their first delivery phase in the middle of December 2008 and are about to start a new phase when we leave the team in January 2009.

Like the company in general, this team consists of co-workers spread out over several worksites in Sweden, Denmark and Norway. The majority of the team's software developers work in Malmö, Sweden. The *director of development* is in charge of several projects throughout Scandinavia: He works from Copenhagen, Denmark. The *project manager* who works from Oslo, Norway, participates in the daily telephone meetings held by the project team and tries to visit the Malmö office once a month. The daily telephone meetings (called stand up-meetings) are managed by the *project coordinator*, who has a professional background as a nurse and also functions as the team's product quality tester and domain expert.

Phase 0: Very early in the life-cycle of the project a plan-driven [32] waterfall-like software development method was used. However, this method in combination with the distributed work environment having three Scandinavian sites generated a lot of severe problems for the project such as missed deadlines and a product with unacceptable (low) quality. Thus the project was in need of a dramatic change in both management and development method and a decision of trying out agile method was taken. This turned out to be a successful move.

Phase 1: The project team switched from a plan-driven software development process to communicating and coordinating their daily work and tasks according to agile processes, thus turning a failing course of action into a successful project. They were now delivering software on schedule and with acceptable quality.

Phase 2: Top management in the company of course took notice of the now successful project that was working across three different sites (Malmö, Oslo and Copenhagen). Based on the team's success the director of development decided to try and integrate offshore outsourcing by adding two Indian developers to the team employed by an Indian subsidiary company working from India. The rationale behind this decision was partly the success in doing work across different sites and partly a company strategy aiming for cost savings through offshore outsourcing (to India).

Thus when going from phase 1 to phase 2 the team started to experience problems. Our data collection and analysis will focus here.

4 Case Analysis

Story Phase 0: From Plan-Driven Chaos to Agile Success

The project team's original work method of plan-driven development [32] in combination with distributed work environment posed a number of severe problems for the project team, which ultimately created an urgent need for change. The developers from the project team felt lost in the overall process. The work climate was stressful work and deadlines were chaotic and often overdue. The result was a system with a design and quality which wasn't acceptable to either the team or the customer. The project manager worked from another location than the other team members and had only met the whole team once. Project management concentrated on creating work breakdown structures, estimates and deadlines, which the project team then time after time failed to meet.

"So we needed to deliver, she (the PM) throttled on and wanted estimates from everybody, estimates, estimates, estimates. And she promised to deliver before Christmas 2007."

The result being a severe breakdown in trust towards the project manager's methods, competence and ability; something had to be done. Thus a new project manager was hired and suggested trying out agile processes.

Story Phase 1: The Use of Agile Processes in Distributed Collaboration is a Success.

The IT company in general as well as the specific project team was used to working virtually, collaborating over geographical distances, linking several worksites together. In spite of this, the project team decided to try to work with an agile development method in their daily work. The way of working chosen was inspired by eXtreme Programming - XP [33, 34] and SCRUM [35]. Even though this type of software development approaches usually prescribes close collaboration and face-to-face-communication as an essential part of the procedure, the project team succeeded in finding alternative ways of communicating and coordinating daily work.

> *PM: "We have pretty good communication, meetings, mails and such. [...] I am supported and collaborating closely with Britt. (the project coordinator)."*

One of the alternative ways of making sure that all team members take part in the development process is to engage in stand up-meetings. Due to the team's distributed work environment where many of the coworkers sometimes are elsewhere (at the customer's supporting or training the it-staff or end-users or simply working from home), they have to transform physical boundary objects [36, 37] used as help tools into digital form and also engage in virtual communication on the stand up-meetings using telephone conference calls with shared desktop. The boundary objects now used are a spreadsheet called a "Cookbook" that contains stories (short specification requirements), a spreadsheet called a "Bank" with finished stories, and the stand up-meetings which play the role of verbalizing and constituting specifications and task assignments.

In fact, the team experienced an increase of productivity and handling of changes after they introduced function points to their stories and as their use of agile processes increased. Overall the team releases better post-release quality shown by customer satisfaction and quicker handling of change requests, even though they often work distributed and have limited possibilities for meeting and working together at the same worksite. This higher productivity in the shift to agile methods coincides with findings from Layman et al. [6] and Fitzgerald et al. [38].

Story Phase 2: Offshore Outsourcing Leads to Breakdown – the Agile Method Fails

Being so used to working distributed, one would think that a single site more or less would not have any major impact on the project team's successful use of an agile method. However, this was not the case. After introducing developers into the team that were working for the Indian subsidiary company from their Indian office, the agile working process gradually broke down. Right after the decision was made to include offshore outsourcing it was known from company experience that socializing into the team was important. Thus two Indian developers are sent on a 2-3 month introduction at the Swedish development site where the majority of the developers work in order to get to know the work environment, the work domain, the work processes, the various aspects of the system, and last but not least their Swedish colleagues in person.

The stand up-meetings works well while the Indian developers are at the Swedish site but when they return to the site in India after their introduction, the team experiences a significant change in productivity, participation and communication from their Indian counterparts.

"Here we have a decline in our function point production. I don't know why, perhaps it's the introduction of the site in Pune?"

The project coordinator tells us about some work tasks which are given to the Indian developers that turn out completely wrong according to what the Swedish site intended. However, she is aware of the difficulties that communication over great geographical distances may cause:

"There are probably a thousand ways of interpreting these kinds of things when you're at the other end of the line. You don't get this ... ping-pong as we call it, when you ask questions and get an answer and then you ask new questions, and then you ask away until you understand how things are. You just don't get that."

This is one of the major challenges in global software development in general and especially for teams working with agile processes, where the close collaboration is dependent on the frequent communication and face-to-face communication is recommended to achieve this. It appears in examining this case study's project team that the step from working distributed across worksites in Scandinavia to working across worksites with greater geographical (and cultural) distances is too large. The concept of communication in this regard is however of great importance. It is peculiar how the type of communication which the project coordinator describes coincides with that which a traditional plan-driven requirements specification method would prescribe.

The Indian developers also remain mostly silent at the daily meetings and are instead engaged in forced communication by the Swedish developers and the stand up-coordinator. This tips power and control in the Scandinavian team's favor and goes against the vision of collaborating closely as one team. We observed stand-up meetings and saw examples of the Indian co-workers getting work tasks appointed to them by the Swedish team members rather than themselves suggesting what they could work on during the workday. This more and more resembles a plan-driven way of communicating and goes against an agile vision of close collaboration as well as the idea that everybody in the team are peers at the same level [35]. Instead it makes it difficult for the Indian developers to understand their work tasks because the team creates a discourse of authority and leadership where questions asked result in more time spent. In continuation of this it becomes a barrier which prohibits the Indian developers in gaining further knowledge of the system and its context because the typical discourse is that the flow of communication and information moves from the Swedish sites to the Indian site. One of the Swedish developers is already aware of this, because it can not possibly be a fulfilling work situation for the Indian developers:

"To sit that far away and not getting everything explained properly, that can't be fun. They are really nice and well-educated boys, so... I think they could get something else, with better working terms."

There are also technical difficulties to overcome as the Indian developers do not use the boundary objects given at their own initiative and sometimes they are not granted access to test environments, databases and even shared screen at the meetings which the rest of the team members always can and do use. There may be a number of reasons for this happening. A Scandinavian developer, who recently had been posted at the Indian worksite for a couple of months, during this time also participating in the stand up-meeting from India, told us that it was difficult to hear the Scandinavian colleagues over the phone, and some of the Swedish co-workers were downright impossible to understand. However, these technical difficulties were not at any time brought up and to attention by the Indian co-workers: Most likely because of the discourse of authority which was being enacted at the meetings. The team members working from India might also have misunderstood or missed out on the information that the content of a certain stand up-meeting would require a shared screen in order to execute the meeting in an effective way. It might also be a combination of misunderstanding or underestimating the work task itself which leads to the Indian developers not being able to evaluate what type of boundary objects they need in order to be able to discuss work tasks at a stand-up meeting in a sufficient and comprehensive way. As a result the gap between Indian and Scandinavian co-workers' knowledge and experience with the systems and its domain grows even wider. This also contributes to the lack of knowledge from the Swedish team about the context of the Indian work site which the Swedish developers realize far too late in the development process.

The project coordinator thinks of the interaction and socialization which naturally takes place at a worksite as one of the factors which might put strains on the communication and coordinating across globally distributed worksites:

"Just think of the amount of information we swop with each other here every day, which isn't... it's just sort of ad hoc. A comment, a question. They (Indian developers) get nothing of that."

As a result of all this there is an unevenly distributed amount of information available for the two work-sites and has a negative, and sometimes even destructive, impact on communication and coordination within the team as a whole. The co-workers in Scandinavia are caught in a difficult work situation where they end up using a lot of time explaining and elaborating work tasks for their Indian co-workers, thus limiting the time they spend on their own work. In some situations they even end up choosing whether they should execute certain work tasks themselves rather than letting the Indian developers try to do it, knowing that the latter option will cost a lot more in terms of time and effort from both sides:

"Interviewer: So it takes the same amount of time for Peter to explain how to solves this task?

Project coordinator: It takes longer time.Interviewer: Maybe even longer time?

Project coordinator: He (Peter) says, this would take me a quarter of an hour to solve, and he (Indian developer) had estimated 14 hours to do this task."

There are several obvious problems in this: Skilled programmers using their time and effort working as communicators and teachers, trying to get co-workers to do some work that they easily could have done themselves. This becomes problematic when resources are not distributed for this purpose. Further there may be potential conflict lying in the fact that it was top management that decided – with a business strategic rationale in mind - to add Indian offshore outsourcing resources to the project (going from phase 1 to phase 2); and maybe the developers themselves never accepted this kind of (changed) work situation and the asymmetry in power between the two groups was facilitated even before they began their collaboration.

There is also the problem of the Indian co-workers never getting a fair chance of learning and understanding the system they work on, as well as its context and domain. If they only get uncritical and sometimes boring tasks to carry out, they will never overcome the skills and knowledge gap between themselves and their Scandinavian colleagues. This renders them in an unfortunate dependency situation where they are dependent on the good will and help from the Scandinavian team members all the time to be able to perform their work, ultimately wasting a lot of time and resources which could have been used instead of sitting idle and wait. It is important to note that the dependency relationship between the work sites in the project team does not go both ways. The Scandinavian team members do not need their Indian colleagues to function in the same way as the Indian team members do. Needless to say, this is not a good platform to build an agile global software developing project team on.

5 Discussion

When we phrased our research question "why is it difficult to get agile processes to work in a distributed environment?", many readers may have thought: That is just because they are not sitting face-to-face! However, as we have explained above agile processes worked very well in a distributed environment with three Scandinavian sites and we aimed at expanding this theory to the antecedents of the distributed environment. Developers at these three sites were obviously not sitting face-to-face. Thus we carried on our analysis digging behind the face-to-face answers.

Based on the story of our analysis, three primary issues emerge that indicate the challenges agile teams must face: (1) the cultural distance after splitting the team is reinforced by the physical distance, in spite of the team meeting virtually through conference calls, (2) different levels of expertise, skills and experience become more obvious due to the limited communication channels available, (3) knowledge asymmetries between both teams where the Indian worksite depends on the communication, information and knowledge of the Scandinavian sites.

The three issues we found were all constituted and reinforced by the way the team communicated at the stand-up-meetings and also from the emerging deadline which drew nearer as time passed.

The list is by far exhaustive but merely represents the empirical findings of our actual case.

One of the reasons this happened was due to an uneven level of domain knowledge which was not properly constituted during the introduction period and as a result of uneven socialization throughout the process which was a result of the geographical distance between the two major work sites. Drawing on power theory from Fairclough, we can characterize the underlying power that the Scandinavian team exerted over the Indian site as a result of this uneven socialization and domain knowledge which was reinforced through their daily interaction [39].

The findings regarding distance and salience of information leading to different interpretations are very similar to the findings of Cramton [17]. Although Cramton studied chats used in study groups with no significant 'developing process' we saw that many of the same problems arose in our study. After some time in the development process, the Scandinavian developers simply had to put their trust in the Indian developers' understanding of the information shared on the stand-up-meetings as the primary means of feedback was the actual software product that the Indian coworkers had to develop.

Our case is an example of distance vs. agile tools that really benefit the most from physical presence. The situation is that we now have available the means of communicating and coordinating technology. However, we have yet to provide an easy way (and even more important, a cheap way) of interacting physically over geographical distances. As a result of this, we saw a reinforcement of the specific work processes and enactments towards one another as time went by that became more or less destructive towards the agile vision of working together as one team.

So far we have mostly seen empirical findings from teams that have implemented agile processes on-the-fly pragmatically and with good reason. The problem of standardizing agile processes is of great importance in this paper, as the theory of agile methodologies often does not resemble the actual work in which they are practiced because of the need of implementing changes [7, 40].

Problems maintaining strict guidelines of agile processes also correlate to the conclusions of Agerfalk [41] where no true answer concerning the performance of agile processes is given. It is even suggested that the hitherto 'pragmatic' method of implementing the agile principles should be discarded completely in favor of adapting the agile processes in their entirety in order to benefit properly from them [41].

David L. Parnas (cited in Agerfalk [41]) simplifies the problem of software development at its core: the problems in software development are not new and the solutions are not agile processes. In our case we saw a classic scapegoat: a belief that it was the communication as a whole that was at fault, since this was obviously the problem and the solution of the development team in the first fiasco project. However, as we dug deeper, we saw that this was not only so. Communication was definitely a problem but not the final and foremost reason for the problems. Instead, communication can be seen as symptoms of other, more physically and deeply grounded problems; cultural distance, difference in experience and expertise of the developers and in the end resulting in an unevenly distributed amount of information resulting in dependency issues from and a change in power leading to a more plan-driven offshore outsourcing strategy.

Indeed, we believe that our study supports the point towards the *potential* benefits of agile offshore outsourcing. Just like the potential benefits of offshore outsourcing were financially grounded in the beginning of the 90's and still not realized to its full extent, the potential benefits of working globally agile are flexibility and speed. The problem is that uneven socialization combined with distance between work sites pose a major difficulty for agile processes because socialization is a prerequisite for successful close collaboration. It is inevitable that each worksite develops and enacts their own social behavior and patterns, resulting in each worksite socializing more with each other internally than with their distributed colleagues.

We argue that this vision of close collaboration poses difficulties so strong that it is not economically feasible. Having two software teams with dedicated project management each would in our case have been more feasible and would most likely prohibit a lot of the 'communication scapegoating' we saw during our study. It could also have prohibited the power asymmetry which was present from the beginning.

Customer location is also a significant issue that must be taken care of through close collaboration and communication in agile methodologies but are very difficult to establish in a distributed environment. One of the primary problems of integrating agile processes in a globally distributed environment is the role and location of the actual customer and end-users and this is a factor which one must not underestimate although a distributed work environment a priori contains challenges of close customer collaboration in the first place.

This finally brings up another issue of the discussion regarding what kind of product is being developed concerning requirements regarding customer's needs and demands. Would an off-the-shelf product be more suited for agile distributed software development? "What are we developing" and "who is the customer" should therefore be trivial yet important questions to ask before, during and after engaging in global software development using agile processes.

6 Conclusion

Using the three categories of observations from the discussion we used grounded theory selective coding (as we explained in the research method section) to derive a theory. It says:

The use of agile processes is made difficult by cultural distance, differences in competencies and knowledge asymmetry. Furthermore cultural distance and differences in competencies will in itself influence the development of knowledge asymmetry. If cultural distance, differences in competencies and knowledge asymmetry becomes too great it will make the use of agile processes impossible.

Our theory is also shown in figure 1. We have *saturated* the theory [26] using all the data available; this means making sure that nothing in our data contradicts the theory (core story) and that no major observation is not explained in the theory.

Cultural distance was derived through the team participants' stories of different interpretations of meaning in their communication or in their lack there of. The cultural difficulties in this instance are also an instance of subcultures between the worksites in the team where both teams create different meanings on their own.

Differences in competencies were a given due to the original Scandinavian team's background of close collaborating and due to the introduction of new coworkers (the Indian worksite) in general. However, the differences became apparent when close physical collaboration was not possible.

Knowledge asymmetry and dependency of information and communication from one site to another, was the not-very-surprising result of cultural distance and differences in competencies. Primarily the Indian site became dependent on the three other sites.

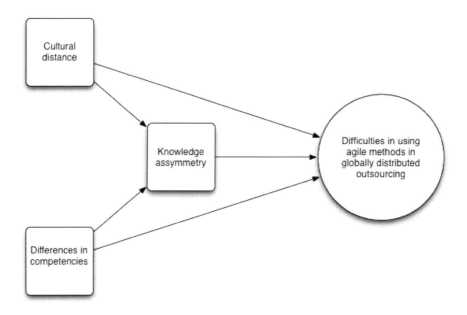

Fig. 1. The resulting theory on what makes use of agile processes difficult

Of course our validation of the theory is based on a single case as well as the concept of saturation from GT. According to Yin [42] and Baskerville & Lee [43], generalizing to statements or theories is more valid through a multiple case study, because a single case study often will have difficulties in generalizing outside its specific, contextual setting. Nevertheless, we deviate from this normative standard of assuming that a quantifiable study result is the best way of creating new knowledge. After all, knowledge and meaning creation in qualitative, interpretative studies is very specific depending on the researcher and the individual as well as the group making up the surroundings of the research.

This means that given enough time and analysis, any case would theoretically deviate from one another and the question remains as to what extra value several cases actually bring? Instead, the theory we produce from this setting is a result of an analytical generalizability process derived not only from the single case but also coded using GT and afterwards compared to current literature through a literature study. The value we add is not that of purely quantifiable results but instead that of a transparent research process and also a proposal of a theory, which other research can benefit from using or testing.

Finally, one of the primary limitations as also discussed in the Discussion is that of practice versus theory. It is difficult to interpret actions and meanings of the use of agile processes because hardly any team proclaiming to use agile processes is actually using it in a rigid (prescribed) way. Thereby leaving behind doubts to whether a more 'strict' use of certain principles and tools - i.e. retrospectives - would have resulted in a different effect than what we found?

References

1. Harter, D., Krishnan, M., Slaughter, S.: Effects of process maturity on quality, cycle time, and effort in software product development. Management Science 46(4), 451–466 (2000)
2. Cusumano, M.A., Yoffie, D.B.: What Netscape learned from cross-platform software development. Communications of the ACM 42(10), 72–78 (1999)
3. Cusumano, M.A., Yoffie, D.B.: Software development on Internet time. IEEE Computer 32(10), 60–69 (1999)
4. Iansiti, M., MacCormack, A.: Developing Products on Internet Time, pp. 108–117. Harvard Business Review (September-October 1997)
5. Pries-Heje, J., et al.: Advances in Information Systems Development: From Discipline and Predictability to Agility and Improvisation. In: Avison, D., et al. (eds.) Advances in Information Systems research, Education and Practice: IFIP 20th World Computer Congress, TC 8, Information Systems, Milano, Italy, September 7-10, pp. 53–75. Springer, New York (2008)
6. Layman, L., et al.: Essential communication practices for Extreme Programming in a global software development team. Information and Software Technology 48(9), 781–794 (2006)
7. Ramesh, B., et al.: Can distributed software development be agile? Communications of the ACM 49(10), 6 (2006)
8. Lacity, M.C., Hirschheim, R.A.: Information Systems Outsourcing; Myths, Metaphors, and Realities. John Wiley & Sons, Inc., New York (1993)
9. McFarlan, F.W., DeLacey, B.: Outsourcing IT: The Global Landscape in 2004, Harvard Business School (2004), doi:9-304-104
10. Dibbern, J., et al.: Information systems outsourcing: a survey and analysis of the literature. ACM SIGMIS Database 35(4), 6–102 (2004)
11. Sauer, J.: Agile practices in offshore outsourcing–an analysis of published experiences. In: Proceedings of the 29th Information Systems Research Seminar in Scandinavia, Helsingborg, Denmark, August 12-15 (2006)
12. Olson, J.S., et al.: The (unique) advantages of collocated work. In: Hinds, P., Kiesler, S. (eds.) Distributed Work, pp. 113–136. The MIT Press, Cambridge (2002)
13. Kussmaul, C., Jack, R., Sponsler, B.: Outsourcing and offshoring with agility: A case study. In: Extreme Programming and Agile Methods-XP/Agile Universe 2004, pp. 147–154 (2004)
14. Paasivaara, M., Lassenius, C.: Collaboration practices in global interorganizational software development projects. Software Process Improvement and Practice 8(4), 183–199 (2003)
15. Moore, S., Barnett, L.: Offshore Outsourcing And Agile Development, Forrester Research (2004)
16. Bloch, M., Spang, S.: Reaping the benefits of business-process outsourcing, McKinsey (2003)
17. Cramton, C.D.: The mutual knowledge problem and its consequences for dispersed collaboration. Organization Science 12(3), 25 (2001)
18. Cockburn, A.: Agile software development: The cooperative game, 2nd edn. Addison-Wesley, Reading (2002)
19. Kiesler, S., Cummings, J.: What do we know about proximity and distance in work groups? A legacy of research. In: Hinds, P., Kiesler, S. (eds.) Distributed Work, pp. 57–82. The MIT Press, Cambridge (2002)
20. Cockburn, A.: Learning from agile software development - part one. Crosstalk - Journal of Defence Software Engineering, 10–14 (October 2002)

21. Conboy, K., Fitzgerald, B.: Toward a conceptual framework of agile methods. In: Extreme Programming and Agile Methods - XP/Agile Universe 2004, pp. 105–116 (2004)
22. Atkinson, P., Coffey, A.: Making sense of qualitative data: Complementary research strategies, pbk edn. Sage Publications, Inc., Thousand Oaks (1996)
23. Fairclough, N.: Peripheral vision: Discourse analysis in organization studies: The case for critical realism. Organization Studies 26(6), 24 (2005)
24. Glaser, B., Strauss, A.: Awareness of Dying. Aldine, Chicago (1965)
25. Glaser, B., Strauss, A.: The Discovery of Grounded Theory: Strategies for Qualitative Research. T. Aldine, Chicago (1967)
26. Glaser, B.: Basics of grounded theory analysis. Sociology Press, Mill Valley (1992)
27. Orlikowski, W.: CASE Tools as Organizational Change: Investigating incremental and Radical Changes in Systems Development. MIS Quarterly 17(3), 309–340 (1993)
28. Urquhart, C.: Exploring Analyst-Client Communication: Using Grounded Theory Techniques to Investigate Interaction in Informal Requirements Gathering. In: Lee, A.S., Liebenau, J., DeGross, J.I. (eds.) Information Systems and Qualitative Research, pp. 149–181. Chapman and Hall, London (1997)
29. Urquhart, C.: Strategies for conversation and systems analysis in requirements gathering: A qualitative view of analyst-client communication. The Qualitative Report (On-line serial), 4(1) (2000)
30. Baskerville, R., Pries-Heje, J.: Racing the e-bomb: How the Internet is redefining information systems development methodology. In: IFIP Working 8.2 Working Conference, Boise, Idaho, USA (2001)
31. Strauss, A., Corbin, J.: Basics of Qualitative Research: Techniques and Procedures for Developing Grounded Theory, 2nd edn. Sage Publications, Beverly Hills (1998)
32. Boehm, B., Turner, R.: Using Risk to Balance Agile and Plan-Driven Methods. IEEE Computer 36(6), 57–66 (2003)
33. Beck, K., Fowler, M.: Planning Extreme Programming. Addison Wesley Longman, New York (2000)
34. Beck, K., et al.: Embracing change with extreme programming. IEEE Computer 32(10), 70–77 (1999)
35. Rising, L., Janoff, N.S.: The Scrum software development process for small teams. IEEE Software 17(4), 26–32 (2000)
36. Gasson, S.: A genealogical study of boundary-spanning IS design. European Journal of Information Systems 15(1), 26 (2006)
37. Levina, N., Vaast, E.: The emergence of boundary spanning competence in practice. Implications for the implementation and use of Information Systems. MIS Quarterly 29(2), 335–363 (2005)
38. Fitzgerald, B., Hartnett, G., Conboy, K.: Customising agile methods to software practices at Intel Shannon. European Journal of Information Systems 15(2), 200–213 (2006)
39. Fairclough, N.: Language and Power, 2nd edn. Pearson Education Limited, Edinburgh Gate (2001)
40. Vidgen, R., Madsen, S., Kautz, K.: Mapping the Information System Development Process. In: IT Innovation for Adaptability and Competitiveness, pp. 157–171. Springer, Boston (2009)
41. Agerfalk, P., Fitzgerald, B.: Flexible and distributed software processes: old petunias in new bowls? Communications of the ACM 49(10), 7 (2006)
42. Yin, R.K.: Case study research: Design and methods, 3rd edn. Sage Publications, CA (2003)
43. Baskerville, R., Lee, A.S.: Generalizing Generalizability in Information Systems Research. Information Systems Research 14(3), 221–243 (2003)

Author Index